THE
RESISTANT
LEARNER

*Helping Your Child Knock Down
the Barriers to School Success*

LAWRENCE J. GREENE

ST. MARTIN'S GRIFFIN ❧ NEW YORK

www.stmartins.com

Design by Level C

Library of Congress Cataloging-in-Publication Data

Greene, Lawrence J.
    The resistant learner : helping your child knock down the barriers to school success / Lawrence J. Greene.—1st U.S. ed.
        p. cm.
    Includes bibliography (p. 299).
    Includes index (p. 301).
    ISBN 0-312-31919-3
    EAN 978-0312-31919-9
    1. Learning, Psychology of. 2. Underachievers—Education. 3. Academic achievement. 4. Education—Parent participation. I. Title.

LB1060.G74 2004
371.9'2—dc22

                                                                    2004056475

First Edition: January 2005

10 9 8 7 6 5 4 3 2 1

For my son, Joshua Ryan Greene

Your spirit and zest still enthrall me.
I shall always be thankful for the joy you
have brought into my life.

Contents

Acknowledgments

Joshua, my nine-year-old son, deserves a heartfelt acknowledgment for letting me use "his" computer. Those many mornings when he entertained himself with construction projects and allowed me to write were a blessing and are much appreciated. Dan and Evelyn Greene, as always, were there for me with their unconditional love and support. And so, too, were Evan and Lisa Greene. Thank you all.

Introduction

Millions of capable students chronically underachieve in school. Despite their sub-standard performance, most of these students are deemed ineligible for learning assistance programs because they don't manifest the classic symptoms of a specific learning disability. Only 3 to 5 percent of the children who do poorly in school actually qualify for special education, and it's obvious that vast numbers of children are essentially being left to sink or swim on their own. That many of these youngsters don't know how to swim, much less tread water, is a harsh reality of life in our overburdened and underfunded educational system. This reality is all the more cruel if you happen to be the parent of one of these drowning children.

Be forewarned that this isn't a book about learning disabilities. I've written several books on that subject already, and I believe that I've covered the territory extensively. Rather, this book is about children who do not fit neatly into the diagnostic-treatment box, children who haven't figured out how to learn productively or who choose for complex academic and psychological reasons not to make a concentrated effort in school. Some of these youngsters are overtly resistant to achieving academically. Others are passively resistant. In either case, the net result is a tragic waste of human potential.

Let me briefly describe my background. During a period spanning more than thirty years, my staff and I provided educational therapy for more than 14,000 underachieving children. I diagnostically tested those marginally performing children, and I developed innovative instructional procedures for getting them on track academically. I've published seventeen books about my clinical experiences, theories, and proprietary procedures, and two additional textbooks are scheduled for publication next year. The methodology and curricula I've developed to meet the needs of struggling learners are being used in elementary, middle, high school, and college classrooms throughout the United States and Canada.

Now let me succinctly state my educational philosophy. I believe that children are born with an insatiable desire to learn and assimilate information about their world, and that they are genetically programmed to develop new skills and abilities. This desire is pounded into the DNA of the human species. Were it not for this genetic programming, symphonies, novels, and philosophical treaties would never be written, skyscrapers and bridges would never be built, new vaccines for treating diseases would never be discovered, and companies such as Microsoft would never be created.

On the first day of kindergarten, excited, wide-eyed and, perhaps, somewhat apprehensive children are ready to get down to the business of acquiring an education. But then something happens to some of them. Learning becomes difficult and unpleasant, and these youngsters begin to lose their enthusiasm for learning. They develop maladaptive behaviors and attitudes. For many, the source of their negative attitudes about school and increasing resistance to learning can be traced to ineptness. I am not talking about the perceptual processing inefficiency associated with learning disabilities, but rather the ineptness that results when children fail to figure out how to use their innate capabilities and fail to acquire the tools that are requisite to academic success.

Fast forward six years, and first graders who were falling behind and who were frustrated and discouraged are now full-blown demoralized, learning-resistant, and learning-aversive pre-adolescents. Counterproductive attitudes and behavior have become entrenched. Self-confidence is shredded. Self-sabotaging behavior is embedded. Enmeshed in a perennially recycling underachievement loop, these children don't know how to learn, and, worse, they don't want to learn. They are in school only because they're required to be there. Their expectations are negative, and their aspirations are for all intents and purposes nonexistent.

I have chosen in this book to focus primarily on underachieving kids in fifth grade through high school. Certainly the parents of younger children can use the information to alert themselves to the red flags and to acquire insight about the dire consequences of not recognizing and heeding these danger signals. Each chapter examines a particular factor that can cause children to learn ineffectually, perform marginally, and become demoralized and resistant to learning. The topics include such critically important factors as determining natural learning strengths and preferred learning modalities, establishing goals, setting priorities, getting organized, recording assignments, managing time, learning how to study effectively.

At the end of each chapter, concrete, practical, easy-to-assimilate methods are presented for reorienting the counterproductive behaviors and attitudes that are causing your child to underperform in school. Depending on your own parenting style and preferences and your child's personality and temperament, you can choose to use either an autocratic or a democratic approach when working with your child. Both approaches are presented clearly and systematically.

Make no mistake about the overriding issue: if your child is striking out in school, you must be prepared to intervene proactively. This book will provide you with the information you need to help your child fix the problems that are undermining his or her attitude, work ethic, and performance. Your child may only hit infield singles at first, but down the road he or she will start hitting doubles, triples, and home runs. Keep an eye on the scoreboard and on your child's reaction to his or her newly discovered skills and abilities. You'll see effort replace laziness. You'll see motivation replace entrenched resistance. You'll see pride replace shoddy work and defensiveness. You'll see positive attitudes and self-confidence replace negativity. With your skillful and proactive intervention, your child will be playing and winning in a new franchise, in a revised lineup, and in a new ball game. Trust me. It's doable.

1

Dancing to the Wrong Music

Jeremy couldn't figure out why the door to his room wouldn't budge. He was certain that it wasn't locked from the inside. Well, there was only one way to deal with the problem. Putting his shoulder against the door, he pushed as hard as he could, but the door only opened about two inches. It was time to get serious. Jeremy took three steps back, put both hands in front of him, and smashed into the impediment with all his strength. He heard a cracking sound, but the door finally opened enough for him to slip through. Once inside, he discovered that his football gear had fallen on the floor behind the door and was wedged against the leg of his desk. Jeremy was glad his mother hadn't seen him smash against the door, and he wondered for an instant if he had damaged the hinges.

Jeremy threw his book bag on his unmade bed. Pushing aside the candy, chewing gum wrappers, and soft drink cans, he began to search through the piles of paper on his desk. He was looking for the science report that had been due today. He was certain the paper was somewhere in his room, but he had no idea where. When he couldn't find the report on his desk, he began to hunt under the mounds of clean and dirty clothes on his bed. Finally, he found the crumpled and creased paper under his grimy gym shorts. It was a bit worse for wear, but it could still be read.

"If I hand it in tomorrow, maybe the teacher will accept it," Jeremy thought to himself as he stuffed the report into his backpack.

As usual, the fifth grader had put off writing the paper until the last minute. He had received the assignment two weeks ago but had waited until the night before it was due to start writing it. Of course, he hadn't had time to proofread the report. Then he forgot to take it to school.

Jeremy knew that his teacher would lower his grade because the assignment was late. Since most of his homework was not submitted on time, he was accustomed to having his grades lowered. He was also accustomed to red marks all over his papers because of spelling and grammar errors.

Spelling had always been a nightmare because so many of the words were not written the way they sounded. He had to admit that the time he had spent in the resource program had helped, but he was still a terrible speller, and he was convinced that he would remain a terrible speller.

Jeremy's sloppy and illegible handwriting made things even worse. Much of his homework was usually done on the school bus on the way to school, and each bump in the road caused a bump in his handwriting.

"So what!" Jeremy thought. "The teacher and my parents can get on my case all they want. I don't care! I can read my reports, and that's what counts."*

ON A COLLISION COURSE

Fact: *A child's attitudes about learning reflect his experiences with learning.* Positive experiences produce positive attitudes, and these attitudes in turn produce positive behaviors. Conversely, negative experiences produce negative attitudes that in turn produce negative behaviors. Stated differently, children who do well in school are generally motivated and diligent, and children who are diligent and motivated generally do well in school. The opposite is equally true. Poor effort produces poor performance, and poor performance produces poor effort. Does this lead inexorably to a confounding "which came first, the chicken or the egg" conundrum? This question, of course, doesn't lend itself to an easy answer, but what we know is that chickens produce eggs, and fertilized eggs produce chickens. The dynamic is circular, and if there's a problem

*Case study from Lawrence J. Greene, *Winning the Study Game* (Minnetonka, Minn.: Peytral Publications, 2002). Reprinted with permission.

with the chickens or a problem with the egg production, the problem must be examined, analyzed, and fixed.

As we read the introductory case study about Jeremy, should we be shocked by his conduct? Should we shift into a judgmental, critical mode, shake our heads, and cluck disapprovingly? Perhaps, as you read the anecdote, you were thinking, "This kid desperately needs a major attitude adjustment!" Or perhaps you were thinking, "This is exactly what my child does, and it drives me nuts!" If you're are a parent who values education, sees school as the means to acquire essential capabilities, and recognizes that good academic skills are stepping stones to a rewarding and remunerative career, you could certainly justify your disapproval of Jeremy's obvious maladaptive attitudes and behavior.

There's a dance in progress here. A resistant, academically deficient eleven-year-old:

- lives in a room that's a disaster area.
- can't find important schoolwork.
- submits late assignments.
- spells atrociously.
- writes illegibly.
- doesn't proofread his assignments.
- is disorganized.
- cannot manage time.
- disregards his academic obligations.
- manifests recurring self-sabotaging conduct.

Certainly, there are underlying academic and psychological reasons that can explain why Jeremy has choreographed this dance, but, nonetheless, the steps are disjointed and the music is loud and discordant. If you have a child like Jeremy at home who is dancing to similar music, be assured that you can take charge of the stereo and change the tune. But first you have to select a new disk, figure out how to insert it, and press the play button. One thing is certain: Unless you intervene proactively and assert yourself, your child's patterns of irresponsibility, resistance, laziness, inadequate effort, disorganization, and time mismanagement are likely to persist, and you don't require a crystal ball to predict the dire consequences.

SURVIVAL INSTINCTS

Fact: *Children who do poorly in school and who feel inadequate consciously and unconsciously develop ways to defend themselves psychologically.* Self-protecting behavior is a natural survival instinct. Difficulty keeping up with the class, frustration, traumatic associations with test taking, learning phobias, negative expectations, emotional scarring, resistance to learning, and diminished self-confidence are common byproducts of the struggling learner's constant battle to keep his head above water.

Children who learn ineffectually and who conclude—consciously or unconsciously—that their academic situation is doomed to failure soon begin to devalue their talents, and by the end of kindergarten, or perhaps first grade, they may already see themselves as being intellectually inadequate. These discouraged learners may not be able to express their feelings of incompetence and may not even be consciously aware of the feelings, but the underlying emotions nonetheless play an instrumental role in shaping their attitudes and behavior. It should not surprise us when children act out their frustration and demoralization in ways that seem expressly designed to undermine themselves and exasperate their teachers and parents. The compelling unconscious agenda of these youngsters is to insulate themselves, and they do so by lowering their expectations and aspirations and by latching onto conduct that they believe is self-protecting. That their defense mechanisms are clearly ineffectual and only call attention to the very deficiencies that they're trying to hide is an irony that defeated, resistant learners rarely perceive. Preoccupied with hiding their vulnerabilities and diverting attention from their shortcomings, the primary objective of these children is somehow to get through another school day without suffering more indignities and without being emotionally bruised and bloodied.

Jeremy represents a perfect example of this psychological circle-the-wagons phenomenon. The fifth grader selects the path of least resistance, one requiring the minimum possible effort and offering the minimum immediate emotional exposure. Faced with fight or flight, he chooses flight. His mindset is simple: "If I don't really try hard, then I'm not really failing." This transparent rationalization is not as illogical as we—responsible and conscientious adults—might think. From the struggling child's perspective, not working diligently makes perfect sense. Why fight when you can run from a battle that you are destined to lose? Why risk additional pain and failure? Why study when you are convinced that you'll get poor grades anyway? In many respects, running away makes perfect sense. Survival of the vulnerable—those scurrying around chaotically like ants on a busy sidewalk—hinges on this instinct to avoid the descending shoe.

As adults with extensive life experience, we realize that running away from problems is a double-edged sword. Flight may temporarily deflect discomfort and unpleasantness, but in most instances it's ultimately a prescription for failure. By evading their academic obligations, resistant children may delude themselves for a while that everything is okay, but the delusion invariably shatters when report cards are sent home. They can no longer run, and they have to pay the piper.

Most parents are keenly aware of the core immutable facts of life, having usually acquired many of their real-life insights through the "school of hard knocks." They realize that a basic cause-and-effect dynamic binds actions with predictable outcomes. *Bills come due, and it's impossible to evade having to pay the bill indefinitely.* Children ensnared in their own coping mechanisms and consumed with protecting themselves do not perceive this inexorable cause-and-effect dynamic.

EMOTIONAL IMPRINTS

Fact: *Counterproductive behaviors and attitudes that originate in elementary school and persist in high school could endure throughout life.* Irresponsibility and self-defeating actions go with the territory when children become convinced that they aren't going to win in school. Some children figure out how to cope. They serve their sentence, tread water for twelve years, and go through the motions of acquiring an education. Others simply give up.

A child's chronic self-sabotaging traits are guaranteed not only to trigger frustration and exasperation in concerned parents, but are also likely to trigger a sense of helplessness and despair. How do you help your child realize that by not working diligently in school he's shooting himself in the foot? How can you help him switch from a subpar performance track to an achievement track? How do you modify his self-defeating conduct? Of course, this conduct is not limited exclusively to boys. Girls struggle with the same issues, but girls are generally less overt in manifesting the resistance, negative attitudes, and acting-out behavior. There are, of course, countless exceptions to this generalization, as you will discover in subsequent chapters.

Fact: *Lectures about responsibility, motivation, and diligence usually are ineffectual in modifying the maladaptive behavior of the resistant learner.* Threats and punishment are also generally ineffectual. Unless academic assistance, clearly defined behavior and performance standards, and on-going emotional support are provided, the defensive behaviors characteristic of the unwilling learner are likely to become increasingly entrenched and problematic. What child wants to study hard for a test when he's convinced in advance that he's going to fail? What child wants to plow through a history unit when the words don't make sense and the information seems incomprehensible? Should we be stunned when a struggling child's negative attitudes about effort and diligence become embedded and enduring? Should we be surprised when maladaptive conduct driven by insecurity becomes a treasured security blanket? Should we be shocked when vulnerable children furrow deeper and deeper under this blanket? This self-protecting reaction, of course, is not limited to children. What emotionally bruised and insecure adult would willingly stretch for the brass ring if he were convinced by his past experiences that he's going to tumble off the carousel?

The last thing academically discouraged children want to deal with is schoolwork. Deluding themselves that they can buffalo their parents and teachers, these youngsters can become masterful at deflecting accountability, denying that they have any problems, and blaming others for their plight. Of course, their excuses are so transparent that they fool no one except themselves. Should it astonish us when an academically defeated youngster argues that school is irrelevant and that he's decided to become a professional skateboarder? To children attempting to escape seemingly impossible academic demands, the improbability of their achieving their fantasy is not something they care to contemplate. Sure, some kids actually do become professional athletes, but the odds are certainly stacked against them. As adults, we realize that children must be consummately talented to even have an outside chance of making it into this elite cadre. Defeated learners who are caught up in their fantasies will do everything possible to avoid having to confront this reality.

It's ironic that children with the greatest need to work conscientiously are typically the most resistant to doing so. The classic litany of excuses includes:

- *"The teacher picks on me!"*
- *"The teacher is a jerk!"*
- *"The work is dumb!"*
- *"I did my homework in school!"*
- *"She didn't assign any homework!"*
- *"The test didn't cover what it was supposed to cover!"*
- *"He never told us that the report was due on Thursday!"*
- *"I did check over my work!"*

These rationalizations, self-deceptions, evasions, and outright lies only magnify and perpetuate the challenges that struggling children face, but this obvious irony is lost on emotionally defended youngsters. The more ensconced they are under their security blanket, the more resistant they are to letting go of it.

THE CLUB IS OFF LIMITS

Fact: *Potentially capable children who learn ineffectually may never gain admission into the elite fellowship of students who are on a track leading to college, expanded vocational options, and rewarding careers.* Students who graduate from high school with first-rate academic skills, a positive attitude, self-confidence, and an ingrained work ethic hold first-class tickets to just about wherever they choose to go in life. In contrast, those who graduate with poor skills, negative attitudes, and entrenched self-defeating behavior and attitudes are holding tokens that can only be redeemed at a penny arcade.

Fact: *Children must be able to function in a world that is harsh and unforgiving of those who lack motivation, skills, and self-confidence.* Youngsters who are in the habit of doing the minimum possible, have a marginal appreciation for the consequences of their actions, and don't recognize that effort, motivation, and good skills produce life's most satisfying rewards are at risk for ending up at the bottom of the food chain. These children are on a path leading to menial jobs and minimum wage. In an even worse case scenario, resistant and defeated learners are candidates for becoming entangled in the criminal justice system. That more than ninety percent of the inmates in American prisons struggled to learn in school is a statistic that our educational system conveniently chooses to overlook. Yes, this is an unsettling thought if you are the parent of a resistant, learning-aversive child, but it is, nonetheless, a fact of life. It certainly doesn't have to end up this way. By intervening proactively, you can play an instrumental role in helping your child change course and in reducing the chances of chronic frustration and demoralization devolving into possible antisocial behavior.

Fact: *Parents can teach children how to prevail over many of the seemingly insoluble challenges and dilemmas they face in school.* You are your child's most important guide, mentor, and monitor. If you see yellow lights flashing and your child is becoming increasingly demoralized and self-sabotaging, it's imperative that you step up to the plate. You must provide your child with viable alternatives to becoming a resistant, defeated learner and shutting down in school. This translates into helping your child confront and fix problems, ideally before they become full-blown, hard-to-manage crises. If sirens are wailing and red lights are flashing and your child is already in major crisis mode, the imperative to intervene proactively is all the more compelling.

THE NUTS AND BOLTS OF ACADEMIC ACHIEVEMENT

Fact: *To be successful in school, children must be capable of mastering basic academic skills.* Children must be able to decipher and comprehend written language, understand verbal and written instructions, write legibly and intelligibly, study productively, identify important information, and assimilate and retain what their teachers consider important.

Those who fail to acquire these core academic skills cannot realistically be expected to work up to their full potential without meaningful learning assistance. The sooner this help is provided, the lower the risk of enduring self-concept damage.

Fact: *Children must develop the capacity to solve problems and think and act strategically.* Problems are a fact of life, and children must be capable of analyzing and handling the challenges and predicaments they encounter in school. They must be able to define personally meaningful short- and long-term goals. They must be able to prioritize their responsibilities and organize their materials. They must be able to develop a practical plan for getting from point A to point B to point C. Whether they're writing a book report, studying for a test, doing homework assignments, or doing a science experiment, they must be capable of figuring out how to get the job done. This capacity to create a strategy and develop specific tactics for attaining defined objectives is the essence of thinking smart, and thinking smart is a requisite to success, not only in school, but also in the world beyond school.

REQUIREMENTS FOR ACADEMIC ACHIEVEMENT

Your child must be able to:

- record assignments accurately.
- create an organizational system.
- manage time efficiently.
- set goals.
- establish priorities.
- plan ahead.
- focus on defined objectives.
- solve problems.
- think logically and rationally.
- recognize and apply basic cause-and-effect principles.
- learn actively (as opposed to passively).

- comprehend the course content.
- study efficiently and conscientiously.
- identify and retain important information.
- anticipate what is likely to be asked on exams.
- think analytically, strategically, and critically.

What can you do if your child lacks these capacities? One thing is patently obvious: If nagging, threats, lectures, sermons, and punishment haven't worked, it's time to change tactics. No reasonable person would dispute the basic soundness of the cliché "If it ain't broke, don't fix it." In many situations, this principle makes perfect sense, but the axiom can also be exceedingly simplistic. Many situations that aren't necessarily totally "broken" can certainly benefit from revisions, tweaks, and improvements. In the case of resistant learners, a second equally valid principle must be factored into the school performance equation: "If it is broken and you need to use it, you must figure out how to make the required repairs." When the breakdown manifests as chronic resistance to learning and chronic demoralization, the need for a repair is imperative.

It's time to learn how to help your child make the repairs. Let's begin by examining the dynamics of academic success.

THE ACHIEVEMENT LOOP

Fact: *Children are programmed by nature to learn.* The desire to acquire insight about how the world works and to assimilate knowledge and skills is one of the most distinctive and consequential characteristics of the human species. This desire provides the quintessential impetus for mankind's remarkable advances and achievements. Most children enter kindergarten primed to learn and with an insatiable craving for knowledge. They are curious about their world, receptive to instruction, eager to acquire new information, and responsive to new insights. When children become resistant to learning, something is profoundly amiss. This resistance is unnatural, and their parents have a solemn responsibility to figure out what's causing the attitudes and behavior and to rekindle the flame before it is permanently extinguished. They must look under the hood, identify the problem, and fix or replace the parts that aren't working. In some cases, the job may involve little more than a simple tune-up. It other cases, a major overhaul may be needed.

Academic achievement is not all that mysterious. The components are bound together in a continuously recycling loop. Good skills, defined goals, motivation, effort, and self-confidence produce success. Success, in turn, generates enhanced skills, new goals, expanded motivation, increased effort, and greater self-confidence. *Stated differently, the more children accomplish, the more they believe in themselves, and the more they believe in themselves, the more they'll want to keep on achieving.*

Fact: *The feelings of accomplishment, pride, and personal efficacy that are produced by achievement are addictive.* Successful children don't want to stop achieving. They like the pleasurable feelings associated with success, and they want to continue to experience this pleasure. It's like eating pistachio nuts. Once you start, most people find it hard to stop. Achieving children are not only certain that they *can* succeed, they are also convinced that they *deserve* to succeed. This mind-set permeates their entire being. Children who feel this sense of power and invincibility are immediately distinguishable. They are convinced that they can attain the personal goals they establish. They appreciate their talents and exalt in the respect and admiration they elicit from others. They radiate self-assurance. They relish new challenges. They delight in testing themselves. They revel in their accomplishments. And they are eager to substitute new goals and challenges to replace those that they have already attained.

The opposite occurs when children are entangled in a nonachievement loop. This loop also continuously recycles itself. Poor skills and no goals produce little success. Little success generates diminished self-confidence, effort, and motivation, which, in turn, guarantee continued marginal performance. In other words, the more children fail, the less faith they have in themselves, and the less willing they are to stretch for the brass ring. These youngsters are like hamsters on a treadmill. No matter how hard they run, they never move forward.

The achievement and nonachievement loops can be represented

graphically. Note that the arrows connecting the interlocking components point in both directions. These bidirectional arrows underscore a
key dynamic in the achievement phenomenon: each component affects
the functioning of the other elements in the loop. This synergy between the parts produces the momentum. When one component is
missing or lacking, the other components are affected. The synergy is
undermined and the energy is diluted.

THE ACHIEVEMENT LOOP

THE NONACHIEVEMENT LOOP

If your child is entangled in a nonachievement loop, the overriding objective is show him how he can change the dynamics of his modus operandi so that he can extract himself from the loop. To help your child make this critically important transition from nonachievement to achievement, you must:

- accurately target the specific deficit areas (e.g., deficient skills, failure to establish goals, inadequate effort and motivation, etc.).
- make certain that effective assistance is provided (e.g., science-based remedial programs for conditions such as dyslexia).
- establish clear and reasonable standards and guidelines.
- furnish consistent guidance and supervision.
- provide acknowledgment and effusive affirmation for effort.

CHANGING THE TUNE

Fact: *To enhance children's performance, attitude, effort, and self-confidence, parents must make certain that their child possesses the tools requisite to achieving in school.* Your child must be taught effective academic, study, strategic thinking, and problem-solving skills. Certainly, this is easier said than done. But you don't really have a choice. The alternatives—mental stagnation, deficient academic skills, negative attitudes about school, diminished self-esteem, and self-sabotaging behavior—are clearly unacceptable. Your child must realize that you're absolutely determined that he acquire a first-rate education and that you're absolutely committed to providing whatever assistance and support that are necessary to make this happen. No ifs, ands, or buts.

DOs

- *Make sure your child is furnished with effective learning assistance.* If your child is in a learning assistance program, you have two basic options: You can trust that the school program will fix the problem, or you can decide to furnish additional after-school assistance. If your child is *not* receiving help in school or is *not* responding positively to the offered help, providing supplemental assistance is not optional.

It's essential! You must find a competent tutor, learning center, or educational therapist (a specially trained LD professional working in the private sector). You must rank your child's educational needs at the top of the priority list. These needs take precedence over gymnastics, karate, scouts, or soccer; although, of course, it's also important for struggling children to have access to nonacademic venues in which they can be successful. The value of each after-school activity must be carefully weighed, and a well-considered judgment must be made about the trade-offs. By helping your child improve his skills, by engineering a turnaround in his attitude about school and his capabilities, and by deliberately orchestrating repeated opportunities for him to experience success, you can pull the strings that will allow him to win academically. In the process, you'll play a key role in changing his attitudes about school, about learning, and about himself, his abilities, and his intrinsic self-worth.

- *Furnish selective homework assistance if you believe that you can do so productively and without losing your patience.* If your child is having difficulty, you can show him how to do a challenging math problem or answer a difficult science homework question, and work with him while he applies what you have taught him to a few problems. Then let him do the rest on his own. Don't get suckered into doing the work for him. Model how to do the work and provide encouragement, guidance, affirmation for progress, emotional support, and structure. If your child asks you to check over his work, it's recommended that you do so randomly, as you don't want him to depend on you to be his on-call proofreader. If you find a mistake, put a check mark in the margin, and ask your child to correct the error. If you believe that he's genuinely confused about how to do the assignment, you'll need to make a judgment call. You may conclude that your child requires additional instruction, or you may conclude that with some extra effort, he can figure out what to do on his own. This latter solution would be the more ideal, because it sends the clear message that you have faith in your child's ability to handle challenges. The key is to provide legitimate and justifiable assistance without creating unnecessary dependencies. Children who conclude that their parents are enablers are far more likely to become helpless.

- *Teach your child how to manage time, schedule obligations, and plan projects.* To do his work, your child must be able to get the job done systematically. (This subject will be examined in detail in chapter 8—Dealing With the Clock).

- *Get as much specific information as possible about your child's skills and behavior from your child's teacher(s).* Explain that you want to take a proactive role in helping your child improve his attitude, effort, and performance. Be forewarned that high school teachers are generally less cooperative than elementary school teachers about providing ongoing feedback to parents. Many of these teachers feel strongly that they aren't responsible for catering to teenagers who are lazy, irresponsible, or uncooperative. Some of these teachers, however, may not realize that your child's counterproductive attitudes and behaviors are not actually the cause of his poor academic performance, but, rather, are symptoms of his travails in school. You may have to employ all of your people skills to enlist the teacher's support and elicit a willingness to provide vital information.

- *Explain to your child that there are going to be changes in his study procedures.* Indicate clearly and unequivocally that specific time slots each day must be allocated for studying. Reasonable assistance will be provided as needed. You expect homework to be completed and submitted on time. You expect work to be proofread for careless mistakes and to be neat and legible. Clearly communicate that desired privileges will be linked to demonstrated effort.

- *Acknowledge your child's struggles and acknowledge the pain associated with these struggles, but stay the course on requiring effort and diligence.* Be very explicit that you will not accept excuses for laziness. Also be very explicit that you expect him to take an active role in getting himself on track in school. This will require hard work on his part. Let him know that you are prepared to provide tutoring, educational therapy, or counseling as needed.

- *Express positive expectations and acknowledge, affirm, and praise effort and progress.* Negative parent–child interactions are common when children are ensnared in a pattern of counterproductive behavior. Buttons get pressed. Frustration and resentment bubble over. You can change these scripts if you are intent on doing so. Examine the

dynamics of your interactions. Identify the triggers and scripted responses. Find areas in which you can compliment your child (e.g.,
sports, arts, popularity, etc.). Express confidence that he can prevail
over the challenges he faces. Be prepared to be an empathetic sounding board and to work with your child on solving problems.

- *Encourage your child to establish short-term and long-term goals.* Goal
setting and achievement go hand in hand and stimulate motivation.
Help your child realize that short-term goals are stepping-stones to
attaining long-term goals. (See chapter 4.) Consider offering selective incentives and rewards for attaining a significant goal (e.g., a B
on the next book report), but be careful to avoid making it appear
that you are offering a bribe. The ultimate objective is for your child
to apply himself for the intrinsic satisfaction of doing a good job,
and not for extrinsic rewards.

- *Limit phone, TV, Internet, and video game access on school nights.* These
activities are restricted to designated and earned blocks of free time.
Children often use diversions and distractions to escape obligations
they don't want to confront. If your child is resistant or refuses to
cooperate, remove the distracting items from his study area.

- *Make punishments reasonable.* Grounding a child for a month because he failed to submit an assignment is unreasonable and is certain to trigger resentment. Positive reinforcement (i.e., praise and
rewards) is generally a far more effective means for modifying counterproductive behavior than is negative reinforcement (i.e., threats
and punishment).

- *Deny privileges selectively and fairly.* If your child is convinced that
your expectations and requirements are unreasonable and unfair,
he'll become resentful and resistant. He's also likely to become more
unwilling to acknowledge transgressions and discuss problems with
you. Explain clearly and unemotionally the reasons for any punishments that are imposed.

- *Resist the temptation to lecture and deliver sermons.* Why continue to do
something that doesn't work? Kids are masters at tuning out when
they don't want to hear something unpleasant.

- *Clearly define the guidelines and consistently enforce the rules* (e.g., no
TV after dinner until your homework is completed). Boundaries dis-

courage manipulative behavior. Be very selective and cautious about permitting deviations from the established procedures.

DON'Ts

- *Don't berate your child for past "transgressions."* The past is the past. What counts is what happens from this point forward.
- *Don't buy into excuses.* If your child usually claims that no homework has been assigned, ask him to document this by showing you his assignment sheet and the completed work. If you still have doubts about his claims, confer with his teacher.
- *Don't get into arguments.* Listen attentively. Discuss issues rationally. Terminate the discussion when it becomes nonproductive, and do not hesitate to assert reasonable and legitimate parental prerogatives.
- *Don't take ownership of your child's problems.* Doing so will send a message to your child that it's okay to be helpless and dependent. Your job is to support, monitor, facilitate, guide, and act as a sounding board. You want to help your child learn how to solve his own problems.
- *Don't compare children.* Your youngest child may be a star student. Reminding your oldest child of his sister's academic talents doesn't accomplish anything, and it could poison the family well.
- *Don't make immediate, draconian changes in your rules and expectations.* It is important that the guidelines be fair. You want to set your child up to succeed, and you want to elicit his active participation in the learning process. To expect him to spend four hours studying every night is probably unrealistic, especially after he has already established a pattern of studying for one hour each evening. The requirement is also a formula for failure. Your child will most likely dig in his heals and become even more resistant. You must be reasonable, and you must develop with your child's participation a methodical plan that will move him from point A to point B to point C. Changes in expectations, rules, and performance criteria should be realistic and incremental.

If you turn back to pages 1–2, you will find a list of the specific maladaptive behaviors and attitudes that describe Jeremy, the protagonist in the introductory case study. Each of these behaviors will be addressed in the chapters that follow. It's one thing to say to your child that he must get organized, record his assignments, manage time effectively, and plan ahead. It's quite another to teach him how to do so. Trust me, it's doable.

2

Identifying and Using Natural Talents

Caitlin felt a wave of anxiety well up in her stomach when her biology teacher announced that the midterm would be given on Monday. The sixteen-year-old's immediate reaction was to mumble to herself, "I'm gonna flunk."

Finding the class boring and the information irrelevant and useless, Caitlin was now faced with what was certain to be a very difficult midterm. To make matters worse, her teacher was infamous for asking really tricky questions and giving lots of Ds and Fs.

Failing tests wasn't a novel experience for Caitlin. She had struggled with reading since elementary school, and despite having been enrolled in a resource program from grades three through six and having ostensibly completed the program successfully, Caitlin still occasionally had trouble deciphering complex words. She also had residual difficulty understanding what the words meant and recalling information when she studied. These problems were compounded by concentration difficulties. Her mind would wander, and she would get confused. Then she would get furious at herself for being dumb. At this point, everything would crash down around her, and she would become dysfunctional.

Unfortunately, Caitlin was not only at risk for failing her biology class, but she also stood a good chance of flunking history and English. The semester was shaping up to be another disaster. With a 2.0 GPA, the sixteen-year-old realized that she might not earn enough credits to graduate with her class in two years, even if she went to summer school. The prospect of another ruined summer vacation infuriated her.

Certain that she couldn't pass the midterm, Caitlin had resigned herself to the inevitable. If she was lucky, she might somehow manage to get a D in the course, but this was unlikely, as she had gotten Ds and Fs on all of her lab reports and on the weekly quizzes. There were too many details to memorize and concepts to understand, and when she took tests she could never remember the phyla and the other worthless information that she was expected to learn.

Biology labs where she had to dissect frogs and look at amoebas and protozoa under a microscope were especially odious. "This is all so disgusting!" she repeatedly exclaimed to her lab partner. "Please tell me who in their right mind would want to spend hours in a dumb lab cutting up a frog when you could be hanging out with your friends?"

True to form, Caitlin put off studying for the midterm until the night before. As she mindlessly turned the pages of her textbook, she kept thinking about Kyle and the party they would be going to on Friday night. Resentful that she had to study at all, she angrily flipped through the pages of her textbook. She could already hear her mother's angry comments about the F that she would undoubtedly get on the midterm. Her mom would then ground her for at least a week. This was her standard punishment when Caitlin received bad grades. It was so totally unfair.

ATTITUDE AND BRAINS

Fact: *Resistant, learning-aversive, and emotionally defended children are incapable of performing academically at a level commensurate with their true ability.* Procuring an accurate assessment of the actual abilities of resistant youngsters who make little effort and seem intent on sabotaging themselves in school is extremely challenging. Energy that should be devoted to academics is diverted and dissipated. Leaving behind a trail of despairing parents and irritated teachers, these students are usually dismissed as having an "attitude" and typically described as lazy, irresponsible, and unreachable. Based on their less-than-stellar performance, it's often simply assumed that they are incapable of achieving in school.

That Caitlin's teachers might conclude that she lacks the where-withal to succeed academically is understandable in view of her grades and frame of mind. Teachers base their assessments of students' capabilities on test performance and on how students function in the classroom. Many teachers, and especially those in the upper grades, have, at best, a marginal understanding of the underlying learning issues that can undermine students' academic performance and trigger maladaptive behaviors and attitudes. This all-to-common lack of awareness about the underlying causal issues is usually attributable to the fact that middle school and high school teachers are content-area specialists, and they may have never been required to take even one graduate-level course focusing on how to teach students who learn ineffectually. As a general rule, teachers in high school aren't concerned about the factors that may cause students such as Caitlin to underperform. Their mandate is to teach the content area, and they expect their students to work hard and perform. Those who are irresponsible, lazy, and unmotivated should be prepared for a harsh reality check.

Middle school and high school teachers usually instruct five classes each day, and they may teach as many as 150 students. Many of these hard-pressed teachers would probably contend that they have neither the time nor the inclination to mollycoddle students who are lazy or noncooperative. They would also probably argue that it's not their responsibility to diagnose learning and attitude problems or to cater to students who aren't willing or able to assimilate the course content. Their responsibilities are to teach the subject matter competently and evaluate students' mastery of the material being taught. That their conclusions about their students' intrinsic capabilities may, in some cases, be inaccurate and myopic are issues that many straight-and-narrow teachers would probably refuse to consider. For these teachers, the dynamic is very basic: *The teacher's job is to instruct. The student's job is to learn. The bottom line—if students work hard and perform in my class, they'll get good grades. If they goof off, they'll get bad grades.*

In fairness, it should be noted that many teachers who appear inflexible and opposed to making adjustments in their grading criteria and teaching style to accommodate students who learn differently are actually highly dedicated. They love teaching. They love the subject matter. They do their utmost to teach effectively. When students are resistant, they take it personally.

Unfortunately, many of these no-nonsense, albeit dutiful, teachers are clueless about factors such as learning styles, teaching styles, learning preferences, and multiple intelligences that can significantly affect students' learning effectiveness and productivity (see pages 28–46). These teachers may also have only a marginal understanding of the complex psychological issues that can undermine a student's efforts and motivation, sidetrack achievement, damage self-esteem, and undercut academic self-confidence.

From a high school teacher's vantage point, Caitlin not only appears incapable of doing the work, but she also has a distinctly negative attitude about learning. Certainly, the teenager seems intent on doing everything possible to scuttle herself academically, and a teacher could justifiably argue that tenth graders must take responsibility for the consequences of their inadequate diligence and unacceptable conduct. These consequences, however well-deserved, can be psychologically devastating. Giving failing grades to a student such as Caitlin who has a long history of learning problems is guaranteed to further undermine her already tenuous self-esteem. The stream of academic debacles is certain to intensify her resistance to learning, reduce her aspirations in life, exacerbate her negative attitudes about school, and confirm her dire expectations. Caitlin's teachers may feel they have no other recourse but to fail her, and they're probably right, given the harsh realities that prevail in the typical high school, where learning-support triage is a daily fact of life. In this flawed system, only the seriously wounded are typically treated. The walking wounded such as Caitlin are usually sent back to the front line without even a Band-Aid. That the minor wounds of these underperforming children are likely to become infected and fester is conveniently overlooked. Absent school-based assistance, the responsibility for fixing Caitlin's problems rests squarely on the shoulders of Caitlin's parents.

Yes, it's true that Caitlin was provided with formal learning assistance in elementary school, and one can reasonably infer that she was dismissed from the program because the objectives had been ostensibly achieved. In some respects, this is analogous to domesticating a wolf and then setting it free in the forest. Unless the transition is handled skillfully, the prognosis for survival in the wild is likely to be guarded.

Caitlin is the classic prototype of a child enmeshed in a nonachievement loop. Her frame of mind guarantees marginal performance, not only in school, but also in the world beyond school. Clearly, the tenth grader is at a critical psychological juncture. If she concludes that she *deserves* to fail, the die is cast and the failure is likely to become a symbolic defeat with enduring emotional implications.

Fact: *Children do not necessarily need to be successful in school to be successful in life.* There are, of course, countless examples of youngsters who struggled academically and who subsequently became highly accomplished adults. These examples notwithstanding, school success does, in fact, generally correlate with later vocational success. When the dynamics of achievement are identified and analyzed, it's clear that motivation, effort, and diligence play pivotal roles in the academic and life success equation. Children who establish the habit of applying themselves responsibly and conscientiously in school are likely to maintain this habit and are likely to apply themselves responsibly and conscientiously throughout life. Their ingrained work ethic paves the way for subsequent accomplishments and career advancement.

Success in virtually any endeavor requires that children be willing and able to focus their physical, emotional, and intellectual energy on attaining their defined objectives. They must also be capable of confronting and handling challenges, solving problems, thinking strategically, establishing priorities, making wise choices, and disciplining themselves. Effort, grit, and determination are the lynchpins in the achievement equation, and it's obvious that Caitlin lacks these lynchpins. Without major attitude, behavior, and self-concept adjustments, she is clearly at risk for having difficulty handling the rigorous demands of a highly competitive world that values and rewards motivation and diligence.

IQ AND ACADEMIC ACHIEVEMENT

Fact: *Intelligence is not the exclusive driving force powering academic achievement.* The traditional assumption is that good students *a priori* possess superior intelligence and that they will, as a consequence, do well in school. This assumption, however, does not explain why unequivocally brilliant people such as Winston Churchill and Albert Einstein struggled in school, and yet made towering contributions to society. Nor does the assumption explain the marginal achievements of some members of Mensa, the elitist organization that limits enrollment exclusively to the highly gifted. Clearly, the commonly accepted cause-and-effect equation that equates intelligence with achievement does not fully account for the many exceptions to the rule.

Fact: *The raison d'être for developing IQ tests was to create an assessment instrument that could correlate innate ability with school performance.* Utilizing a range of subtests that generate statistically based verbal, nonverbal, and full-scale scores, IQ tests were originally designed to predict the potential for academic achievement. The tests equate intelligence with the ability to perceive relationships, understand concepts and abstractions, solve problems, apply logic, and recall information. The operating premise is, the higher the IQ score, the greater the likelihood of school achievement.

That capabilities in the areas of logic, problem solving, recall, and conceptualization can facilitate a child's ability to handle the academic curriculum successfully is beyond question. Bright children can grasp information more easily, and they can more easily apply and retain this information. These capacities furnish them with a significant advantage in the classroom. Intelligent children who are also conscientious, motivated, emotionally stable, and focused are the pride of the academic litter and have a virtual lock on scholastic achievement.

Despite the obvious advantages of being bright, the many exceptions to the *superior IQ = superior school performance* equation raise doubts about the validity of the traditionally accepted achievement equation. Some children with average IQ scores perform outstandingly in school, and other children who test in the superior range on IQ tests perform marginally. Are these "anomalies" exclusively attributable to effort, motivation, diligence, and focus, or are there indeed intrinsic limitations in the intelligence-testing procedure? Other key questions must also be raised about the function and validity of intelligence testing as a valid predictor of academic success. These questions include:

- Are there valuable learning capabilities that standard IQ tests fail to assess?
- Are there types of intelligence that are not typically acknowledged or rewarded in the typical classroom?
- Is one type of intelligence intrinsically superior to another?
- Is it possible for children to be intelligent but not be "school-smart?"
- How do you differentiate intelligence from smartness?
- Can children be taught how to identify and apply their natural learning abilities so that they can learn more effectively and productively, and, in effect, become smarter?
- Can children be taught to think more tactically and strategically, and can this developed capability help them function at a level that is more commensurate with their true potential?
- Should a child's capacity to apply his or her intelligence be factored into predictions about the likelihood of achievement in school and in life?
- Do IQ tests measure only a narrow and limited range of intellectual capabilities?
- Do the traditional criteria used to measure intelligence disregard a range of innate talents that can be instrumental in determining academic and vocational achievement?

As you read the case study about Caitlin, you may have consciously or unconsciously concluded, on the basis of her performance and attitude, that she was not particularly bright. Would you have been surprised to learn that her IQ was 132 and that she was gifted? If you learned that her IQ was 92, would you have been more willing to accept her poor school performance and behavior as "par for the course"? Could Caitlin's attitude, resistance, and diminished effort, or her lack of rapport with the examiner, skew her performance on an IQ test, and, if so, does the impact of a child's state of mind when taking the test raise questions about the reliability of the score? Is it possible to assess accurately the true ability of children who are fearful, insecure, highly defended, resistant, and/or oppositional?

There is a general operating assumption that a child taking an IQ test is trying to do well on the test.* What if for psychological reasons the child is unconsciously intent on sabotaging herself? Under such circumstances, would the score be valid? The answer to this question is self-evident—the score would have virtually no validity.

APPLIED INTELLIGENCE

Fact: *Intelligence is a multifaceted phenomenon.* The equation that produces scholastic success is comprised of overlapping variables, and the many exceptions to the *superior IQ = superior school performance* formula not only raise questions about the limitations of IQ tests in predicting academic success, but they also raise questions about how to define intelligence.

Differentiating IQ from DAI (demonstrated applied intelligence)[†] might explain some of the anomalies. Whereas IQ is primarily genetically based—psychologists generally believe that IQ is 70 to 80 percent inherited and 20 to 30 percent influenced by environment—demonstrated applied intelligence is primarily acquired through observation, experience, training, and practice. Kids who think strategically use what they've been given. They closely watch and copy others who possess qualities and abilities they admire. They model their behavior on that of a respected parent, older sibling, teacher, sports hero, or peer, and they are intent on becoming equally smart and capable.

To underscore the distinction between IQ and demonstrated applied intelligence, imagine that a standard IQ test is administered to:

---

*In California, IQ tests cannot be used to determine the placement of African-American students in public school special education programs because of concerns about cultural and racial bias.
[†]A term coined by the author.

- a musician who performs brilliantly or composes outstanding music.
- a coach who is an superb teacher, an accomplished tactician, and a skilled motivator.
- a businessperson who is a consummate manager and inspirational leader.
- a sculptor who creates world-renowned works of art.

It's conceivable that all of these exceptionally talented people might score in the average range on an IQ test. This, of course, raises the issue of whether IQ scores correlate reliably with capability, and, in the above-described cases, with exceptional capability. What then is intelligence? Does the traditional IQ model fail to acknowledge the full range of abilities and aptitudes that should rightfully be factored into the process of measuring intelligence? Does the traditional model need to be expanded? Certainly, in the hypothetical situations described above, the traditional model used to determine intelligence is unquestionably too restrictive.

This issue of correlation between IQ scores, classroom performance, and demonstrable or latent ability has particular relevance if your child is doing poorly in school, is resistant to learning, and has concluded that she's unintelligent. The questions also have particular relevance if your child's teachers have similarly concluded that your child is *a priori* lacking in ability because she's not performing well in class and on tests.

CRITICAL QUESTIONS ABOUT YOUR CHILD'S ABILITY AND PERFORMANCE

- Have I identified my child's natural talents and aptitudes?
- Is my child aware of her natural talents and aptitudes?
- Could my child be far more capable than anyone realizes or acknowledges?
- Could my child achieve at a significantly higher level if she were able to identify and capitalize on her innate capabilities?

- Could greater insight about her natural talents enhance my child's self-esteem, self-confidence, and motivation?
- Could greater insight about her natural talents play a pivotal role in extricating my child from a nonachievement loop?
- Can my child be taught how to develop and apply her intelligence?

The answer to all of these critically important questions is *yes*— unequivocally *yes!*

MULTIPLE INTELLIGENCES

Fact: *Traditional IQ tests are not designed to assess a comprehensive range of invaluable talents and capabilities.* Recognizing the inherent limitation of traditional IQ assessments, a Harvard professor named Howard Gardner has developed a more expansive model for defining intelligence. Gardner contends that there are many different types of intelligence. Coining the term *multiple intelligences,* he has identified eight major areas of ability, which include:

- *Verbal/Linguistic Intelligence:* If your child possesses this type of intelligence, she has good auditory and verbal communication skills and uses language to help her assimilate, comprehend, and retain information. She excels in classes that emphasize class discussions, verbal presentations, cooperative study groups, debates, and writing assignments, and she enjoys telling stories and expressing her conclusions and insights. Children who capitalize on their natural verbal/linguistic intelligence often gravitate to careers in areas such as law, writing, journalism, acting, teaching, or politics.
- *Visual/Spatial Intelligence:* If your child possesses this type of intelligence, she has a facility for creating graphic images in her mind and on paper. Because she can visually conceptualize and mentally imprint what she sees, she prefers to assimilate, comprehend, and retain information by reading books and viewing charts, demonstrations, videos, maps, and movies. She does well on tests that emphasize the recall of written information. Children who capitalize on their natu-

ral visual/spatial intelligence often gravitate to careers in areas such as engineering, mechanics, medicine, interior design, graphic arts, fine art, scholarly research, or architecture.

- *Logical/Mathematical Intelligence:* If your child possesses this type of intelligence, she feels most comfortable and capable when applying logic and reason. She tends to be more rational than emotional and has a questioning mind. She delights in solving problems, doing puzzles, and figuring out "brainteasers." She thinks conceptually, is adept at using numbers, and has a talent for linking together pieces of information to form a whole. She enjoys classifying and categorizing data, doing calculations, and handling abstractions. Intrigued by the physical world, she enjoys doing experiments that help her understand the dynamics of what is happening and the underlying concepts causing these events. Children who capitalize on their natural logical/mathematical intelligence often gravitate to careers in areas such as mathematics, engineering, geology, astronomy, theoretical science, applied and theoretical physical science, scientific research, teaching, medicine, computer hardware and software development, programming, or accountancy.

- *Interpersonal Intelligence:* If your child possesses this type of intelligence, she is adept and comfortable in social situations. She's empathetic, tries to see issues from another person's perspective, and is sensitive to what others think and feel. She finds it easy to establish relationships, organize events, mobilize people to work toward a common goal, resolve conflicts, build trust, maintain harmony, and encourage cooperation. Children who capitalize on their natural interpersonal intelligence often gravitate to careers in areas such as sales, marketing, human resource development, management, advertising, psychology and counseling, or politics.

- *Intrapersonal Intelligence:* If your child possesses this type of intelligence, she is likely to be introspective and keenly aware of her feelings. She is contemplative, interested in acquiring insights about herself and others, and intent on understanding the dynamics of her relationships. Children who capitalize on their natural intrapersonal intelligence often gravitate to careers in areas such as clinical psychology, counseling, writing, religion, and teaching.

- *Body/Kinesthetic Intelligence:* If your child possesses this type of intelligence, she's naturally coordinated and enjoys and excels in sports. She can control her movements (as in gymnastics, dancing, karate, ice-skating, or basketball), has great gross-motor coordination and fine-motor dexterity, and excels in physical pursuits. She uses movement to imprint information such as complex dance steps, karate kicks, or gymnastic routines). Children who capitalize on their natural body/kinesthetic intelligence often gravitate to careers in areas such as dance, athletics, acting, martial arts, sculpture, choreography, or coaching.

- *Music/Rhythmic Intelligence:* If your child possesses this type of intelligence, she has a natural talent for performing or composing music. She is highly responsive to rhythm, lyrics, melodies, and tonal patterns. She enjoys singing, playing musical instruments, performing on stage, marching in a band, and rehearsing. Adept at recalling melodies, the words to songs, and the notes in musical scores, she thinks in musical patterns and responds primarily to sounds. Children who capitalize on this type of natural intelligence often become singers, musicians, composers, conductors, disc jockeys, record producers, or music impresarios.

- *Naturalist Intelligence:* If your child possesses this type of intelligence, she enjoys interacting with animals, nature, and wildlife. She is interested in ecology, the environment, and the biological, chemical, and physical principles and phenomena that affect rain forests, oceans, jungles, seasonal cycles, animal reproduction, food chains, and species survival. Children who capitalize on this type of natural intelligence often gravitate to careers in botany, biology, oceanography, conservation, zoology, ecology, exploration, animal husbandry, veterinary medicine, zoo management, and forestry.

Children, of course, may possess more than one type of intelligence. For example, a child may have exceptional body/kinesthetic intelligence and may be a very talented natural athlete. She may also possess exceptional naturalist intelligence. In high school she may excel in competitive volleyball, basketball, and tennis, and in college, she may play varsity sports while majoring in biology. Upon completing college, she may pursue a career in veterinary medicine while continuing to play competitive sports whenever possible.

Fact: *Children who recognize and deliberately use their natural intelligence have a distinct advantage over those who are unaware of their capabilities and fail to capitalize on them.* You want your child to recognize that kids have different talents and learn in different ways. You also want your child to realize that a particular academic subject may be easier for a student to master because she possesses a particular type of intelligence, while her classmates may excel in other subjects because they possess different types of intelligence. The key message that you want to communicate is that there is nothing intrinsically superior about mathematical/logical intelligence versus verbal/linguistic intelligence or tactile/kinesthetic intelligence. The distinctive capabilities associated with each type of intelligence allow children to excel in particular areas. The same principle applies to vocations and professions. One career may favor a certain type of intelligence, while another may favor a different type of intelligence.

The likelihood of your child improving her performance in school and in the world beyond school can be significantly enhanced if you:

- help your child figure out what she can do well.
- encourage your child to use the tools in her tool bag.
- affirm your child's natural abilities.
- praise your child's accomplishments.

THE BASIC PRINCIPLES OF SUCCESS IN SCHOOL AND IN LIFE

- Knowing who you are
- Knowing what you do well
- Knowing what you want

- Knowing what you enjoy
- Knowing how to compensate for your weaknesses by capitalizing on your strengths
- Knowing what is required to attain your goals
- Knowing how to get the job done efficiently and effectively

Children equipped with self-knowledge, goal-directed purpose, strategic thinking skills, critical thinking skills, motivation, and a work ethic are sitting comfortably in the saddle and cantering confidently down the trail. They are in control, and they will find their path in life. Can resistant, defeated students be taught how to saddle and bridle their horse, mount, and ride? You bet they can! They just need assistance, guidance, and monitoring. They need their parents to help them identify their talents, and they need their parents to provide consistent boundaries, encouragement, acknowledgment, and affirmation for effort and progress.

The nine types of intelligence identified by Gardner significantly expand the traditional IQ testing paradigm. His extended model acknowledges and affirms capabilities that have never before been formally factored into an assessment of intelligence. Despite this amplification, IQ tests in the traditional format are still administered, and, as yet, there is no standardized and quantified protocol for assessing IQ based on Gardner's encompassing definition of intelligence. Clearly, such a testing instrument is needed.

Gardner's insights have particular relevance in the case of resistant learners. By helping underperforming children discover their distinctive talents, by validating these talents, and by acknowledging and applauding them for their distinctive capabilities, parents can play a direct and proactive role in enhancing their child's self-concept. Armed with new insights, children who previously perceived themselves as inadequate can begin to reappraise their self-worth. Resistant, learning-aversive youngsters can discover that they are, in fact, far more capable than they ever thought possible. This realization can reshape the course of their lives.

LEARNING PREFERENCES

Fact: *Students who identify and capitalize on their preferred learning strengths are far more likely to study productively and achieve academically.* Just as a child's recognition of her distinctive intelligence type can play a pivotal role in the scholastic success equation, so, too, can her recognition of her natural learning strengths and preferences (i.e., auditory, visual, tactile, kinesthetic, and/or experiential) play an equally pivotal role.

Multiple intelligences and preferred or dominant learning modalities are overlapping and interrelated. The child who possesses superior verbal/linguistic intelligence would probably prefer to use the auditory modality when learning, and the child who possesses superior visual/spatial intelligence would probably prefer to use the visual modality. A tactile or kinesthetic learner would most likely have superior body/kinesthetic intelligence and whenever feasible would probably prefer to capitalize on these capacities. In each instance, the child's dominant learning modality is likely to correspond to the student's distinctive intelligence type.

Most achieving students intuitively identify and apply their dominant learning modality or modalities when they learn. In contrast, underachieving students typically fail to make this basic cause-and-effect connection between achievement and the utilization of their natural abilities. Unaware of how to use what they've been given, these children continue to underperform.

In much the same way that your child has preferences about colors, food, and clothing, so, too, is she likely to have preferences about how to learn. Unfortunately, if she's struggling academically, it's likely that she's not consciously aware of these learning preferences. The vast majority of underachieving students do not realize that they can assimilate information and master skills far more effectively if they deliberately identify and methodically utilize their dominant learning modality. They also don't realize that they can use their learning strengths to compensate for their learning deficits. Although their study system may be failing miserably, underperforming students typically persist in using the flawed methods, oblivious to more viable alternatives. The effect of their continuing to use these ineffectual study procedures is predictable: They will continue to underperform.

APPLYING DOMINANT AND PREFERRED
LEARNING MODALITIES

Auditory Learners
assimilate information best by listening.

Characteristics: Auditory learners have a facility for comprehending and remembering verbal information. They recall best by "recording mental audio tapes" on which they register orally communicated data that may include facts, instructions, descriptions, and explanations. Auditory learners have an advantage in conversation-oriented foreign language classes because they have a facility for remembering spoken dialogues, idiomatic expressions, vocabulary, grammar, and verb conjugations. These students enjoy class discussions and learn best by participating in study groups and debating issues. They remember the words to songs and the content of previous discussions, and they typically possess good verbal communication skills. If a sentence or paragraph doesn't *sound* right, they will typically edit and revise the material until it does. They prefer to master course content by vocalizing or subvocalizing the data. Whenever possible, they will use their auditory memory to compensate in courses that require the mastery of a great deal of "visually loaded" information such as science formulas, math equations, and historical dates.

Tips for maximizing studying and learning effectiveness: Auditory learners should recite information aloud until it's assimilated. During lectures and class discussions, they should focus intently on the teachers' words and be conscious of deliberately creating a mental audio tape of the key data (i.e., a tape that allows them to hear the data in their mind).

Visual Learners
assimilate information best by seeing it.

Characteristics: Visual learners have a distinct advantage when it comes to recalling data written in textbooks and notes. Their visual recall capabilities are especially useful in courses such as history that often emphasize recalling facts. Because they can "see" the correct spelling of words in their mind, visual learners are usually good spellers. When they proofread, they can catch many of their own misspellings because the word just doesn't "look" right. They also are adept at recalling written telephone numbers, math facts, people's faces, written directions, data in diagrams and graphs, and information in newspaper and TV ads.

Tips for maximizing studying and learning effectiveness: Visual learners should read and reread content in their textbooks and notes. It can be helpful for them to make a conscious association between learning information and using a camera to take a picture. Using this analogy, they can perceive their brain as a digital camera and their eyes as a camera lens. When they press the shutter button, they can imprint a visual image of the information they are studying. Whenever possible, visual learners should use diagrams, illustrations, graphs, charts, and flash cards as study tools.

Tactile Learners
assimilate information best by touching
and manipulating materials.

Characteristics: Tactile learners learn most effectively when they are able to handle concrete objects. They enjoy doing dissections in a biology lab, experiments in a chemistry or physics lab, and classification activities, and they excel when constructing and deconstructing mechanical components and designing and building three-dimensional projects. Whenever possible, they translate abstract information into hands-on materials. For example, they might utilize or build a model of what they are required to learn. They might use a three-dimensional construct of an atom to understand the internal structure and the way in which the nucleus is bound to and interacts with the electrons. A note of caution: making information tangible may not always be feasible or sufficient, especially when children must assimilate large quantities of data in their textbooks and notes. For this reason, tactile learners must also learn to use other learning modalities if they are to be successful in most academic subjects.

Tips for maximizing studying and learning effectiveness: Whenever possible, tactile learners should assimilate information through hands-on manipulation of tangible materials and should translate data into concrete representations.

Kinesthetic Learners
assimilate information best by linking
the data with movement.

Characteristics: Kinesthetic learners excel when activities involve physical movement. They can recall and understand information better when they involve their body in the learning process. They imprint information and directions best through movement. They learn athletic plays by running them, and they learn how to do projects through experimentation and hands-on use of tools. Swinging a golf club, making a layup, or putting top spin on a tennis ball are mastered by repeated practice, become automatic and visceral, and appear to bypass conscious thought. This impression, however, can be misleading. Physical movements such as making a seemingly effortless jump shot or throwing a perfectly executed touchdown pass actually reflects hours of intense practice and repetition. Despite the speed and fluidity of the physical action, the mind of the kinesthetic learner has methodically imprinted vital information about how to perform each movement that the brain deliberately applies when directing her body to perform the associated movements.

Tips for maximizing studying and learning effectiveness: Whenever possible, kinesthetic learners should assimilate information through movement. They should do "walk-throughs" and "run-throughs" to learn techniques, routines, and procedures, and they should incorporate physical movements to master academic content. For example, they might tap out the beat of poem written in iambic pentameter or create a physically based pattern for learning facts in a history or science textbook.

Experiential Learners
assimilate information best by doing.

Characteristics: Experiential learners excel when they are involved in hands-on learning, and as such, they share key characteristics with tactile learners and kinesthetic learners. They enjoy experimenting, and they make it a point to derive insight from their positive and negative experiences. Learning as they proceed, they might characteristically begin to build or assemble something without bothering to look at the instructions. They thrive in physical science, technology, and mechanical engineering classes that involve working in a lab or using a workbench. Whenever possible, they try to make written or spoken information more tangible. Hands-on experiences help them understand, link, and recall concepts and abstractions. Despite their natural proclivity for dealing with the concrete, experiential learners must also develop the capability of using other learning modalities to understand, recall, and apply the contents of textbooks and class lectures.

Tips for maximizing studying and learning effectiveness: Experiential learners should make every effort to assimilate information through experimentation and trial and error. Combining experiential learning with tactile and kinesthetic learning (for example, taking something apart to figure out how the pieces fit together) is consonant with their learning style and can enhance content mastery. Experiential learners are apt to practice a foreign language by intentionally seeking out and speaking with native speakers. They are likely to learn how to play golf or tennis by whacking the ball and figuring out how to get it to do what they want it to do. A note of caution: learning exclusively through direct hands-on experience may not always be feasible or sufficient, and experiential learners must also learn how to use other learning modalities if they are to handle the academic curriculum successfully.

USING MULTIPLE MODALITIES

Fact: *Most successful students are capable of utilizing multiple learning modalities and will select the modality that can help them most effectively master the particular material that they are required to learn.* Despite their personal learning preferences, these children realize that it may be strategic to capitalize on a nondominant modality. For example, an auditory learner may prefer to learn French conjugations by reciting them aloud and incorporating the conjugations in spoken sentences (an auditory process). She may conclude, however, that it's more effective to learn math formulas by putting them on flash cards and repeatedly reciting them aloud while also reading them silently (a procedure that combines both auditory and visual learning). The ability to select the right tool to do a particular job is a classic example of pragmatic thinking. Strategically minded students do what works. They realize that sometimes you need a wrench and sometimes you need a screwdriver or a hammer.

Being able to select the right tool for the job and apply the appropriate skills so that the tool works effectively is a capability that children can acquire. Auditory, tactile, kinesthetic, and experiential learners can deliberately develop their visual skills by training themselves to take visual pictures when they study. They can do so by looking intently at a block of information, closing their eyes, and trying to visualize the data. With sufficient effort and practice, they will begin to "see" a chemical formula or a Spanish irregular conjugation imprinted on the inside of their eyelids. By so doing, these students are, in effect, developing, enhancing, and utilizing their visual memory skills. In the same way, visual learners can intentionally enhance their auditory capabilities. For example, they might imagine that they're "burning" an audio CD as they recite Spanish dialogues aloud. By making a concerted effort to vocalize and hear in their mind their voice as they rhythmically recite the dialogues, they are deliberately developing, enhancing, and utilizing the auditory modality to assimilate the assigned material. So, too, might visual and auditory learners enhance their tactile and experiential learning skills and learning effectiveness by using a skeleton in their biology classroom to help them remember the bones in the hand. In chemistry class, they might manipulate the configuration of an atomic model and in this way better understand and assimilate the physical principles that they are required to master.

The goal is for your child to learn how to capitalize on her natural learning talents. At the same time, you want her to be able to use other methods when it's strategic for her to do so. This ability to utilize multiple learning resources is one of the primary benchmarks of the academically achieving child.

IDENTIFYING YOUR CHILD'S PREFERRED LEARNING MODALITY

Fact: *Children can easily identify their preferred learning modality.* The following inventory is designed to help your child better understand how she prefers to learn. The goal is for her to realize that she can use her innate natural talents to achieve in school at a level that she may never have thought possible. This deliberate application of learning preferences can play a central role in enhancing academic performance and self-confidence.

If your child is in grades three through six, you may need to explain some of the statements on the Learning Modality Inventory. Other statements that are not relevant for younger children should be selectively skipped (for example, statement #1, about taking notes).

The Learning Modality Inventory is likely to be of limited application for children in grades one and two. You may, however, wish to complete age-appropriate sections of the inventory based on your observations of your child's learning modus operandi. Any conclusions reached about the preferred or dominant learning modality or modalities of young children, however, should not be considered definitive.

If your child completes the inventory on her own and you disagree with her response to a particular statement, wait until she has completed the entire assessment procedure before discussing your differing perceptions. Be careful not to communicate disapproval with words, facial expressions, or body language, and do not say to your child that her response to a statement is wrong. Simply say, "Okay. Let me tell you what I've observed. If you don't agree with me, then go with your original response. But keep an open mind."

Setting the stage: *To introduce the Learning Modality Inventory, you might find it advantageous to communicate the following explanation to your child. It's recommended that you read the paragraph first to get a gist of the content and then translate the key points into your own words.* **Explanation:** "All students have natural learning preferences that can help them study more effectively. Some kids prefer to listen because they can understand and remember best when they hear information. Some kids prefer to read information because they can understand and remember best when they see something written on a piece of paper, in a book, on a computer monitor, or on the chalkboard. Others prefer to touch what they are learning, and others would prefer to learn through movement. In basketball they would rather run through and practice a play than look at a diagram of the play. This inventory will help you better understand how you prefer to learn and how you learn best. Take a few minutes to complete it. I'll be in the next room if you have questions." (Please note: A reproducible copy of this inventory can be found on pages 261–262 in the appendix.)

LEARNING MODALITY INVENTORY

	Yes	No	Not Sure
1. I learn best by reading information in textbooks, textbook notes, and lecture notes.	___	___	___
2. I can recall and understand information best when I can look at it.	___	___	___
3. Seeing a science experiment or a class demonstration helps me understand and learn the information.	___	___	___
4. I can remember information better when it's in diagrams, graphs, charts, and pictures.	___	___	___
5. When I can see information, it increases my interest, motivation, and involvement in what I am learning.	___	___	___
6. I learn best by listening to lectures, audio tapes, and spoken explanations.	___	___	___
7. I can understand and remember information better when I hear it.	___	___	___

	Yes	No	Not Sure

8. Class discussions help me understand and learn what's being taught. — — —

9. I can remember jokes and the words in songs when I hear them. — — —

10. Hearing information that I'm expected to learn stimulates my interest, motivation, and active involvement. — — —

11. I learn best when activities are physical. — — —

12. I can recall and understand information better when I can move things around. — — —

13. Doing experiments, drawing pictures, plotting graphs, making diagrams, or building models helps me understand what's being taught. — — —

14. I can usually learn the steps to a dance or athletic plays by practicing them once. — — —

15. Physical activities stimulate my interest, motivation, and involvement in what I am learning. — — —

16. I learn best when I am touching, holding, or manipulating what I need to learn. — — —

17. I can put something together without instructions. — — —

18. I can understand and recall how things work by handling them. — — —

19. I enjoy mechanical projects, and I can disassemble and reassemble objects with little difficulty. — — —

20. Hands-on activities stimulate my interest, motivation, and active involvement in what I am learning. — — —

21. I like to learn by figuring out how to do something on my own. — — —

22. I enjoy learning through trial and error. — — —

23. I don't like to follow written or verbal instructions. — — —

	Yes	No	Not Sure

24. If I make a mistake, I learn from it and
    make adjustments so I can get it right
    the next time.   ___ ___ ___

25. I like to work independently.   ___ ___ ___

Interpreting the Survey

Statements 1–5:   These statements relate to visual learning. If your child
                   has responded primarily "Yes," his/her learning prefer-
                   ence is probably visual.

Statements 6–10:   These statements relate to auditory learning. If your
                   child has responded primarily "Yes," his/her learning
                   preference is probably auditory.

Statements 11–15: These statements relate to kinesthetic learning. If your
                   child has responded primarily "Yes," his/her learning
                   preference is probably kinesthetic.

Statements 16–20: These statements relate to tactile learning. If your child
                   has responded primarily "Yes," his/her learning prefer-
                   ence is probably tactile.

Statements 21–25: These statements relate to experiential learning. If your
                   child has responded primarily "Yes," his/her learning
                   preference is probably experiential.

Please note: This inventory may reveal that your child possesses more than one preferred learning modality. This can be a distinct asset in much the same way that being a switch-hitter in baseball can be an asset. Your child possesses multiple learning resources and learning options.

After your child has completed the inventory and you've discussed how to interpret her responses, it would be beneficial to read the brief descriptions of the different types of learning modalities (see pages 34–37).* Read the descriptions slowly and encourage a discussion. The more involved your child is in the discussion, the more impact it will

---

*The olfactory/gustatory modality is not addressed in this book, as this modality has highly specialized vocational applications (e.g., culinary arts, wine tasting, perfume or flavor development, etc.)

have on her. Encourage your child to react. Ideally, you want to elicit an "I'm just like that!" response. Provide concrete examples of tactile and kinesthetic learning (i.e., touching and manipulating the pieces of a puzzle or dribbling a basketball during a lay-up). Then ask your child the following questions (You may prefer to have your child write the answers to the questions or you may prefer to pose the questions orally. If you do decide to have your child write out the answers before discussing them, you can find a reproducible form that she can use on page 262 in the appendix.)

USING PREFERRED LEARNING MODALITIES

- Do you agree with what the inventory indicates about your preferred (or most natural) learning modality?
- Five primary learning modalities are described: *auditory, visual, tactile, experiential,* and *kinesthetic.* List these modalities in the order of your personal preference. Begin with your most preferred.

_____

_____

_____

_____

If you needed to study material that might require combining learning modalities, what would be your *preferred combination*? (Younger children may have difficulty handling this question. You will need to give concrete examples of how more than one modality might work in tandem.)

- visual/auditory
- visual/tactile
- visual/kinesthetic
- visual/experiential
- auditory/tactile

- auditory/kinesthetic
- auditory/experiential
- tactile/kinesthetic
- tactile/experiential
- kinesthetic/experiential

To confirm the accuracy of the inventory, observe your child's learning style. If she tends to reach out to manipulate or touch objects when learning something, it would be reasonable to conclude that she's probably a *tactile learner*. If she seems most comfortable learning through physical movement, it would be reasonable to conclude that she's probably a *kinesthetic learner*. If she prefers to study diagrams or drawings, prefers to read information in order to understand it, and likes to make up flash cards when learning facts, it would be reasonable to conclude that she's probably a *visual learner*. If she's inclined to listen intently to what is being said and to repeat what she hears, it would be reasonable to conclude that she's probably an *auditory learner*.

Another important clue in identifying learning preferences is your child's choice of vocabulary. If she tends to say "I *see* what you mean," she is more likely to be a visual learner. If she tends to say "I *hear* you," she is more likely to be an auditory learner. If she tends to say "That *feels* right," she is more likely to be a tactile learner.

Learning preferences are powerful assets when channeled and harnessed. An important key to improving your child's learning efficacy is to help her recognize her strengths and to encourage her to deliberately use these strengths as a counterweight to any academic deficiencies that are impeding her progress in school.*

ADJUSTING TO THE TEACHER'S TEACHING STYLE

Fact: *Many teachers emphasize their own preferred or dominant learning preferences when they teach.* Just as students have different preferred learn-

---

*The material describing learning preferences and learning modalities is modified from Lawrence J. Greene, *Study Wise* (New York: Pearson/Prentice Hall, 2003). Reprinted with permission.

ing modalities, so, too, do teachers have their own preferred teaching modalities. Most teachers teach the way that they themselves learn best. Some lecture and want their students to take notes. To get good grades, students are expected to study these notes and diligently assimilate the written data (emphasis: *auditory input/visual learning*). Some teachers write extensive information on the chalkboard and prepare comprehensive handouts and lecture notes for students to study (emphasis: *visual input/visual learning*). Some utilize class discussions and small cooperative learning groups (emphasis: *auditory input/auditory learning*). Some do daily demonstrations and experiments (emphasis: *visual input/visual learning*). Others structure repeated opportunities for hands-on learning (emphasis: *concrete input/experiential, tactile, and/or kinesthetic learning*).

If you conclude that your child's teacher is primarily visually oriented (i.e., wants students to assimilate information found in textbooks, handouts, graphs, and diagrams), you want to help your child adjust to the teacher's teaching preference. This can be particularly challenging if your child is primarily an auditory, tactile, kinesthetic, or experiential learner. You want to encourage your child to capitalize on her preferred learning modality (for example, reciting information aloud), but at the same time you want to encourage her to develop a functional strategy for learning content that requires visual learning (for example, chemical symbols). To do so, your child must be taught how to improve her visual memory skills, even though the visual may not be her preferred learning modality (see strategies for developing visual memory skills, pages 34–35). Successful students are pragmatists. They accommodate themselves to the realities of the situation, and they do what they need to do to win the game.

It would be unrealistic to expect resistant learners to abandon their defense mechanisms and phobic associations with learning and studying until they become convinced that they can succeed academically. The more your child understands about her own distinctive "learning fingerprint," the more likely she will develop self-confidence, acquire motivation, and generate effort. As your child begins to capitalize on her own intelligence type and preferred learning style, and as she experiences the rewards that accrue from deliberately using her natural talents, she's likely to become less resistant to learning. You want to communicate clearly and unequivocally a core message: *Successful students who think strategically deliberately use the gifts with which they have been blessed to make the job of learning and studying easier and more productive.*

STEPS FOR MAXIMIZING LEARNING

- Help your child identify the specific information she must learn to get a good grade in each course and help her create a practical strategy for learning this information.
- Help your child identify her aptitude and distinctive intelligence and encourage her to capitalize on her natural abilities.
- Help your child identify her preferred learning modality and encourage her to apply her preferences when studying.
- Help your child identify material that might best be learned using a nonpreferred modality (e.g., the visual modality for memorizing formulas).
- Encourage your child to develop learning skills in nonpreferred modalities that can be "put in the vault" and withdrawn when needed.
- Encourage your child to compensate for her learning deficits by capitalizing on her learning strengths.
- Help your child make tactical adjustments in her study procedures if it is clear that her current procedures aren't producing positive payoffs.

Rest assured that all of these vital issues will be addressed in subsequent chapters.

3

Drowning in Chaos

After another heated argument, Lucas grudgingly went to his room to start his homework. As usual, he had put it off until the last possible minute, partially from habit and partially because he found homework so distasteful.

Lucas sighed as he sat down at his desk and turned on his desk lamp. He realized that he couldn't delay the inevitable any longer. After years of battling with his dad about doing his homework, he could tell from his father's scowl and from the bulging veins on his temples that he had reached the boiling point. Further noncompliance would push his father over the edge and would result in him being grounded for the weekend. That would be even more intolerable than having to do his homework.

Shoving the papers, candy wrappers, and empty soft drink cans to one side, the twelve-year-old put his book bag on his desk and reached inside for his social studies textbook. He always knew which one it was without even looking. It was the biggest and the heaviest book in the bag.

As Lucas pulled out his bulging binder, a mass of wrinkled papers fell onto the floor. Lucas smirked. For the umpteenth time, he had forgotten to snap the binder rings closed. Getting down on his knees, he scooped up the tangle of creased papers, dropped them in a heap on top of his backpack, and began shuffling through the pile. He was certain that somewhere in the heap was the piece of paper on which he had scribbled his social studies assignment. After fifteen minutes of searching, he finally found the assignment scrawled on a page of doodles. Lucas had forgotten all about the artwork that he had drawn during English class, and he spent the next several minutes scrutinizing his masterpieces. "Not bad," he concluded with pride. Now if he could only find where he had scribbled his math, English, and science assignments, he would be set.

Lucas took a bite of the half-eaten bagel with cream cheese he found at the bottom of his book bag. Not being sure how long the bagel had been there, he decided to eat around the tiny green spots. He wasn't certain if these were chives or something nasty. "A little hard," he thought, "but still okay." When he had eaten what he thought were the edible parts, Lucas attempted to toss the remainder in the basket that was near the door. He missed, and the bagel landed on the floor about six inches from the lip of the basket. "Air ball. Too bad. No points," he muttered to himself. Leaving the bagel where it fell, the sixth grader turned his attention to rummaging through the desk drawers for a piece of notebook paper and a pen. By this point, he had been "working" on his homework for twenty minutes. Feeling exhausted, he was ready for a break. The fudge brownie ice cream in the freezer had his name on it and was beckoning him. It just wouldn't be fair to disappoint a bowl of ice cream that's calling out to you.*

THE PRICE OF CHRONIC DISORGANIZATION

Fact: *Organization is an essential element in the academic achievement equation.* Students who possess good organizational skills invariably study more effectively than those who spend their time searching for the materials they need to do their work. These children have assimilated a core fact of life that chronically disorganized children either don't recognize or are intent on denying: Achievement, productivity, and organization are joined at the hip.

Well-organized students manifest a predictable pattern of behavior. They know where things are. They plan ahead. They have a system for recording their assignments, and they use the system consistently. If

---

*Case study from Lawrence J. Greene, *Winning the Study Game* (Minnetonka, Minn.: Peytral Publications, 2002). Reprinted with permission.

they don't have a written study schedule, they have at the minimum a mental to-do list that allows them to sequence and complete their daily homework responsibilities. At the end of the school day, they make sure they take home their assignment sheet, textbooks, and binder. When they sit down to do their homework, they have pens, pencils, paper, ruler, and dictionary to do their complete assignments. Their schoolbooks are accessible. They've signed off from the Internet, turned off the TV, and have quit any X-Box games they may have been playing. Their study area is orderly, and they can find what they need to do their homework. Their binder is organized and divided into subject areas. Their class notes, textbook notes, previously graded tests, homework assignments, handouts, essays, and reports from each course are inserted in the corresponding and clearly labeled subject areas and are readily accessible. These ingrained organizational habits facilitate enhanced learning efficiency and productivity.

It's obvious that Lucas resides at the opposite end of the organization, self-discipline, efficiency, and productivity spectrum. Seeming to delight in the chaos with which he surrounds himself, the twelve-year-old is quite willful about being disorganized, and his "I couldn't care less" attitudes and behavior make a clear and compelling statement about his disdain for academic responsibility and achievement.

The consequences of Lucas's flippancy and indifference are clearly foreseeable and include inferior work, incomplete assignments, missed deadlines, ineffectual studying, and poor grades. That he will pay a price for his maladaptive behavior is a foregone conclusion. Lucas is fated to ricochet from crisis to crisis as he proceeds through school, and unless there's a major shift in the sixth grader's attitude and behavior, his irresponsibility, disorganization, disinterest, and shoddy work habits will prove to be his academic undoing. Down the road, these same qualities could also prove to be his vocational undoing.

Fact: *Resistant learners, and particularly those with ADHD (attention deficit hyperactivity disorder), are often disorganized, and this counterproductive behavior compounds their academic difficulties.* As is the case with successful students, chronically disorganized children such as Lucas also manifest predictable patterns of conduct. In their case, however, the conduct is irresponsible and self-sabotaging. They characteristically "forget" to bring home required textbooks and important papers. Their desk is invariably a mess, and their room is a disaster area. Papers, books, game cubes, DVDs, and dirty clothes are strewn everywhere. The floor is often littered with discarded candy wrappers, soft drink cans, and snacks that are now spoiled and moldy. Every corner is cluttered with haphazardly stacked possessions. Their backpack more often than not functions as a convenient trash bag. Their binder is in disarray, and they have no idea where to find the essential materials they need to do their work. School papers are creased, ripped, and stained, and previously graded assignments and tests are missing or misplaced. If by some miracle they actually have an assignment sheet, the information on it is usually incomplete, inaccurate, and illegible, and their homework is typically sloppy, substandard, and submitted late, assuming, of course, that they even bother to complete and hand in their assignments.

If you have a child at home who is drowning in clutter, you know the routine by heart. Your child probably spends more time looking for things than he does actually doing his work. "I can't find my math assignment!" is the standard plaintive cry. The repercussions from the chronic disorder include not only poor grades, but also infuriating stress for everyone in the family who is directly and indirectly affected by the chaos.

In all probability, you've discovered that lectures, sermons, and admonitions about the value of organization are a waste of time. So, too, are nagging and punishment likely to prove ineffectual. Children who have the greatest need to alter their self-defeating behavior are generally the most resistant to doing so. Associating parental advice with nagging, they react by tuning out the sermons and insisting on doing it "their way." Unfortunately, their way is a recipe for disaster, and every day they dig the hole they're in a bit deeper.

No one needs to remind you about the downside of chronic disorganization. You're undoubtedly acutely aware that patterns of disorder established in childhood are likely to become hard-to-break habits that persist throughout life. You're also aware that the vocational marketplace where your child must ultimately sell his skills can be harsh to those with chronically poor work habits. This marketplace may make occasional exceptions for the brilliant disorganized physicist or the quirky disorganized computer software developer, but unless your child possesses extraordinary talents, his disorganization is likely to erect major impediments not only to his career advancement, but also to his simply being able to get and keep a job.

As you witness the repercussions from your child's poor organization, inefficiency, and ineffectual wheel spinning, your basic instinct is most likely to step in and fix the problem. If you're like most parents, you probably feel like yelling, "Don't you get it? Don't you see that this chaos is sabotaging you in school?" After repeated failed attempts to reorient your child's behavior, you may have concluded that your efforts are little more than an exercise in futility. Frustrated and repeatedly rebuffed, you may have reluctantly resigned yourself to the fact that your child will forever remain a slob. Well, teaching your child how to be more organized is, in fact, eminently doable, assuming you have patience, are willing to persevere, and are committed to applying a practical and functional behavior modification strategy.

In many respects, altering a child's maladaptive behavior is akin to breaking in a new baseball glove. The glove must be oiled, kneaded, and shaped until it fits right, feels comfortable, and becomes pliant and fully functional. Fortunately, children are, in some respects, like baseball gloves. They, too, are malleable. They're designed by the "manufacturer" to be molded, and with deliberate, methodically conditioning, they will become more pliant and more functional.

COGNITIVE BEHAVIORAL CHANGE

Fact: *Modifying children's counterproductive behavior is an ongoing instructional process that must be carried out patiently, systematically, and consistently.* Most parents of a chronically disorganized child can "do the math." They realize that their child's maladaptive behavior is playing a major role in his substandard academic performance. They can plainly see that precious time that should rightfully be devoted to studying is being wasted looking for things. These parents are also cognizant of the fact that the daily searching ritual is a primary source of stress for the entire family.

With focused and systematic instruction, your child can be taught how to create a practical system for establishing more order in his life, and with sufficient practice, he can integrate this system into his everyday procedures. The first step in the instructional process is for you to help your child acquire insight into his own behavior. The second step is for you to provide him with tangible, specific, and easy-to-apply procedures for creating an organized study environment. The final step is for you to engineer repeated opportunities for your child to practice the organizational procedures until he fully masters and assimilates them and until the procedures become automatic.

The instructional methods utilized in this book are based upon an instructional model called *cognitive behavioral change* (also commonly referred to as *cognitive behavior modification*). The methodology incorporates seven fundamental teaching principles:

- *Relevancy*—You systematically teach your child pragmatic skills that directly relate to the challenges and problems that he confronts every day.
- *Insight*—You help your child understand the underlying issues and guide him to the realization that the skills being taught can make school and life easier, more productive, and more rewarding.
- *Instruction*—You present the methods and skills methodically and sequentially so that your child can comprehend and assimilate them.
- *Reinforcement*—You provide your child with repeated opportunities to practice.
- *Feedback*—You continually assess your child's progress and advise, critique, and affirm your child's efforts and improvement.
- *Behavior Modification*—You orchestrate repeated opportunities for success and effusively acknowledge and praise positive changes and productive behavior.
- *Application*—You make certain that your child consistently uses the skills that have been taught until they become automatic.

The term *cognitive behavioral change* may sound terribly erudite and off-putting, but the teaching methods actually parallel the way human beings master any new skill (for example, learning to put topspin on a tennis ball or do research on the Internet). The academic-sounding semantics can be translated into everyday language and distilled into a sequence of simple, practical, down-to-earth, and easy-to-apply procedures:

- You help your child define what he wants or needs to do (i.e., setting goals).
- You teach your child how to break objectives down into smaller and more manageable parts (i.e., applying divide-and-conquer principles), and you help him figure out how to develop the necessary skills to attain his objectives (i.e., applying strategic thinking).
- You teach your child how to identify and sidestep potential land mines (i.e., applying analytical and critical thinking).
- You help your child develop step-by-step techniques or progressing from point A to point B to point C (i.e., applying tactical thinking).
- You have your child practice and use the newly learned skills until they become second nature (i.e., achieving mastery and assimilation).
- You provide effusive affirmation for progress and achievement (i.e., furnishing extrinsic reinforcement).
- You encourage your child to derive pleasure and pride from his accomplishments (i.e., promoting intrinsic reinforcement).

You've undoubtedly applied these procedures countless times without necessarily realizing it. If you've ever taught your child how to water-ski, play chess, hit and catch a baseball, swim, bake a cake, or build a birdhouse, you've utilized the principles of cognitive behavioral change. The effectiveness of your instruction directly reflects your success in applying the basic cognitive behavioral change procedures.

By providing clear organizational guidelines, by helping your child develop a personalized organizational system, and by demonstrating that improved organization can save time, enhance performance, and free up time for pleasurable pursuits, you can fundamentally alter your child's mind-set. Once he begins to experience the benefits of organization, he'll be far more likely to become a "convert" than if you subject him to a diet of daily lectures, sermons, or diatribes. Certainly, your child will require supervision and reminding during the transition from disorder to order, but when he realizes that organization is actually an ally and that your efforts to teach him organizational skills are not a sinister plot designed to make his life miserable, he'll be less resistant to altering his behavior. Your goal is to engineer this realization.

The starting point in the cognitive behavioral change procedure is to teach your child practical hands-on techniques for organizing his binder, study area, and room. You must actively involve him in cleaning up the mess, praise his progress, and elicit his cooperation.

You may be thinking, "easier said than done." Well, let's see how to make it happen.

A PROCEDURAL BLUEPRINT

Fact: All children can learn and assimilate enhanced organizational skills if properly taught. You're about to examine two different approaches for altering your child's maladaptive attitudes and behavior. The first approach is autocratic. The second is more democratic and incorporates a "let's analyze this problem together and come up with a solution" methodology. You will have to decide which approach feels right and fits for you and your child. You must factor into your choice not only your own temperament, personality, and preferred modus operandi, but also the distinctive personality characteristics of your child. If his style is to dig his heels in and resist at all costs any attempt to reason with him, then the autocratic approach may prove most effective. As you will see, autocratic does not translate into an "I will tolerate no discussion" dictatorial imposition of your will, nor does it translate into ominous threats of punishment. Rather, the style parallels that used in a benevolent monarchy. Your goal is to communicate clearly and unequivocally that certain counterproductive behaviors must be changed. You want your child to conclude, "This is the way my parents want it to be, and I can tell that they really mean business." You don't need to be harsh, but you do need to be firm and communicate explicitly that you're absolutely committed to his making key behavioral changes. Your role is akin to that of a wise and caring sovereign who refuses to brook any nonsense. Your child must be guided to the unambiguous conclusion that when it comes to his becoming better organized, you expect him to be an obedient "subject." You must also unequivocally communicate that you fully expect him to implement the procedures that you're teaching him.

You'll also discover that the democratic approach as modeled in this book does not translate to "I'm your pal, and let's have fun playing with this disorganization problem." Certainly, this collegial approach can work with some children, but it's generally ineffectual with resistant and emotionally defended children. For the democratic method to work, you must assume the role of guide and mentor. You must express your concerns and underscore the necessity for making positive behavior and attitude changes. You must be empathetic and affirming, but at the same time firm and clear about the intended objective. Implementing the democratic approach can be tricky until you get the hang of it. As you become more adept and comfortable with the techniques, the modeled problem-solving procedure will be easier to use and will become automatic for both you and your child.

A second option is to experiment using each approach with a different issue and then select the methodology that works best and feels the most natural and comfortable. A third option is to borrow portions of each method and synthesize your own individualized approach. In some situations, you may feel the autocratic procedure is more appropriate, and in other situations, you may conclude that the democratic or synthesized approach is more appropriate. This is roughly the equivalent of using a menu in a restaurant to customize your meal and choosing one dish from column A, one from column B, and one from column C.

The words used in the following dialogues are not sacred, and please do not attempt to memorize them! The dialogues are intended only as a model. Change the words if they don't feel right, and use language that fits your personality and communication style when you're feeling calm and poised. What counts is not the specific words, but, rather, the content, formatting, intonation, and style of your communication. Additional pitfalls to avoid include:

- **Don't fall into the trap of continually lecturing or admonishing your child.**
- **Don't come across as being highly critical. (You probably already have ample evidence that expressing continual disapproval is ineffectual and usually counterproductive.)**
- **Don't lapse into delivering repetitive sermons about the benefits of organization.**

Your goal is to have a frank, nonemotionally charged interchange with your child about an important issue and to model a process for dealing with the problem. Being condescending and judgmental and wittingly or unwittingly expressing exasperation and disapproval will destroy any chance of producing meaningful behavioral changes. Despite any previous negative history in dealing with your child's counterproductive conduct, you must deliberately disregard these past experiences and communicate positive expectations. The attitude you want to convey is: "You're about to turn to a new page and become more organized, and I'm absolutely convinced that the methods you're going to learn will allow you to make important changes." The alternative is to communicate with words or facial expressions, "I'm going to teach you these new procedures, but I know it will be a waste of time because you'll refuse to learn them." This attitude is guaranteed to result in failure.

Please note that when you present the following organizational procedures, you should use the *first person singular* to describe your own feelings and issues (e.g., "*I* have a problem with the clutter in your study area, and *I* get upset when *I* see you continually searching for things." Avoid statements such as, "*You* make me mad when *you* insist on surrounding yourself with clutter, and *you* are causing stress for the entire family.") You should also consistently use the *second person singular* when referring to your child's behavior, problems, and issues, especially if you're using the more autocratic approach (e.g., "*You* are about to turn a new page.") **It's very important that you not use the first person plural** (e.g., "*We* are about to turn a new page.") This deliberate pronoun usage clearly communicates to your child that **you** own your upset and that **he** owns the disorganization problem and that it is **he** who will be turning the new page. This is a vital distinction. You don't want to give your child the impression that you share ownership of *his* problem. Parents who make statements such as "*We* have a disorganization problem" are signaling that they've acquiesced to an unhealthy codependency. What parents actually "own" is their justifiable frustration and upset about being at the mercy of their child's disorganization. For this reason, you must explicitly communicate that *he*—and not you—is the one who must fix *his* disorganization problem.

IMPROVING ORGANIZATION
The Autocratic Approach

> ### Guidelines
>
> - Create a conducive context for interaction.
> - Check out your child's perceptions (see checklist).
> - Define the problem.
> - Examine the evidence.
> - Provide functional organizational procedures.
> - Supervise implementation of behavioral changes.
> - Affirm your child for effort and progress.

Let's see how the autocratic approach works.

Scenario: You ask your child to come into the kitchen or the dining room. You are calm. Any siblings in the area should be instructed to leave. You ask your child to sit in a chair facing you so that you can establish and maintain eye contact. Your tone of voice is friendly and nonthreatening, but, at the same time, firm and decisive.

You: "I have a problem. Let me tell what my problem is. I don't like being a police officer at home. I don't like nagging you about homework. I don't like arguing with you or punishing you. Before I examine my problem and find a solution, I want you to take a few minutes to complete this checklist. Be honest and don't try to say what you think I want to hear. Here's the checklist. I'll leave the

room while you complete it. Tell me when you're done." (A reproducible copy of this checklist can be found on page 264 in the appendix. By photocopying this form in advance, your child will not see
that the checklist comes from a book you are reading. As previously
stated, this could be a turn-off for some highly resistant children.)

If your child has significant reading problems, you'll need to sit next
to him and help him read the checklist statements. Depending on your
child's age and the extent of his reading difficulties, you may need to
patiently explain how to use the code. If you do help your child, do not
express verbally or with facial expressions any reaction—positive or
negative—as he responds to the statements. Once he completes the
checklist, you will have an opportunity to examine his responses to the
statements.

ORGANIZATION CHECKLIST

Code: 1 = Never 2 = Rarely 3 = Sometimes 4 = Often 5 = Always

My study area is neat and uncluttered. ＿＿

My room is neat and uncluttered. ＿＿

I make certain that I bring home the books and materials
　I need to do my homework. ＿＿

I have all the materials that I need to complete my homework
　(pen, paper, dictionary, etc.) on, in, or near my desk. ＿＿

I have a system for filing previous tests, homework
　assignments, book reports, etc. ＿＿

I have labeled dividers in my binder for each subject. ＿＿

I insert all returned papers in my binder in the correct
　subject section. ＿＿

I keep my assignment sheet in my binder. ＿＿

I make certain before I go to sleep that I have put all
　the materials I will need for school (completed
　homework, textbooks, etc.) in my book bag. ＿＿

I neatly place my books and other materials in my
　backpack so that I can find what I need when I get to
　school and when I return home after school. ＿＿

Scenario: After allowing your child sufficient time to complete the checklist, you should return to the kitchen or dining room. You pull up a chair and ask your child sit next to you.

You: "Let's take a look at your responses to the statements on the checklist. Before beginning, I want to say that you are entitled to your opinions, and I am entitled to mine. If there are differences, we need to discuss them calmly. OK. You indicate that your study area is *sometimes* neat and uncluttered. My impression is very different. In fact, let's go into your room and check out your study area. We'll take the completed checklist with us."

Scenario: You are now in your child's room.

You: "What I am seeing is a lot of papers crumpled on your desk. I see two empty cans of soda. I see half a chocolate chip cookie, three candy wrappers, a comic book, two game disks, and four DVDs scattered on top of your desk. I see your school books on the floor. I see an overflowing trash basket, and I see two skate-boarding magazines on the floor near your desk. I see underpants and a shirt draped over the back of the chair that you use to study. In my opinion, this is the way your study area always looks. If I filled out the checklist, I would have to mark a 5 after this statement. Do you think it would be unreasonable for me to give you a 5? And, if so, tell me why."

Allow your child to express his feelings, even if his position contradicts what you have both just observed, but to avoid an argument or showdown, refer back to the tangible evidence when you respond.

You would then go through the entire checklist while being careful not to be demeaning. Examine the observable facts. Make it clear that you don't want to argue, but that you just want to observe and compare responses based upon the evidence. When you've completed this procedure (it should take no more than ten minutes), it's time to proceed to the next step.

Scenario: You're at the kitchen or dining room table. Your child is sitting next to you. You've asked him to get his binder and backpack, and they are on the table.

You: "Okay. As I said at the beginning of this discussion, I have a problem with having to be a police officer at home. And it's clear to me that you also have a problem. Your problem involves disorganization. There's no need for us to argue about this. The evidence is in your room, in your binder, on your desk, and in your backpack. Now if you reject this evidence and refuse to see that you have a problem with organization, things get more complicated. If you do reject my conclusions about your being disorganized, then you're simply going to have to trust me that you do, in fact, have a problem. You're going to have to bow to my wishes that you solve this problem before you completely torpedo yourself in school."

Allow your child to respond, but make it clear—without expressing frustration or anger—that he will have to address and solve the organization problem whether or not he concurs with your conclusions. No arguments.

You: "You aren't going to solve the entire organization problem now. You're going to break the problem down into manageable pieces. You'll start tonight with the first piece—organizing your binder. Your binder has to be organized so that you can find what you need to do your schoolwork. If you look inside this bag, you'll see that I've bought dividers, tabs, labels, hole reinforcements, and plastic sleeves. Step one is for you to insert your assignment sheet at the front of your binder. If you don't have an assignment sheet that's organized into subjects, you'll take care of that down the road. For now, take a sheet of blank paper, write *Assignment Sheet* at the top, and insert it. This is where you'll write your assignments until you create a formal assignment sheet [see chapter 4]. I want you to print legibly and clearly on the label inserts the names of the courses you're taking. Why don't you start with English? When you're done, I want you to insert a course label into the tab on each divider. Good. Now I want you to go through your binder and separate your papers according to subjects. Once you've sorted out the papers, you'll place them in the appropriate section of your binder. Order them according to the dates at the top of each page. You'll want to put reinforcements on the important papers that you can't afford to lose. When you're finished, we will go up to your room, and you'll sort through the papers on your desk."

You're now in your child's room and you've cleared off a workspace on his desk, the floor, or his bed.

You: Let me show you how to get started. Put all of your English assignments and tests in one pile, and all of your social studies papers in another pile. Now separate each pile into graded tests and graded homework assignments. Using the dates at the top of each paper, put each paper in the proper chronological order. You'll follow the same procedure with your math papers, science papers, and Spanish papers. These will go into separate piles that will be organized. Once you've finished, you can place the papers you should take to school into the corresponding folders that you insert in the appropriate sections of your binder. You'll place the papers that you don't need to take to school in course folders that you will leave at home. You'll then put course labels on these files and place the papers inside. You'll put these folders in alphabetical order inside this desk drawer. This is where they will remain when not in use, and you'll always know where to find them." (You may want to put a hanging file system in the drawer if it will accommodate one.) "Good. You're done for today. I'm pleased with what you've accomplished and with your effort. Tomorrow, you'll tackle the task of organizing your desk."

Please note: these interactive sessions should be relatively short and last from twenty-five to thirty minutes. The duration should be geared to your child's developmental maturity and attention span. Overkill will make the interaction intolerable and will trigger unnecessary resistance and resentment. If your child cannot complete this first phase in a twenty-five minute session, have him finish tomorrow.

HANDLING FALLOUT

- **Your child communicates verbally or nonverbally that he resents your "meddling."** *Response:* Acknowledge the negative reaction and clarify your prerogatives. ("I can tell that you're unhappy with my getting involved in this problem. It's my responsibility to help you get on track. To do so, you must make changes in the way you do things, or your grades will suffer. I can't allow this to happen. I have a responsibility to make certain that you do the best you can do in school.")

- **Your child actively or passively resists using the organizational procedures.** *Response:* Point out your child's resistance and communicate unequivocally that this behavior is unacceptable. ("I can see that you're resistant to acknowledging or fixing the organization problem, and this distresses me. Nonetheless, I insist that you use the procedures you've learned. By improving your organization, you can improve your grades, reduce the stress at home, and make both of our lives easier. How you do in school is not only your business, but it's also my business.")

- **Your child is applying the organizational procedures inconsistently.** *Response:* Communicate your observations about your child's inconsistency and ratchet up your supervision. ("I am determined that you consistently apply the organizational methods you've learned. I want these techniques to become an automatic habit. To ensure that you get into this habit, I'm going to have to supervise you more closely. Once it's apparent that you're consistently using the methods, I'll begin to back off. (If you subsequently observe a slack-off or a return to the old maladaptive habits, simply say, "I can see that you're getting careless about using the organization methods that you've learned. This is unacceptable. I want you to place these papers in the appropriate section of your binder, and I want you to keep your study area neat and organized. It's clear that I'm going to have to monitor you again more closely until I'm convinced that you're using the organizational methods consistently.")

IMPROVING ORGANIZATION

The Democratic Approach

Guidelines

- Create a context conducive to interaction.
- Check out your child's perceptions (see checklist).
- Model problem-solving procedure (DIBS).
- Have child apply the procedure (DIBS).
- Furnish practical organizational methods.
- Supervise implementation.
- Affirm your child for effort and progress.

Scenario: *The first two steps of this method are the same as those used in the modeled autocratic approach.* Your child has now completed the checklist. You've both gone to his room with the completed checklist to do a visual inspection. You've reviewed his responses on the checklist, compared the evidence of disorganization in his room, and expressed your observations. You're now sitting at the kitchen or dining room table. Your child is sitting next to you. (*Please note:* The democratic approach lends itself to your using both the first person singular [*I*] *and* the first person plural [*we*] when discussing methods for dealing with problems.)

You: "I told you that I have a problem that I want to solve. I want to solve my problem with you observing the procedure that I use. I'm going to apply a powerful problem-solving method called **DIBS**. The word DIBS is an acronym made from the first letter of the four steps in this problem-solving system. Let's write the four steps on a piece of paper. If we list the letters that make up the acronym vertically, it will look like this:"

(You'll find a reproducible DIBS form on page 265 in the appendix. It's recommended that you have several photocopies of the form available.)

DIBS

Define the Problem: _____

Investigate the Causes of the Problem: _____

_____

_____

_____

Brainstorm Solutions to the Problem: _____

_____

_____

_____

Select a Solution to Try Out: _____

You: "You can see how the acronym is formed. Since I'm familiar with DIBS, I'll use it to solve my problem. You can follow along. I'll start by defining the problem. I actually already did this when we first started talking, but now I'll write it down."

> **D**efine: I* don't want to be a police officer at home, and I don't want to have to continually nag, threaten, and punish you.

---

*As previously stated, when applying DIBS, use "I" statements as opposed to "you" statements (e.g., "*I* get upset and angry when you're disorganized" versus "*You* drive me crazy and make me angry when you're disorganized." This less-accusatory communication style can significantly reduce resistance.)

You: "Now I'm going to investigate the causes of my problem."

Investigate: I get upset when I go into your room and see the mess.

I'm convinced that your disorganization is having a negative effect on the quality of your school-work.

I'm experiencing a great deal of stress because I'm convinced that you're torpedoing yourself in school.

Brainstorm: I could accept your disorganization.

I could avoid entering your room.

I could let you sink or swim on your own in school.

I could help you become more organized.

Solution: I could help you become more organized.

"I hope that you can see that the first three brainstormed solutions are either impractical or unacceptable for the following reasons:

- I wouldn't be meeting my responsibility to prepare you for success in life.
- I must go into your room occasionally to dust, get your dirty laundry, and return your laundered clothes.
- I can't allow you to do poorly in school because you are disorganized.

"The only choice that I have is to help you become better organized. I would now like you to use the DIBS method to help you solve your problem. If you're unwilling to admit that you have a problem with organization, that's your choice. Based upon the evidence, I'm convinced that you do indeed have an organization problem. OK. It's time to define the problem accurately. You can use this form to write in the information."

Give your child a second form with the steps of the DIBS procedure (on page 265 in the appendix), and patiently guide him through the four-step process. It's very important that you help your child define the problem accurately and precisely, namely: *I am disorganized.* This first step can be very challenging for children.

In step two, one of the possible causes of the problem that your child lists could be: *I have developed some bad habits.* Make suggestions, but resist the temptation to fill in the blanks for your child. To do so would discourage him from developing his own thinking skills and would dissuade him from becoming actively involved in the problem-solving process. Allow your child to include heartfelt reasons that you might consider off target such as: *I am disorganized because I hate school.* These should be acknowledged, listed, and discussed. (Please note: Your child may still resist acknowledging that he has a problem. In this case, you'll need to assume a more active role in helping him complete the DIBS procedure.)

In step three, permit your child to list brainstormed solutions that you may be convinced are unreasonable or impractical. These should be examined with sensitivity. By means of discussion and suggestions, make sure that he also includes on his brainstorming list words to the effect: *I need to develop a system for getting organized.* Suggest that he select this solution as the first one to try out. Once he makes this selection, discuss specific procedures to achieve the objective. You can make suggestions and provide appropriate guidance. Keep in mind, however, that the objective is for your child to come up with the specific ideas that can solve the problem. These should ideally include: *organize my binder by inserting dividers, label the sections, put my schedule in a plastic sleeve at the front of the binder, organize my papers according to course and dates,* etc. Remember to acknowledge and affirm his insights about how to deal with the problem. You also want to reassure your child that, with practice, using DIBS will become easier and easier. At this juncture, you should say: "I picked up some supplies. Let's see what you can use to get started on this project."

REVIEWING THE STEPS FOR ORGANIZING A BINDER

(A reproducible copy of these steps can be found on page 266 in the appendix.)

#1. Insert your assignment sheet in the front of your binder.

#2. Use dividers for each of your courses.

#3. Label each subject.

#4. Label a section "Completed/Corrected Assignments."

#5. Label a section "Assignments To Turn In."

#6. Label a section "Miscellaneous."

#7. Place all school materials you want to keep (quizzes, tests, reports, course syllabi, reading lists, notes) in the appropriate subject section.

#8. Put dates on all material and insert them in chronological order.

#9. Tape your study schedule on the inside front cover of your notebook. (You'll create a study schedule later.)

#10. Put another copy of your study schedule in a plastic sleeve and insert it in the front of your notebook.

#11. Punch holes in any papers you want to keep that do not have holes. Use reinforcements for important papers so that you don't lose them.

TWO METHODS, ONE OBJECTIVE

Fact: *A parenting strategy that may work with one child may not work with another child.* Adjusting your strategy so that it fits comfortably with your personality and values and meets your child's needs significantly improves the likelihood of your being able to successfully modify your child's counterproductive behavior.

The two procedures and the interactions modeled above are obviously very different stylistically. The autocratic approach makes no attempt to involve your child creatively in the process of developing a solution to his disorganization problem. The procedure represents expedient and forceful crisis intervention. Having observed your child's counterproductive behavior, you recognize that, unless the issues are quickly addressed and resolved, his conduct could become entrenched and is likely to produce ongoing negative repercussions. Given the urgency of the situation, you have every right to assert your parental prerogative to intervene. After being apprised of the irrefutable evidence (i.e., the checklist and the tour of his room), your child will ideally acknowledge the validity of your position. If he doesn't, he'll simply have to accept your conclusions and submit to your guidelines and directives.

The more democratic and participatory approach can achieve the same objective with certain children. As you can see, this procedure can be more challenging to use, but once your child masters DIBS, he will have acquired a powerful problem-solving tool that he'll be able to use throughout life.

Raising a child sometimes lends itself to a democratic approach and sometimes to an autocratic approach. You must autocratically tell your young child to hold your hand and look both ways when crossing a street. You must autocratically tell him when it's time for bed on school nights. On weekends, however, you may be willing to negotiate bedtime more democratically. You may also decide to involve your child democratically in the process of deciding where to go for your summer vacation.

Continual self-sabotaging behavior often demands an autocratic response, especially when children are highly reactive to reasonable suggestions. If you intuitively conclude that this behavior is driven by compelling underlying psychological factors, you should be prepared to consult a mental health professional. This is an important point. Chronically angry, exceedingly resistant, demonstrably maladjusted, and profoundly unhappy children require counseling. These children are unconsciously expressing their internal conflict through their counterproductive and self-sabotaging behavior.

Autocratic parental intervention is obligatory when children are chronically resistant and appear intent on shooting themselves in the foot. Kids may complain bitterly about their parents' rules and guidelines (for example, the dictum that homework must be completed before the TV is turned on), but they respect parents who lay down the law, especially when these laws are fair and appropriate. Children desperately require reasonable boundaries and consistently applied discipline. It may be human nature for children to search for wiggle room when it comes to resisting parental authority, but on key issues such as lying, honesty, hygiene, bedtime, safety, smoking, liquor, drugs, etc., they must realize and accept that deviation from the house rules is simply not an option.

Encouraging children to figure out on their own how to solve problems through a process of trial and error is vital to the development of self-confidence, ingenuity, character, grit, and independence. This notwithstanding, standing by passively and allowing your child to live immersed in chaos and disorder does nothing to stimulate the development of these critically important traits. The disorganization impedes achievement and this, in turn, impedes the development of the very qualities you want your child to develop. After carefully weighing the pros and cons of intervention versus nonintervention, you may conclude that a laissez-faire response is ill-advised and that your proactive intervention is imperative.

APPLYING EFFECTIVE COGNITIVE BEHAVIOR-MODIFICATION PROCEDURES

DOs

- **Assert your prerogative to intervene proactively when you identify a problem that must be addressed.** Examine each roadblock or risk from the perspective of the potential consequences that might result if your child fails to address and resolve the problem expediently. How could you not intervene if you discover that your child is being terrorized or extorted by a bully every day on the way home from school? How could you not intervene if you discover that your child is not submitting his assignments? How could you not intervene if your child is engulfed in clutter that is undermining his performance in school? The urgency, the level of risk, your child's level of maturity, and your child's judgment track record must be factored into each decision about the appropriateness of intervention or nonintervention.
- **Communicate clearly and unequivocally.** To alter your child's counterproductive behavior, you don't need to continually nag, cajole, scream, threaten, or punish (although at times, these responses may be justified). Nor do you have to become embroiled in contin-

ual showdowns and shoot-outs. The alternative is to present clear evidence that a problem exists that must be resolved and to do so in a manner that your child can understand, recognize, and acknowledge. Through your choice of words, your tone, and your facial expressions, let your child know that with your help he is going to fix the presenting problem. Whether you choose the autocratic or democratic approach, your child needs to realize that chronic disorganization is unacceptable. The modeled procedures for dealing with a disorganized notebook can be used to help your child organize his desk, room, closet, and book bag. Cliché or not, practice does make perfect. Practice will help you teach the methods, and practice will help your child learn the methods.

- **Help your child achieve insight.** Explain the rationale for your involvement and/or intervention in terms your child can understand. If your child dismisses your concerns, denies he has a problem, or refuses to acknowledge the logic of your position, so be it. This should not deter you. You must remain focused on the overriding objective—to alter your child's counterproductive behavior.

- **Underscore the relevancy of the process.** Your intervention should address tangible issues and should be motivated by legitimate concerns. Crumpled papers stuffed in a book bag, dirty clothes strewn around the room, discarded food and drinks left on the floor, and incomplete homework assignments on a child's desk can obviously diminish academic performance and justify your proactive intervention.

- **Provide instruction and guidelines that are clear, unequivocal, and easily assimilated.** Apply *divide and conquer* principles, and methodically break procedures down into parts that can mastered. Making generalizations about the need for better organization is far less effective than providing tangible, hands-on procedures for systematically getting organized. Help your child develop specific, concrete methods for dealing with problems and provide guidance, consistency, feedback, support, encouragement, and affirmation for effort and progress.

- **Structure repeated opportunities for practice.** Mastery of any new skill hinges on repeated application. Children who conclude that they can actually do what's being asked of them are far less likely to be resistant.

- **Set up your child to succeed.** Success is a platform for building self-confidence. Achievement generates pride and the desire for more success.
- **Acknowledge and praise success and effort.** Kids crave and thrive on affirmation from their parents. They may feign that they don't care, but this is a defense mechanism, albeit an often very convincing defense mechanism. Provide affirmation whenever you see progress.

DON'Ts

- **Avoid nagging, lecturing, admonishing, and threatening, as these tactics are generally ineffectual in modifying counterproductive behavior.** Children tune out what they don't want to hear. When subjected to what they perceive as tyranny, they typically become either actively or passively resistant. Don't fall into this bottomless pit. Far more effective alternative strategies have been modeled in this chapter.
- **Avoid protracted interactive sessions.** A child's attention span is limited. This is, of course, especially true in the case of children with Attention Deficit Hyperactivity Disorder. Whenever possible, break the instruction down into small components that can be easily assimilated. Don't expect your child to digest the "whole enchilada" in one sitting.
- **Do not communicate negative expectations.** Regardless of your child's past track record, give him the benefit of the doubt. Children can read your facial expressions, tone of voice, and body language. If you communicate negative expectations, refer to past transgression, or say something that's perceived as a putdown (i.e., *"I know you're probably going to disregard what I'm telling you."*), your child is likely to respond by becoming more resistant and resentful.
- **Do not compare siblings.** Asking your son why he can't be more organized like his younger sister is certain to trigger bitterness. It's also certain to negatively affect the relationship your son has with his sister, and the resentment could endure throughout life.

One doesn't need to be clairvoyant to recognize that chronic disorganization diminishes efficiency and productivity and erects major obstacles to achievement. These barriers add to the already considerable challenges that resistant, learning-aversive, and underperforming children face. Teaching your child how to create more order in his environment is a gift that will serve him throughout life.

4

Targeting Goals and Plotting a Trajectory

Darnel was doodling on a sheet of paper when Mr. Petrocelli announced that the mid-term exam was scheduled for the following Wednesday. Looking up, the eleventh grader saw the other students furiously writing down the clues that the history teacher was providing about what would be covered on the exam. Darnel smirked and yawned loudly, and this caught his teacher's attention. "Am I boring you, Darnel?" Mr. Petrocelli asked sarcastically. Feigning contrition, Darnel began writing in his binder, but he knew that he wasn't fooling his teacher with his sudden effort. At least once every week, Mr. Petrocelli would remark, "I've got your number, mister." Then he would threaten to kick Darnel out of class if he continued to make snide comments and disrupt his class, and he had actually done so on two occasions.

Corry, who sat at the next desk over, grimaced and shook his head disapprovingly. Darnel was his best friend, and they had been going to school together since first grade. For as long as Corry could remember, Darnel had been the class smart aleck and the one who always played the clown and made the other kids laugh. Throughout elementary school, Darnel had been repeatedly sent to the principal's office for acting out in class, and he had been suspended on several occasions. He didn't seem to care about getting in trouble or about the Ds and Fs on his report cards, the missed recesses during which he had to write "I will not misbehave in class" one hundred times on the chalkboard, and the after-school detentions. It pained Corry to see Darnel on a collision course with the history teacher, and he feared that his friend was setting himself up to be suspended again.

"Hey, man, it's not smart to aggravate him," Corry whispered when Mr. Petrocelli had turned back to the chalkboard.

Darnel yawned again. "This class is such a drag!" he whispered back. He must have whispered too loudly, for Mr. Petrocelli turned around and glared at him again. "One more time, Darnel, and you're out of here!" he shouted. Darnel immediately looked down again at his binder where he had just written in big block letters, "TEN MINUTES TO GO!!!"

"Thank God this is the last period before lunch," Darnel whispered, this time in a much lower voice. "I have to get out of here before I go ballistic."

Later, Darnel joined up with Corry and Sarah in the cafeteria. "I totally hate this school, and I especially hate Petrocelli," he exclaimed as he set his tray on the table. "What a total idiot he is. He acts like the stuff he's teaching really matters to anyone. One more year and I'm out of here forever. I just hope I can get through the last year without going totally nuts."

"If you don't go to college, what will you do?" Sarah asked.

"Don't know. Right now I'm just trying to get through the next two months until summer vacation starts. I'm not ready to think about what I'm gonna do a year from now."

"Will you have enough credits to graduate?" Corry inquired.

"Who knows. All I do know is that if I flunk history I'm definitely not going to summer school. I don't care what my parents say. June, July, and August belong to me. No more dumb summer school."

"I'll bet your parents will really hassle you if you flunk and refuse to go," Corry commented.

"I don't care! No way they can force me. No way. And I don't need their money. I'll bus at the Burger Pit if I have to."

Corry looked at Sarah who rolled her eyes. Darnel saw her expression of disapproval, and he was clearly annoyed.

"Hey, I've got enough problems with my parents leaning on me," Darnel said bitterly. "I don't need my friends to get on my case, too. My dad keeps asking me, 'What do you want to do with your life?' Hey, I'm seventeen. Duh. Who needs a 'career path' at seventeen? Like he's really doing something important with his life. He's an accountant and works all day in a little office with no windows. He has a boss who he has to suck up to every day. Who wants to spend the rest of your life going to a job that you hate, putting on the storm windows every fall and the screens every spring, mowing the lawn, and shoveling snow? My dad's life is a total boring drag. He never does anything fun. He goes to work every day, and then he comes home and does more work around the house. You call that a life? What I want is a car and an apartment where I can party whenever I want to without my father giving me a dumb lecture about ending up 'at the bottom of the food chain.' I want to get outta here and I want to have fun. I want to drink beer and party!"

KIDS WHO SHOOT THEMSELVES IN THE FOOT

Fact: *Unmotivated, learning-aversive, and psychologically defended children are characteristically resistant to establishing personal academic goals that require effort, commitment, and diligence.* Defeated learners realize that if they target challenging objectives, they significantly increase the likelihood of subjecting themselves to more frustrations and failure. Why take the chance? It's far safer for them to set their sights low, or not to set them at all.

Darnel is a perfect case in point. The teenager is clearly intent on disregarding the basic cause and effect principles that link personal goals and achievement. Indifferent to the role that motivation, focused effort, and self-discipline play in the success equation, Darnel does little more than take up space in the classroom, disruptive and contentious space at that. The repercussions from his oppositional behavior and apathy are predictable: minimal skills, poor grades, and the likelihood of negligible achievement in life.

We can only speculate about the factors that might be responsible for Darnel's self-sabotaging behavior and attitudes, as these factors are not enumerated in the case study. The likely culprits include unresolved learning problems, family problems, emotional problems, generalized hostility toward authority figures, and an inability to think critically and act smart. Whatever the underlying causes, Darnel's sullen attitude, disavowal of basic standards of school decorum, disrespect for authority figures, disdain for his father, disregard of consequences, and myopia about his future herald the monumental challenges that lie ahead for him. If Darnel pursues the path he's on, his prospects in life are likely to be as stunted as his current motivation and effort.

Fact: *The maladaptive behavior of dysfunctional adults can invariably be traced to patterns of maladaptive behavior that were first established in childhood.* Self-defeating behavior is habit-forming. Most adults who regularly shoot themselves in the foot first began pointing the gun at their toes when they were children. Their chronically flawed choices guarantee failures that inexorably damage their self-esteem. This self-concept damage, in turn, guarantees additional flawed choices. Over time, the self-destruct loop assumes a momentum of its own and becomes self-perpetuating.

Darnel's penchant for making poor decisions clearly testifies to his inadequately developed analytical thinking skills. It's obvious that the seventeen-year-old cannot see the forest for the trees. Having zoomed in on the trees, he seems incapable of zooming out and perceiving the whole picture. If he could adjust the lens, he would see that the forest in which he is wandering aimlessly is seeded with mines and bounded by a cement wall and coils of razor wire.

Even if Darnel does earn enough credits to graduate from high school, he's destined to arrive at the end of the line with few, if any, marketable talents. His father's acerbic prognostication about the looming consequences may have been harsh, but the warning was also prescient. Darnel is indeed at serious risk for ending up as a bottom feeder.

Fact: *Continual reproaches and dire warnings are generally counterproductive and often exacerbate children's self-defeating behaviors and attitudes.* Perceiving parental admonitions as another adult excuse to make their life miserable, resistant, learning-aversive children often respond to the criticism and censure by digging in their heels and becoming even more intransigent and resentful. Given the inevitable negative consequences of this mind-set, it's imperative that parents develop a more effective means for modifying their child's conduct that doesn't resort to continual reproaches and censure.

Certainly, Darnel is an extreme example of the resistant, self-sabotaging, and learning-aversive child, but his nihilism underscores the consequences of parents not heeding the red flags that signal significant behavior and attitude problems. Darnel's "attitude" didn't suddenly emerge in eleventh grade. The danger signals were almost certainly present in elementary school, perhaps even as early as first grade. If these warning signs were overlooked or disregarded, the grim repercussions from this neglect make a compelling case for identifying problems and proactively intervening before serious emotional damage occurs and maladaptive behavior becomes entrenched. In Darnel's case, timely intervention would probably have prevented the subsequent downward spiral.

Fact: *Children often use misconduct to camouflage feelings of inadequacy.* Darnel acted out in class to draw attention to his disobedience and deflect attention from his personal problems and insufficiencies. The wise-guy role he cultivated was a coping mechanism, and the attention that his misconduct elicited somehow made him feel less incompetent and vulnerable. The scheme that he used to hide his inadequacies probably fooled no one. His behavior made them laugh, but his classmates and teachers realized that he was essentially the classroom equivalent of a court jester. Darnel didn't grasp that he was actually an object of ridicule. For him to recognize this would have required that he take a long, hard look at himself, and he was obviously too psychologically defended to be introspective. Instead, he contented himself by getting his classmates to respond to his acting out behavior and to laugh at his wisecracks. This produced an illusory sense of power that was a surrogate for achievement. As time passed, Darnel's misbehavior became an ingrained component of his personality and shaped his public persona. Ultimately, the misbehavior became his persona. Just as a serious student who wants to impress his teachers would deliberately craft an identity of conscientiousness, so, too, had Darnel deliberately crafted an identity, but in his case this identity was one of flippancy and disobedience. By the time he entered middle school, Darnel had become a confirmed defiant learner.

Darnel had settled into the role of class clown in the early grades of elementary school. Although the specific factors that caused him to assume this role are not detailed, we can reasonably infer that the factors included inattentiveness and impulsiveness, behaviors typically associated with ADHD. It's also conceivable that Darnel had diagnosed or undiagnosed learning problems that were never adequately addressed. And certainly the disdain that Darnel feels for his father suggests the likelihood of family problems. Whatever the source of his self-sabotaging behavior, Darnel is, in the final analysis, an angry teenager, and his conduct is unconsciously intended to camouflage his inadequate self-esteem and to provide an outlet for his hostility. That his misbehavior draws attention to the failings and feelings that he is trying to hide is an irony that Darnel is psychologically unprepared to recognize and acknowledge. For him to achieve this insight, he would undoubtedly require professional counseling.

The alert system obviously failed in Darnel's case. His parents and teachers and the school psychologist, the school counselor, and the school administrators either didn't see or didn't feel obligated to respond to the blinking red lights. Of course, this assumes that his school was actually equipped to provide help for resistant, oppositional, and learning-aversive students such as Darnel. Unfortunately, most schools are woefully ill prepared to address these types of deportment problems. Their typical responses to misconduct is limited to detention, suspension, and, in extreme cases, expulsion. Relatively few school districts have social workers and clinical psychologists on staff or on call, and, tragically, more and more schools have been forced to eliminate school counselors altogether because of their dire financial straits.

In hindsight, we may conclude that Darnel required counseling and/or after-school tutoring when he first began to struggle and misbehave in school. Perhaps he had a learning dysfunction and should have been enrolled in a learning assistance program, or if he was enrolled in a program that proved ineffectual, perhaps the remedial strategy needed to be revamped or supplemented with additional after-school help. Perhaps Darnel required firmer and more consistent rules and guidelines at home about doing homework, establishing goals, and working conscientiously. Perhaps he required treatment for ADHD. Perhaps he required all of these interventions. Absent more detailed information, we can only conjecture.

Fact: *Parents have a compelling obligation to identify and fix their child's learning and attitude problems before they deteriorate into full-blown crises.*

Proactive parental intervention is imperative when children are at risk for becoming defeated learners. Certainly, it's possible that Darnel's parents did, in fact, recognize the danger signals and that they did everything conceivable to help their son when his problems first began to manifest. More likely than not, however, there were missed opportunities to intervene with a determined commitment to finding solutions.

OPPOSITIONAL TEENAGERS

Fact: *Dealing with a teenager's entrenched resistant behavior can be one of a parent's worst nightmares.* Unable or unwilling to come to grips with their school difficulties, many defeated learners choose instead to latch onto fantasies and escapist illusions. They may convince themselves that having a car, an apartment, independence, and endless parties are all that they need to make their life work. Most of these youngsters never consider how they're going to pay for these perks. With few, if any, saleable skills, little ambition, and an unrealistic understanding of how the real world works, their vocational prospects are as grim as their earning potential. Cautioning these self-deluding teenagers about the harsh facts of life rarely proves a successful strategy for altering their behavior. In most instances, they will defiantly hold onto their illusions until reality crashes down around them.

Fact: *America is the land of second and third chances.* All is not necessarily gloom and doom when youngsters appear intent on making flawed choices in elementary, middle, and high school. Resistant, learning-phobic students may ultimately find their path in life. At some point, they may discover an interest or vocation that appeals to them and at which they can succeed. They may take stock and realize that they want to do something worthwhile with their life. They may begin to establish personal goals that significantly improve their prospects and the quality of their life. Assuming that they haven't already done irreparable damage to themselves, they may ultimately get it right. Of course, this possibility of later "redemption" doesn't lessen parents' compelling responsibility to proactively address the causative factors for their child's maladaptive behavior when the symptoms first begin to manifest.

One of the major advantages of living in this country is that young adults can avail themselves of a broad range of excellent community college and trade school programs that provide opportunities for self-advancement. Most of these programs furnish tutorial services for students who have learning difficulties. Some late bloomers who excel in these community college and trade school programs may subsequently elect to transfer into four-year college programs. Some may even go on to earn graduate degrees and pursue professional careers. Vocational training opportunities are also, of course, available in the military, and there are countless examples of underperforming high school students who achieved outstanding success in private-sector careers after receiving technical training in the military.

DON'T TELL ME WHAT TO DO!

Fact: *Some children need to acquire their own truths about life from the school of hard knocks.* These youngsters insist on doing it their way, even if their way seems patently flawed from their parents' perspective. The children demand the right to make their own mistakes and, if need be, they are prepared to suffer the consequences. Averse to accepting and acknowledging their parents' wisdom or society's collective wisdom, they insist on creating their own personal learning curve, often to their parents' grave consternation. At issue, of course, is whether these youngsters are able to analyze their miscalculations and learn from these mistakes.

The strains on parents who are confronted with a determined child's "don't tell me what to do or think" mind-set can be palpable. Realizing that egregious mistakes, such as those involving smoking, experimenting with drugs, acting promiscuously, or taking mindless risks, can literally destroy their child's life, these parents may be faced with a heartrending dilemma. Their child may insist on having the right to plot his own course in life and make mistakes. He may also profess that he's willing to suffer the consequences for these mistakes, but he may, in fact, be unaware of the very real and perilous implications of certain defective decisions, and despite his assertions, he may not be prepared to deal with the actual repercussions.

It's obviously risky for parents to simply hope that a resistant, learning-aversive child will one day figure out how to get his life un-tracked. The epiphany may never occur, and the child may be sucked into a vortex of failure and despair. Given this frightening possibility, early parental intervention when potentially serious problems first manifest is clearly the safest course of action.

Fact: *Children whose counterproductive behavior is deeply embedded will not easily relinquish their compensatory mechanisms.* Unfortunately, the cognitive behavioral change procedures described in this book may prove inadequate in reorienting the entrenched attitudes and conduct of highly resistant and highly defended teenagers such as Darnel. Their knee-jerk unwillingness to acknowledge that they, in fact, have a prob-lem, their refusal to accept help and guidance, and their self-defeating attitudes, smugness, hostility, and oppositional behavior may be too ingrained, and counseling and tutoring may be the only viable re-course. Parents who realize that they need professional help in dealing with their child's problems are not failures. They're simply manifesting sound judgment.

Fact: *Effecting meaningful changes in the conduct of teenagers who are resistant, defended, and learning aversive requires a well-conceived interven-tion strategy.* For such a strategy to be effective, it must:

- convince children that their situation can be rectified.
- identify and address children's specific academic and study skills deficiencies.
- identify children's aptitudes, intelligence type, and preferred learn-ing style.
- encourage children to capitalize on their natural talents.
- orchestrate repeated opportunities for children to be successful.
- show children how to handle problems and setbacks.
- teach children how to think strategically and act tactically.
- provide children with practical and functional skills that are essen-tial to completing their education and to finding and keeping a job.

Fact: *Children do not necessarily need to be academically oriented to be successful in life.* All children are not cut out to go to college. To find re-warding and remunerative work, youngsters don't necessarily need to study calculus and physics. Our society abounds with self-actualized adults who, despite never having earned a college degree, have become successful business owners, sales reps, chefs, hair stylists, musicians, photographers, artists, clothing designers, dancers, mechanics, electricians, and technicians.

The foregoing notwithstanding, all children, irrespective of their personal interests, natural abilities, and vocational objectives, must acquire basic academic skills. They must be able to read with decent comprehension, identify and retain important information, establish goals, set priorities, plan ahead, organize, evaluate the pros and cons of choices, manage time, budget finances, fill out forms and applications, and express themselves comprehensibly. They must also be receptive to learning new skills. For some, this may involve learning how to use a computer. For others, it may involve learning how to repair a broken pipe, cook beef Wellington, make pastry, lay bricks, read music, shingle a roof, rebuild an engine, fix a computer, or make a sales call. To achieve in life, these young adults must be willing to target personally meaningful goals, work conscientiously, acquire pertinent proficiencies, solve problems, learn from mistakes, bounce back from defeat, and develop strategies for attaining their objectives.

Darnel is on a very different path. In little more than a year, he'll find himself smack in the middle of the real world. He'll need to find a job, and, at some point, he'll need to move out of his parents' home. If he wants to do more than work in a fast-food restaurant, he'll have to acquire vocational skills. Despite his conviction that his life will work once he finishes school, he's obviously in for a sobering reality check. He'll discover that the price tags for owning the car he covets, renting an apartment, getting insurance, buying food, and throwing parties are well beyond what he'll be able to afford if he's flipping burgers and earning minimum wage.

It's conceivable that Darnel will ultimately come to grips with the facts of life and make the requisite changes in his attitude and work ethic. It's also conceivable that he may never do so. In much the same way that he has become a defeated learner, he could also easily become a defeated worker. Logic suggests that psychological and vocational counseling while Darnel is still in high school would reduce the risk of this happening and could make the learning curve less torturous. Of course, convincing a highly resistant and defended teenager such as Darnel to accept the idea of counseling would in all likelihood prove to be a major challenge.

HANDLING THE COUNSELING ISSUE

Fact: *The most effective way to convince a resistant, self-sabotaging, defiant teenager to agree to the need for counseling is for parents to be completely forthright about the issues.* Once parents are convinced that they must find a mental health professional to assess the situation and address their child's resistance and self-sabotaging behavior, the next step is to find the right therapist. This person should have experience working with children and with family systems. Sources for referrals include the family physician, school psychologist, school counselor, and friends and associates who have had positive experience with a particular therapist.*

Once the person is selected, the next challenge is to get the child to accept the ideal of going to a counselor. Parents should express their concerns about what's happening without being accusatory or derogatory, and they must admit that they cannot objectively deal with the issues. They must also clearly communicate that they're determined to find a solution to the problems and conflicts. If they anticipate a knee-jerk negative reaction from their child to the idea of counseling, they might ask the therapist about how best to broach the subject. Another option is to consider presenting the idea as follows:

Parent: "As you know, in labor disputes, the parties who are in conflict often agree to mediation when the issues can't be resolved and a strike is imminent or has already occurred. Each side has its position and viewpoint, and the problem is that the respective positions and viewpoints don't mesh. A professional mediator listens carefully to both parties, helps sort out the issues, and suggests reasonable compromises that can resolve the disagreements. Families

---

*See Lawrence Greene, *Finding Help When Your Child is Struggling in School* (New York: St. Martin's Press, 1998).

sometimes face the same situation when issues can't be resolved. To solve the conflicts, someone outside of the family must objectively analyze what's going on. Otherwise, the conflicts will never be settled. Just as a factory can shut down because of a labor dispute, so, too, can families shut down because of a dispute between parents and children. If the disagreements aren't resolved, they could conceivably destroy the family. Everybody will begin to feel more and more resentful and angry. No one wins and everyone suffers. We're a family that needs an outside, objective mediator to examine what's going on and to advise us about how to proceed. This person will be fair and won't take sides and will fashion a win-win solution as opposed to a we win and you lose or a you win and we lose solution. If you diagram this problem-solving principle, it would look like this." [A reproducible copy of the following diagram can be found on page 267 in the appendix.]

HANDLING ARGUMENTS AND CONFLICTS

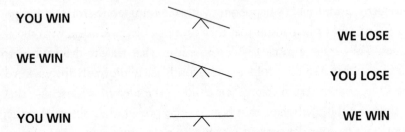

YOU WIN		WE LOSE
WE WIN		YOU LOSE
YOU WIN		WE WIN

"We've been given the name of a skilled counselor who can help us reduce the conflicts that are causing stress and unhappiness in the family. We have an appointment to meet with her as a family next Thursday at five o'clock."

As you can see, the issue has been handled calmly and rationally. You've presented a logical explanation for procuring therapy. You've said nothing derogatory. Although your child may react defensively, you've clearly communicated that his opposition will not deter your decision to seek an objective assessment of the family dynamic and find solutions to the family conflicts. The first session is scheduled at a certain time on a specified day. The matter is settled. Certainly, there are other ways to broach the subject, and the preceding modeled explanation may not work for you. If so, develop a plan that is better attuned to your personality and your child's personality. The objective is to communicate unequivocally to your child that you are committed to the counseling process and that the issue can be discussed but not debated.

STRATEGIC PLANNING AND ACHIEVEMENT

Fact: *Achieving children understand the basic cause-and-effect principles that link achievement and strategic thinking and planning, and they consistently apply these principles both inside and outside of school.* Successful students who think analytically, critically, and strategically are in the habit of carefully weighing the pluses and minuses of their options and carefully considering the potential consequences of their decisions. Morality aside, these youngsters would reject any temptation to steal from a store because they don't want to pay the price if they were caught. They would also take into consideration the impact of their attitudes and behavior on those who have control over their life. They may not like a particular teacher, but they would scrupulously avoid doing anything to intentionally alienate the teacher or show disrespect. They realize that this person will be giving them a grade at the end of the semester.

The basic inclination of strategically minded children is do everything they can to improve the odds of success. They may not enjoy a subject, but they'll deliberately develop a study plan that assures them a decent grade in the course. They learn from their past mistakes and use the data they derive from their positive and negative experiences in life as a guide when they confront similar situations. When they miscalculate, their credo is simple: *Been there. Done that. Don't want to make that mistake again.*

Fact: *Achieving students intuitively recognize the vital role that establishing personal short- and long-term goals plays in the school success equation.* Successful children realize that goals impel effort and that effort fuels achievement. They set their sights on a defined objective, plan astutely, apply themselves conscientiously, and persevere until they attain the desired goal. Whether the target is a B+ in English or a spot on the varsity basketball team, they recognize that developed skills, hard work, and dedication are the core factors that will influence the ultimate outcome. It's a simple equation: You aim for what you want. You plan. You work hard. You vector in on the target. You sustain your effort and resist temptations to abandon your goal. You attain the objective. You establish a new goal and start over again.

THE FUNCTION OF GOALS

- Provide a sense of direction and purpose
- Stimulate motivation
- Galvanize effort
- Inspire diligence
- Encourage commitment
- Fuel achievement
- Provide a context for experiencing success and pride
- Create opportunities to enhance self-confidence

Fact: *Achievement is a function of goal-focused strategic and tactical thinking, clarity of purpose, and efficiency of effort.* Children who establish personally meaningful academic goals have a distinct advantage over those who meander through school with no sense of direction or purpose. Having assimilated this vital achievement-producing principle, goal-directed students consistently function at a level commensurate with their abilities.

Achieving children do everything possible to stack the odds in their favor. They define the target, formulate a practical step-by-step plan for getting from point A to point B to point C, organize their resources, and focus their intellectual and physical energy on successfully handling the associated tasks. Even first and second graders can grasp these fundamental principles and can learn to discipline themselves so that they can proceed systematically and sequentially to their destination. Were it not for this capacity to develop and implement a functional plan of action, book reports would not be written, art projects would not be completed, math problems would not be done, spelling words would not be learned, and completed homework assignments would not be submitted on time.

Of course, even strategically minded children occasionally miss the target and occasionally have lapses in judgment, but more often than not they succeed in making it to the finish line. Because they consider the potential consequences of their actions, they realize that if they choose to play basketball or watch TV instead of studying for a test, their grade is likely to suffer. This crucial concept of voluntarily suspending immediate gratification to attain more meaningful down-the-road gratification is often lost on kids who chronically underperform in school.

GOAL SETTING AND INEFFECTUAL LEARNING

Fact: *Many struggling learners are consumed with simply making it through another day without getting bruised and humiliated and feeling incompetent.* As children with deficient skills battle with daily crises, long-range planning is usually the furthest thing from their minds. Compelling here-and-now considerations usually preoccupy them, restrict their perspective, and render them myopic. Their immediate gripping concerns may include:

- How can I possibly complete this history assignment on time?
- How do I do these math problems?
- How do I write this essay?
- How can I get a C on this science test?
- How do I answer the question about constitutional checks and balances?
- Why did the teacher circle the word *sargent* in my essay and write *sp* in the margin?
- What does she mean by a run-on sentence?
- What is the subjunctive tense, and why does the regular Spanish conjugation change when you are using it?

When basic academic survival is the order of the day, long-range objectives such as raising your GPA or getting into college are often little more than abstractions. Handling immediate pressing challenges such as doing tonight's biology homework assignment or learning the newly assigned vocabulary words are the highest priorities. Having to think about and plan for long-range projects such as completing a term paper that is due in two weeks or studying for a U.S. government final that they will be given in three weeks can cause overwhelmed youngsters to go into meltdown.

The reasons why ineffectual learners frequently have difficulty planning and completing complex, multifaceted projects are basic. Many of these students have never been taught how to systematically establish long-term academic goals, nor have they been taught how use short-term goals as stepping stones for attaining their long-term goals.

This instructional failure is unfortunate. Goal-directed children are more likely to develop practical timetables for attaining specific academic objectives, and they are also far more likely to devise pragmatic strategies and tactics for attaining these objectives than students who simply lurch from task to task and from academic crisis to academic crisis. Their goals function as a catalyst for effort, a stimulus for diligence, and an incentive for achievement.

When deficient skills are compounded by the absence of goal-directed motivation, inadequate effort, and passive learning, the scholastic challenges children face are magnified exponentially. The obvious solution is to show resistant learners how to target personally meaningful objectives and to condition them to raise the achievement bar in small increments after they attain each defined objective.

Fact: *Resistant children who learn ineffectually are often resistant to developing a utilitarian study plan.* Ironically, struggling children with poor skills and inadequate academic self-confidence are the very ones who could most benefit from establishing goals and creating a functional action plan. Unfortunately, the benefits of establishing short-term goals (e.g., getting a B– on the next Spanish quiz) and using these goals as stepping-stones for attaining a long-term goal (e.g., a C+ in the course) may never register on crisis-driven students. On either a conscious or an unconscious level, defeated learners are likely to conclude that setting challenging personal goals would only produce additional burdens.

Why add more obligations when they're already feeling overpowered and their compelling desire is to reduce the potential for more failure? These youngsters want to limit the challenges, not increase them.

Of course, there's a fundamental flaw in this "limit the risks" reasoning. Many struggling children are too entangled in their seemingly insoluble problems to recognize a fundamental cause-and-effect principle, namely, that by prevailing over the challenges and by attaining their objectives, they can significantly enhance their performance and academic self-confidence.

Fact: *Parents must help their underperforming child realize he must deal with the daily challenges and crises he faces in school and that he must develop a functional long-range strategy for extricating himself from these predicaments.* Parents must help their child understand that if he falls into a pit, he must devise a plan for climbing out. He must focus on reaching the daylight. This is the goal. Each carefully planned movement represents an interim goal. If he is to get out of the pit, he must methodically scoop out footholds and search for ledges and handholds, and step by step he must work his way to the top. The alternative is for him to focus exclusively on whether he has enough candy in his pocket to keep from getting hungry and on whether the water dripping from a stone in the pit will be sufficient to quench his thirst. Certainly, these factors must be considered, but focusing exclusively on survival is not going to get him out of the hole and into the daylight.

Fact: *The antidote for the counterproductive, self-protecting instincts of goal-aversive children is to encourage them to initially establish modest and attainable goals.* Urging a child who is reading two years below grade level to aim for a B+ in history is likely to set the child up to fail. It would be far more realistic to encourage the child to aim for a C or C+. If he gets a B, that's great, but if he ends up with a C, he should be acknowledged, praised, and affirmed for both his effort and his accomplishment. As his reading improves, so, too, will his grades, assuming that he's willing to target improved grades as his goal and assuming that he's willing to make the requisite effort.

Children who are in the habit of doing the minimum possible should certainly be urged to stretch for the brass ring (i.e., good grades, college, rewarding careers, etc.). They shouldn't, however, be prodded into stretching too far at first, as this might cause them to fall off the carousel. If they have too many spills, they're likely to become phobic about getting back on the horse.

Encouraging children to establish new and more challenging goals as their academic skills improve plays a critically important role in the academic achievement equation. These new goals should be reasonable and reachable. As children attain them, their self-confidence and motivation will inexorably increase. They'll realize that they have control over their academic destiny, and they'll begin to voluntarily establish more demanding goals. This sense of empowerment will provide the impetus for continued achievement.

TEACHING YOUR CHILD HOW TO ESTABLISH GOALS

Fact: *The sooner children establish the habit of setting goals, the better*. Even children in first grade can be encouraged to work toward goals. These goals may involve finishing ten reading units by December, learning how to do two-place addition problems, or finishing an art project for open school night. Ideally, these procedures will become automatic. You'll know that your child has assimilated the concept of goal-setting when you hear the following:

- "I want a B on the next math quiz."
- "I want a minimum of B+ on my science project."
- "I want a part in the school play."
- "I want the teacher to pick my art project for display in the school office."
- "I want to make the varsity baseball team in my sophomore year."
- "I want to save enough money to get a new skateboard."
- "I want to get a summer job working as an assistant in our vet's office."
- "I want to go to the University of Wisconsin."
- "I want to become a criminal law attorney."

Both the autocratic and the democratic approaches can be used to teach your child goal-setting procedures. As stated in preceding chapters, the determining factors that will influence your choice of methods should include your child's personality, his cooperation track record, your own personality, and your parenting style preferences. If appropriate, you may want to borrow components from both approaches and synthesize your own personalized cognitive behavioral change instructional methodology (see pages 52–53).

Let's first examine how the autocratic approach can be used to teach your child how to establish motivational goals.

ESTABLISHING GOALS

The Autocratic Approach

Guidelines

- Create a conducive context for interaction.
- Check out your child's perceptions (see checklist).
- Define the problem.
- Examine the evidence.
- Provide functional goal-setting procedures.
- Supervise implementation.
- Affirm your child for effort and progress.

Now let's put the autocratic approach into action.

Scenario: You ask your child to come into the kitchen or the dining room. You are calm. Any siblings in the area should be instructed to leave. You ask your child to sit in a chair facing you so that you can establish and maintain eye contact. Your tone of voice is friendly and non-threatening, but, at the same time, firm and decisive.

You: "I'm concerned about something, and I want to discuss my concern with you. I don't feel that you're in the habit of establishing goals in school. Before we go any further, I want you to take a few minutes to complete this checklist. Be honest and don't try to say what you think I want to hear. I'll leave the room while you complete the checklist. Let me know when you've finished filling it out." [A reproducible copy of the following form can be found on page 267 in the appendix.]

GOAL-SETTING CHECKLIST

CODE: 1 = Never 2 = Rarely 3 = Sometimes 4 = Often 5 = Always

I aim for a specific grade on tests, essays, reports, and
    homework assignments.   ____

I target the specific grade I want to get in each
    class at the beginning of the semester.   ____

I develop a strategy for getting what I want.   ____

I carefully plan the steps I must take to achieve
    my long-range goals.   ____

I make these steps my short-term goals (for example,
    a B– on the next math test).   ____

I use short- and long-term goals to motivate me
    to work hard.   ____

I periodically review my goals to remind myself
    about what I want to achieve.   ____

I periodically review my goals to make certain they're
    current, realistic, challenging, and attainable.   ____

I set new goals to replace the ones that I've already achieved.   ____

I carefully examine and make revisions in my
    step-by-step plan (short-term goals) if I fail to
    achieve a particular goal.   ____

I am proud when I attain my goals.   ____

Scenario: After giving your child sufficient time to complete the checklist, you return to the kitchen or dining room. You pull up a chair and ask your child to sit next to you.

You: "Let's look at your responses to the statements on the checklist. As I've said before, we're each entitled to our opinions. If we disagree, we need to discuss the differences calmly. OK. I see that you've indicated that you often aim for specific grades on tests, homework, reports, etc. and that you often target the specific grade you want to get in each course. I'm curious about what grades you targeted for this semester. Have you written down these goals anywhere? What about last semester? For example, what grade did you target in English and math? It's my impression that you didn't actually go through a grade-targeting process at the beginning of this semester or last semester. I don't want to get into an argument about this, but if I were filling out the checklist for you, I would have to give you a 2 in the area of targeting specific goals. All right, let's go through the rest of the checklist and see where we agree and disagree."

As you examine your child's responses on the checklist, carefully temper your reactions and tone if you disagree with his assessments. The objective is not to assert that your child's assessments are wrong, but rather to enhance your child's awareness of his own modus operandi. If you come across as hostile or overly aggressive, you'll cause your child to become defensive, resentful, and resistant. Make it clear that you don't want to argue but that you simply want to understand how he views the issues raised in the checklist, and you want to express how you view the issues. When you've completed this procedure, it's time to move onto the next step.

You: "I believe that it's very important for you to have clearly defined goals in your life. Even if you think you are already in the habit of setting goals, I want us to work together on developing a goal-setting system. Do you have any long-range goals right now? These are goals that you want to achieve when you are an adult. For example, you may want to be a video game developer. You may want to be a clothing designer. Another goal may be to make a lot of money, own a sports car, or travel around the world. You may want to play college basketball. List your personal long-range goals below."

Please note: The goals your child lists in the following exercises will be used in the next chapter, which deals with learning how to prioritize.

You should save your child's completed lists. Reproducible copies of all of the following forms can be found on pages 268–270 in the appendix.

MY PERSONAL LONG-RANGE GOALS

Date:_____

1. _____

2. _____

3. _____

4. _____

5. _____

6. _____

You: "Now I want you to list your short-term or more immediate goals. These might include goals such as getting a certain grade on your next science test, scoring two goals in your next soccer game, buying a hot new DVD, or saving enough money to buy a new trail bike."

MY SHORT-TERM GOALS

Date:_____

1. _____

2. _____

3. _____

4. _____

5. _____

6. _____

7. _____

8. _____

9. _____

10. _____

You: "Now I want you to list four specific long-term goals that have to do with school. These might include the GPA you're aiming for at the end of this academic year, the GPA you want when you graduate, or the college you want to attend."

LONG-TERM SCHOOL GOALS

Date:_____

1. _____

2. _____

3. _____

4. _____

You: "Now I'd like you to indicate the specific grade you are aiming for at the end of this semester in each course you are currently taking. These targeted grades will be your short-term goals."

SPECIFIC ACADEMIC SHORT-TERM GOALS

Subject	Most Recent Report Card Grade	Grade I Want on My Next Report Card
Math	_____	_____
_____	_____	_____
_____	_____	_____
_____	_____	_____
_____	_____	_____

You: "OK. During the next two weeks, I want you to write down a specific weekly goal and specific daily goals. I want you to do this experiment for two weeks. You'll use this form. As you can see, there's a place to indicate whether you attained your goal for the week and for each day." (Complete a form for each subject.)

GOAL-SETTING IN SCHOOL

Goal Attained?

Week #1:   Yes   No

Weekly Goal: _____ ____ ____
Daily Goals:
Monday: _____ ____ ____

Tuesday: _____ ____ ____

Wednesday: _____ ____ ____

Thursday: _____ ___ ___

Friday: _____ ___ ___

		Goal Attained?	
Week #2:		Yes	No
Weekly Goal:	_____	___	___
Daily Goals:			
Monday:	_____	___	___
Tuesday:	_____	___	___
Wednesday:	_____	___	___
Thursday:	_____	___	___
Friday:	_____	___	___

You: "You've listed your long-term, weekly, and daily goals. I'm certain that if you work conscientiously you'll achieve them and your grades will improve. As you attain your goals, you'll feel proud of yourself, and you'll want to set new goals. Your daily goals are stepping-stones to achieving your weekly goals. And your weekly goals are stepping-stones to achieving your long-range goals. Later, we'll examine another function of establishing goals, and you'll learn how to use goal setting to solve problems. So, starting today I want you to begin putting the goal-setting system into action. I want goal setting to become a daily habit in your life, one that you will use automatically."

Now, let's examine the more democratic approach.

ESTABLISHING GOALS
The Democratic Approach

Guidelines

- Create a conducive context for interaction.
- Check out your child's perceptions (see checklist).
- Define the problem.
- Examine the evidence.
- Provide functional goal-setting procedures.
- Supervise implementation.
- Affirm your child for effort and progress.

Scenario: You are seated facing your child at the dining room or kitchen table.

You: "I need to share one of my concerns. I have the impression that you aren't in the habit of establishing personal short- and long-term goals. My own experiences in life have convinced me that having goals provides focus and motivates us to achieve. I'd like you to take a few minutes to fill out the following checklist. I want you to be forthright in responding to the statements." [Refer to the checklist on page 92. A reproducible copy is found on page 267 in the appendix].

"After you've completed the checklist, we'll discuss your responses." (Once your child has finished responding to the statements on the checklist, you would examine his responses and share your own impressions. Calmly discuss any discrepancies in your respective perceptions about the issues that are raised in the checklist. You might examine the issues as follows:)

"Do you believe that you're in the habit of setting personal goals on a regular basis? If so, could you give me some examples of short-term and long-term goals that you've established? Do you write down your goals and remind yourself of them? Well, it's my impression that you don't regularly establish goals. You may, of course, disagree with this observation. Even though you may not agree with me, follow along as I deal with my concern. As I've done before, I'll use the DIBS problem-solving method. Pay close attention as I go through the DIBS steps." [Reproducible DIBS forms can be found in the appendix.]

DIBS

Define the problem:	I'm concerned that you aren't establishing goals.
Investigate the causes:	I believe that without goals you will be less motivated.
	Unless you define the interim steps or short-term goals (for example, a B on the next book report) you'll have difficulty achieving long-term goals (for example, a B in English).
	Without specific goals, your efforts are likely to be unfocused and scattered.
	Unless you deliberately set personally meaningful goals, you'll deny yourself the opportunity to experience pride and satisfaction in your accomplishments.
Brainstorm solutions:	I could accept the fact that you are not in the habit of setting goals.
	I could show you how to establish short- and long-term goals.
Select:	I'll show you how to establish short- and long-term goals.

You: "As you can tell, I believe that it's very important for you to have clearly defined goals in your life. You may be convinced that you do set goals, but I would like to work with you on developing a more formal goal-setting system. This system will help you to indicate not only your long-term goals, but also the short-term or interim goals that will permit you to attain your objectives."

At this juncture, you would use the same goal-targeting procedures described in the more autocratic approach (see pages 91–97). You would probably want to soften the language. Instead of saying, "I want you to . . ." you could substitute, "I would suggest that you . . ." or "What do you think about this idea?" As needed, make other appropriate modifications so that the tone of the interaction appears less authoritarian. You might finish the interactive session with the following statement: "I'm sure that this new system of identifying long-term goals, weekly goals, and daily goals will produce a significant improvement in your schoolwork. Once goal-setting becomes a habit, you won't even have to think about it. You'll do it automatically."

Goal-setting and ambition fuel achievement. Your child's desire to attain specific personally significant objectives will stimulate his ingenuity and strategic thinking and will provide him with a tangible motive for focusing his intellectual, emotional, and physical energy. Once he begins to experience the pride and sense of accomplishment that accrue from being successful, goal setting will become increasingly automatic. He'll be hooked, and he'll want to have more of these pleasurable feelings. Achievement is habit forming. Unlike other less wholesome cravings, this particular addiction is healthy, constructive, and productive.

5

Figuring Out the Priorities

Courtney felt like she was caught in a riptide and was being pulled out to sea. Her book report was due in four days, and she still had one hundred pages to read before she could begin writing it. Of course, she had another option. She could write about what she had finished reading and ask her friend Lisa about how the book ended. Courtney realized this would be risky, as her English teacher was really smart and had been teaching forever. Courtney was certain that over the years students had tried just about every conceivable trick on Ms. Dominguez, and the sixteen-year-old considered her chances of getting a decent grade without actually finishing the book to be a long shot.

Courtney's problem was compounded by the fact that she also had to take a big U.S. government test on the same day the book report was due, and she hadn't yet started studying for it. She had also promised to help Tanya buy supplies for the party that they were throwing at Tanya's house on Friday night. And then there was the matter of shopping for new clothes for the party. Some friends had told her that Keith was coming to the party, and Courtney really wanted to dazzle him. A junior and the star wide receiver on the varsity football team, Keith was one of the most popular boys in school. Courtney made no secret about having a big crush on him, and she was determined to get him to ask her out. A new outfit would be just the ticket, and she had no reservations about spending the baby-sitting money she had saved to buy something spectacular. Courtney smiled when she thought how jealous her friends would be if Keith actually asked her for a date.

Unfortunately, shopping for a new outfit would take up an entire afternoon, and Courtney didn't have time to spare in view of the looming book report and government test. Her immediate concern was finding something special at the mall before she had to take the bus home for dinner. If she wasn't in the house by six, her mom would be furious. For some weird reason, her mother insisted that everyone had to be seated at the dinner table at precisely six o'clock. If she came in late and didn't have a really good excuse, she was certain that her mom would ground her, and this would pull the rug out from under the party. Her mother would already be more than a little curious about why she hadn't come directly home after school, and Courtney knew that she would have to make up some sort of plausible story. Getting home late would just put the frosting on the cake and would undoubtedly lead to her being restricted for the entire weekend.

Because of the time constraints, Courtney realized that she would only have about an hour and a half to shop. If she was lucky, she might find what she was looking for in her favorite store, but if she didn't locate something quickly, she would only be able to check out a few other stores before she would have to head home. She would then have to return to the mall the following day, and she would lose another afternoon of studying. This would make it absolutely impossible for her to finish reading the book and complete the report on time.

"I'll just have to take a chance and fake it. Maybe I'll get lucky and put one over on Ms. Dominguez," Courtney thought. This halfhearted attempt to reassure herself that she could pull off the deception was not very comforting. And then, of course, there was the matter of having to study for the government test. On top of that she still had to finish all of her regular homework in science, math, and Spanish. "No way I can get everything done," Courtney thought dejectedly. "My goose is cooked." To her dismay, she realized that she had used one of her mom's favorite expressions, an expression that Courtney actually hated. Ugh!

ESTABLISHING A HIERARCHY OF IMPORTANCE

Fact: *The ability to identify what's important and determine the proper order for sequencing and completing tasks plays a major role in the achievement equation.* Children are faced with a myriad of in-school and at-home responsibilities that include doing homework, completing chores, and participating in after-school activities. As youngsters progress into the upper grades, the academic demands they face expand, and those who cannot categorize, organize, and order the components of their homework and study obligations are at risk for becoming overwhelmed. Because they don't know where to start and how to progress logically and sequentially from task to task, their efforts are likely to be disjointed and ineffectual, and their performance will suffer accordingly. Book reports are typically left to the last minute and then are done in a hurried, slipshod manner, assuming they're done at all. Studying for tests is hit or miss, and critically important steps in multifaceted projects such as writing a term paper are often overlooked. The net effect of this failure to systematically prioritize tasks and obligations is diminished achievement and diminished self-confidence.

Any parent reading the introductory case study would probably conclude that Courtney's predicament is of her own making. She runs out of time because of poor planning and procrastination, and her scheduling ineptitude produces a crisis. It's clear that if Courtney doesn't buckle down and get her work done, she'll get failing grades on her book report, government exam, and homework assignments. On the other hand, if Courtney does buckle down and fulfill her academic responsibilities, she could scuttle her plan to entice the popular football player to ask her out.

At the core of Courtney's predicament is her obvious unwillingness to prioritize her academic obligations over her social life. Had she decided to forgo the shopping trip and instead work intensively on her book report, she might have conceivably finished reading the book and writing the report. She might have also conceivably carved out enough time to study for the government exam and complete her other homework assignments. This would have necessitated a marathon, last-minute effort, and it's apparent from the description of Courtney's attitude about school that she would refuse to make this intensive effort. Instead she chose to go to the mall to buy a new outfit to dazzle the star football player. There's an obvious irony here. Courtney does, in fact, establish her priorities and acts on them. Unfortunately, from the perspective of academic diligence, these priorities are fundamentally flawed.

Certainly, one can almost understand a sixteen-year-old's temptation to choose shopping and preparing for a party over doing homework, especially when the student doesn't seem to care about her grades. Courtney is, after all, a teenager, and as any parent of an adolescent can attest, social life can be a consuming preoccupation for many high school students. At the critical decision point, Courtney has to select what matters most to her. She decides to prioritize the party over doing her work, realizing full well that she'll have to pay the price for this decision, a decision that also necessitates her having to lie to her mother about her whereabouts after school. As a consequence, Courtney faces a potential triple whammy: bad grades, the erosion of trust if her mother finds out that she has lied to her, and likelihood of being grounded if she receives failing grades on the book report, the exam, and her homework assignments.

Fact: *Underperforming students often have a distorted interpretation of the principle of relative value.* What chronically resistant, learning-aversive children prioritize is rarely what their parents and teachers would have them prioritize. Play typically takes precedence over diligence, and fun typically outranks responsibility. For these academically cavalier youngsters, little of what happens in school has much intrinsic significance. They endure sitting in the classroom for five hours every day because they're required to do so, and while they're "incarcerated" they do little more than go through the motions of being educated. They may grudgingly do the assigned class work and homework, but their efforts are more often than not minimal and purposeless. Having no personally meaningful long-term academic goals and no strategic plan of action, they rarely, if ever, think in terms of using short-term goals as stepping-stones for fulfilling their scholastic obligations and getting good grades. Instead, they float through school in a cerebral haze, oblivious to the practical scholastic benefits of systematically establishing goals and priorities. For them, the concept of assigning a higher order of importance and urgency to scholastic obligations and tasks is little more than a nebulous abstraction.

Achieving students operate very differently. They define their academic objectives and then develop a pragmatic, methodical, and sequential plan for attaining these goals. The systematic ranking and ordering of their obligations, needs, and desires form the underpinnings of this strategy. When necessary, these children are willing to make hard choices that may require sacrifices and involve foregoing immediate pleasure. These choices may severely test their resolve and may make them temporarily unhappy, but more often than not, goal-directed youngsters can resist temptations that underperforming children cannot resist. Whereas the implicit credo of successful students is *work hard and then play,* the implicit credo of resistant, learning-aversive students is *play first, and if by some miracle there's time left over, perhaps do some work.*

Courtney epitomizes the *play now and work later* ethos. She wants instant gratification despite her realization that there will be immediate consequences for her decisions in the form of failing grades on her book report, government exam, and homework assignments. The long-range repercussions—Ds or Fs on her report card, a lowered G.P.A., and fewer educational options when she completes high school—simply do not concern her.

Of course, even serious students have occasional lapses. Although they may from time to time prioritize their social life or other pursuits over studying, they generally act in consonance with their academic goals and priorities. When they're tempted to succumb to temptations that could distract them from their studies, they usually remind themselves of the long-range payoffs they covet. The internal monologue might go something like this: "I desperately need an A in this course so that I can qualify for advanced-placement English next year. Acing this book report is more important to me than shopping for a new party outfit."

FIGURING OUT HOW TO PRIORITIZE

Fact: *Youngsters who think and plan strategically either intuitively recognize or have learned from experience that they must develop a logical sequencing system for handling the multiple scholastic obligations that vie for their attention and effort.* Students must understand and assimilate three basic "get the job done" precepts if they're to be successful in school, namely:

- Some responsibilities are more immediate, urgent, and/or imperative than others.
- Certain tasks must be completed before beginning other tasks.
- Academic obligations take precedence over social diversions.

Elementary school teachers expect children as young as six to be able to apply basic prioritizing principles. First graders must recognize that they have to put away the materials on their desks before they can line up to be dismissed at the end of the day. Second graders must understand that their teacher requires that they complete worksheets in a specified order. Third graders must realize that doing their homework takes precedence over watching television or playing games on the computer. Fourth graders must grasp that they have to learn their multiplication tables before they can do division problems. Tenth graders must realize that they have to prioritize studying for tomorrow's Spanish test before they begin studying for next week's biology exam. They must also understand that studying for next week's biology exam takes precedence over blocking out the weekend for a Friday-night concert, an all-day excursion to the beach on Saturday, an after-the-basketball-game party on Saturday night, and a volleyball game on Sunday. By defining their priorities, planning astutely, working intensively, and exercising good time management, they may be able to participate in some of these extracurricular activities, but it's unlikely that they'll be able to indulge in all of them if they're determined to get a good grade on the exam. *You can't always have it all* is a harsh fact of life, but it's a fact that all children who want to be successful in school must learn, and the sooner the better.

LINKING GOALS AND PRIORITIES

Fact: *For children to derive the benefits of an effective ordering system, they must remain focused on their objectives and be willing to exert self-discipline.* At critical junctures, children must be capable of saying "no," even though saying "yes" may be far more appealing. Those who aspire to more than a menial job and minimum pay after completing high school must learn this essential *I sometimes have to say no* lesson.

The nature and scope of children's personal goals will determine the extent of the sacrifices that they may need to make. The higher they aim, the more extensive the demands for self-sacrifice and self-discipline. If they are aiming to go to West Point, they had better be prepared to sacrifice certain pleasurable pursuits in high school. This basic *if you aim high, you'd better be prepared to work diligently* axiom applies in all arenas of life. Anyone familiar with the grueling training requirements for becoming a Navy Seal, a world class gymnast, an Olympic ice-skater, a black belt in karate, a neurosurgeon, or a classically trained musician recognizes the pivotal role that clarity of purpose, effort, motivation, and self-regulation play in the achievement equation. Yes, some of these stellar accomplishments may appear to have little relevance when discussing resistant, learning-aversive children, but there's a core underlying principle that is relevant. Marginally performing children can dramatically alter the course of their lives if they target personally significant goals, establish priorities, and then work diligently to attain their objectives. Of course, there is a caveat: Marginally performing students must also acquire the essential academic, study, and self-management skills that they require to win in school. In tandem with motivation and effort, this amalgam of goal-setting, prioritizing, self-regulation, and developed academic skills provides an invincible resource that virtually guarantees achievement.

The conscientious high school student who is determined to become a veterinarian realizes that getting a good grade on a book report and on an exam in her U.S. government class can improve her chances of getting an A in her English class. She also realizes that an A can raise her GPA and improve her chances of being admitted into a good college and earning a scholarship. Recognizing that the satisfaction she'll derive from attaining these long-range objectives far exceeds any immediate gratification that she might derive from attending a party, she decides that her schoolwork takes precedence over her social life. This hierarchy of relative value stands in stark contrast to Courtney's hierarchy.

Fact: *Goal setting is a catalyst for efficient learning.* Children who define what's important, target their objectives, and strategically and methodically sequence their efforts usually make a surprising discovery: They don't necessarily have to make monumental sacrifices and forfeit all pleasure to achieve academically. By carefully plotting a course and by being well organized, managing time wisely, planning effectively, working productively, and thinking and acting strategically, students can usually strike a reasonable balance between fulfilling their scholastic obligations and their social and recreational needs. Yes, from time to time, they may have to pass up going to a movie or taking a Saturday excursion with their friends to an amusement park because they have to study for an important test. And yes, they would certainly prefer to be able to cram in everything—the studying and the fun—but life teaches them that this isn't always possible. To get where they're headed, they must pick and choose and sometimes make tough choices. This axiom is applicable not only in school, but also in the demanding world beyond school.

HANDLING COMPETING DEMANDS

Fact: *Children who enter middle school unable to rank their obligations in order of logical sequence, importance, and urgency are likely to be in a constant crisis mode.* The demands that a conscientious student in the upper grades faces can be staggering. These obligations include completing daily homework assignments in five subjects, developing a schedule for writing reports, essays, and term papers, and budgeting adequate time to study for daily quizzes, weekly tests, chapter exams, and midterm and final exams.

On any given night, a high school student may have to complete fifteen math problems and read and take notes on twenty pages in her history textbook. She may also need to memorize the conjugations of five irregular French verbs, learn five new idiomatic French expressions, write ten sentences incorporating the irregular conjugations, memorize ten new English vocabulary words and use them in sentences, read the second act of *King Lear,* and answer the questions at the end of a chemistry unit. In addition, she may need to begin studying for a French test that's scheduled in three days, do research for a history report that is due in two weeks, read ten pages of the next chemistry unit before her next class, and prepare for a math test that's scheduled for the following Tuesday. She may have karate class on Tuesday and Thursday evening, basketball practice after school every day, a church youth group meeting on Wednesday evening, and an audition on Friday evening for a forthcoming community theater play. Any teenager faced with these seemingly impossible-to-meet responsibilities who doesn't carefully assess her goals and priorities and who doesn't develop a logical plan of action is at risk. Her academic and emotional survival hinges on her being able to eliminate, or temporarily suspend, certain less essential commitments. If she thinks rationally, she would probably decide not to audition for the play, as getting a part would entail daily time-consuming rehearsals. Given the volume of her obligations, temporarily suspending participation in karate may also be necessary. If the student's highest priority is to do well in school, she'll undoubtedly have to make some very tough choices.

Students who profess that their goal is to do well in school, but who are unwilling to accept that academic success requires that they prioritize their studies and are unprepared to make the necessary difficult decisions and sacrifices to attain their objectives are in for a harsh reality check. By not putting their schoolwork at the top of the obligations pecking order, they leave themselves vulnerable to a host of dire consequences. These include:

- Being overwhelmed by academic responsibilities.
- Being stressed.
- Being in crisis.
- Functioning ineffectually.
- Underperforming in school.
- Getting lowered grades.

Children who aspire to good grades must be able to define and sequence the specific steps involved in each assigned academic obligation, apply basic divide-and-conquer principles, and break down complex tasks into manageable pieces. They must also be able to create a schedule and establish a flowchart of tasks and subtasks. For example, if they're assigned a term paper, they must develop a practical progression for doing the required library and Internet research, taking notes, transferring notes and citations onto index cards, and organizing the index cards. They must realize that these steps precede writing the first draft, revising the draft, writing the second draft, and proofreading the final draft.

Students who can't figure out the proper order for completing the steps and who can't adhere to this order are at risk for being overpowered by complex projects. As they become increasingly frustrated and discouraged, they're likely to procrastinate, and as the deadline approaches, they're likely to scurry frenetically in several directions at once. Like cars on an icy road, they will spin their wheels, fishtail from side to side, and generate little forward momentum. The subsequent substandard quality of their work will testify to their inability to order their efforts efficiently and effectively.

GOALS, PRIORITIES, TIME MANAGEMENT, AND ORGANIZATION

Fact: *Children who can coordinate goals, priorities, time management, and organization are invariably more productive, self-reliant, and self-confident than children who aimlessly wander through school.* Most achieving children automatically develop a plan (a prime example of strategic thinking) and a logical progression for handling each academic challenge (a prime example of tactical thinking). Based upon their past experiences with similar academic challenges, these successful students allocate realistic blocks of time to complete each assignment, and when each assignment is completed, they check it off. Their task completion procedure is methodical, consistent, and efficient.

Strategic students also anticipate potential problems and develop contingency plans to deal with these problems. They'll most likely build a buffer into their schedule to handle these contingencies, and if they run out of time, their ordered priority list may allow them to defer on certain tasks until a later date. For example, they may want to do their assigned chemistry problems on Monday evening, even though the problems may not need to be submitted until Wednesday. Their English essay, however, may take longer to complete than they anticipated, and they may be forced to put off doing the chemistry problems until Tuesday evening. This may necessitate their allocating more time for homework on Tuesday, but if they're on top of the situation, they should be able to make this adjustment with relatively little difficulty.

Whether children prioritize intuitively or must make a deliberate conscious effort to establish a hierarchy of needs, desires, and tasks, those who can logically sequence their academic responsibilities have a significant advantage over children who lurch thoughtlessly from task to task. Clearly defined goals provide children with a compass, and clearly ordered priorities provide the roadmap.

PRIORITIES AND LEARNING DIFFICULTIES

Fact: *Difficulty planning and sequencing obligations and difficulty differentiating the relative significance and urgency of their obligations invariably compounds the challenges that ineffectual learners face.* Struggling students are often preoccupied with simply being able to make it through the day. For these beleaguered children, every assignment may appear to be the highest priority. Should they study for tomorrow's science test first and then use whatever time is left over to begin writing their English essay that is due in two days, or should they switch the order? If it's clear that they're running out of time, should they read the assigned pages in their history textbook or should they complete their math problems and try to read the history textbook in the car on the way to school? Making these types of sequencing and scheduling decisions can be overpowering for children with learning problems.

Despite their learning difficulties, many teachers expect struggling students to complete their in-class assignments within the announced time constraints. Despite their distractibility, impulsiveness, and difficulty concentrating, teachers expect them to pay attention in class, record their assignments accurately, take notes, participate in class discussions, and carefully proofread their work. Despite their decoding and comprehension problems, teachers expect them to understand what they're reading and follow verbal and written instructions. Despite their time-management and organizational difficulties, teachers expect them to do their homework assignments, study for tests, write essays, and complete reports. However unrealistic these expectations may be, they're facts of life, and if struggling students are to cope with the curriculum demands they must be taught how to create a functional, pragmatic, and logical order for doing their work. The alternative is to allow them to become increasingly frustrated and demoralized. Academic shutdown is then all but inevitable.

Fact: *Struggling learners who are not taught how to rank and sequence obligations and tasks in a logical order are at risk for either falling further and further behind or for becoming increasingly reliant on their parents to continually monitor and supervise them.* The reaction of many parents when they see that their child is becoming overwhelmed and is unable to manage her competing academic responsibilities is to intervene. In some instances, this intervention translates into parents becoming on-call task managers. Their desire to assist their child may be laudable, but parents should be prepared to pay a steep price for taking ownership of their child's problems. The child on the receiving end of continual monitoring, supervision, and assistance is at risk for becoming increasingly helpless, dependent, and dysfunctional.

Teaching struggling children practical, hands-on methods for ranking, ordering, and scheduling their academic obligations clearly represents a far better alternative to parents taking over the job. Wise parents want their child to become fully functional, independent, and self-reliant. This objective is defeated when children conclude that their parents will always be there to rescue them.

Unfortunately, many teachers assume that children will figure out on their own how to prioritize effectively, and because of this flawed assumption, these teachers may not devote the requisite time to systematically teaching children step-by-step prioritizing procedures. In view of this all-too-common failure to provide this instruction in school, the onus for teaching children how to prioritize often rests on parents' shoulders. Fortunately, basic ordering and sequencing skills can be taught and mastered with relative ease.

STEPS FOR ESTABLISHING PRIORITIES

- List all responsibilities, assignments, projects, tasks, or items that must be handled.
- Number the list in order of importance or necessity, putting the most urgent, immediate, and essential needs, obligations, and tasks at the top of the list.
- Stack in descending order less urgent, immediate, and essential needs, obligations, and tasks.
- If the list is lengthy and time is in short supply, eliminate or defer on less important items at or near the bottom of the list.

Let's examine two methods for teaching your child to establish priorities. We'll begin with the autocratic approach.

ESTABLISHING PRIORITIES
The Autocratic Approach

Guidelines

- Create a conducive context for interaction.
- Check out your child's perceptions (see checklist).
- Define the problem.
- Examine the evidence.
- Provide functional priority-setting procedures.
- Supervise implementation.
- Affirm your child for effort and progress.

Scenario: You ask your child to come into the kitchen or the dining room. You are calm. Any siblings in the area should be instructed to leave. You ask your child to sit in a chair facing you so that you can establish and maintain eye contact. Your tone of voice is friendly and nonthreatening, but, at the same time, firm and decisive.

You: "We've already worked on establishing long-term and short-term goals. There's another related issue that I want us to take a look at. This issue involves establishing priorities. Establishing priorities means creating a logical order for meeting obligations and completing tasks. It also involves figuring out what's most important and urgent on your to-do list. Achieving goals is much easier when you set your priorities and you figure out how to get the job done. Before we go any further with this discussion, I want you to complete this checklist. Be honest and don't try to say what you think I want to hear. I'll give you a few minutes to fill it out. Let me know when you're done." [A reproducible copy of this checklist is found on page 271 in the appendix.]

Please note: the concept of establishing priorities may be difficult for younger children to grasp at first, and it may be advisable to sit with them while they complete the checklist so that you can explain the language and, if required, provide concrete examples. Resist any temptation to influence or judge your child's responses while she is completing the checklist.

PRIORITIES CHECKLIST

Code: 1 = Never 2 = Rarely 3 = Sometimes 4 = Often 5 = Always

I know what I need to do to meet my obligations in school.   ___

I identify the tasks that are most immediate or urgent.   ___

I identify the steps that are required to achieve specific goals.   ___

I order the steps required to achieve a goal in a logical sequence.   ___

I create a ladder of importance when I am faced with
    making choices about my priorities.   ___

I create a logical and practical sequence for completing
    tasks and obligations.   ___

I place the most significant tasks at the top of my to-do list
    and list the less important tasks below in descending order
    of importance.   ___
I eliminate the less important or urgent tasks at the bottom
    of my to-do list when it's clear that I can't do everything.   ___
I remind myself of my goals and priorities to avoid any
    temptation to procrastinate or become lazy.   ___
I check off each task or obligation when completed.   ___
I periodically evaluate my priorities to make sure that they
    are properly ordered and will help me achieve my goals.   ___
I make adjustments in my priorities when targeted goals
    are attained or when my goals change.   ___

Scenario: After giving your child sufficient time to complete the checklist, you return to the kitchen or dining room. You pull up a chair and ask your child to sit next to you.

You: "Let's take a look at your responses to the statements on the checklist. As I've said before, we are each entitled to our opinions, and if we disagree, we need to discuss the differences calmly. I see that you've indicated that you order the steps required to achieve a specific goal in a logical sequence. I have a different impression. When you have assignments such as writing a term paper, I've observed that you have trouble getting started and figuring out what to do. I've also observed that you don't identify the required steps and that you don't create a logical and ordered plan for getting the project done efficiently. Because of this lack of careful planning, you don't proceed properly from step A to step B to step C. If you recall, this happened with your last science report. You also procrastinate, and when you can't put the project off any longer, you become upset, and then you panic because you realize that you may not be able to complete the report on time. If I were filling out the checklist, I would give you a 1 or a 2 in these two areas. Feel free to respond to my observations, but I don't want to get into an argument. I just want you to know how I see things. All right, let's go through the rest of the checklist and see where we agree and disagree."

As recommended in parent-child interactive sessions in previous chapters, you should be careful to temper your reactions and tone if you disagree with your child's responses on the checklist. Your objective is not to assert that your child's assessments are wrong, but rather is to enhance your child's awareness of her modus operandi. You don't want to come across as contentious or hostile, as this will cause your child to become defended and resistant. Make it clear that you want to understand how she views the issues raised in the checklist and that you also want express how you view these issues. When the review procedure is completed, it's time to move onto the next step.

You: "We've already dealt with the issue of establishing goals. It's now time to deal with establishing priorities. The two procedures are directly related, as it's difficult, if not impossible, to attain your goals without getting your priorities straight. Your priorities are a roadmap for achieving your goals. They have to be in a logical and practical order so that you can get the job done efficiently. This applies to ordering the steps to finish a history report and to ordering the steps to make the varsity soccer team.

"You recently identified and listed your personal long-range goals. You listed six specific goals. Let's take a look at your list. [Refer to the list that your child completed in chapter 4. See page 94.] I want you to carefully consider each goal on your list in terms of how important it is to you. Certainly, there are some goals that mean more to you than others. I would like you to renumber your list in terms of personal importance. The most important goal will be # 1 on the revised list, and the remaining goals will be ranked in descending order of personal importance.

"Okay. Now I want you go through the same procedure with your short-term goals. Inasmuch as you've changed the order of importance or priority for your long-range goals, this will undoubtedly require that you change the order of priority for your short-term goals.

"Now, I want you to go through the same prioritizing procedure with your long-range school goals. Take a few minutes and reorder your original list in terms of importance, need, desire, or urgency.

The most important goals should be at the top of the list. Later, as you attain each goal on your revised priority list, I want you to put a check in front of the goal. This will help you keep track of what you've achieved and what remains to be achieved. You'll obviously be periodically adding new goals to your priority list. This will require that you reorder your list from time to time. The key to achieving long-term goals is to make certain that your list of short-term goals will allow you to attain your long-term goals and that the order of your priorities is logical and practical. With practice, this procedure of establishing, ordering, and sequencing priorities will become automatic. You'll have a ton of things to do, and you'll be able to set up a logical procedure for doing the tasks."

Please note: The next activity is relevant only if children have been taught the steps involved in writing a term paper. An alternative activity for younger children can be found on page 118.

You: "To make certain that you understand the principles of prioritizing, I want you to prioritize the steps involved in writing a term paper. You have some options in how you order certain steps. For example, some students might prefer to complete their bibliography as the last step before handing in their term paper, while other students may prefer to complete this step before writing the second draft." [A reproducible copy of the following form can be found on page 272 in the appendix.]

PRIORITIZING THE STEPS FOR WRITING A TERM PAPER

___ Write first draft

___ Choose a topic

___ Write notes on index cards

___ Go to the library

___ Make up bibliography

___ Go online to find relevant information

___ Write down quotations on index cards

___ Examine relevant books about subject

___ Read material about topic in the encyclopedia, using either the actual volumes or CD encyclopedia software

___ Turn in the paper on time

___ Proofread for spelling and grammar mistakes

___ Revise and edit first draft

___ Put index cards in order

___ Incorporate quotations into first draft

___ Write final draft

(The recommended order is: 9, 1, 6, 2, 14, 3, 7, 4, 5, 15, 13, 11, 8, 10, 12)

ALTERNATIVE ACTIVITY FOR YOUNGER CHILDREN

You: "To practice establishing priorities, I want you to do the following activity. Pretend that we're going on a camping trip to Yosemite Park. Imagine that I put all the camping gear we'll need for the trip in the driveway, and then I ask you to pack the gear in the trunk of the car. Let's pretend that we'll be staying at a motel on the way to Yosemite, and that we won't start camping until we get to the park. I want you to create a logical order for putting the items in the back of the trunk that we'll need when we get to the campsite. I want you to place the items we might need during the drive to the park nearest the front of the trunk. The items that we'll need during the drive should be easy to get to. Okay. Here's the complete list of gear. The item that you'll put in the trunk first should be #1. Other items that we'll need at the campsite will also have low numbers. The items you place in the trunk last—things we'll need to use during the trip—will have the higher numbers." [A reproducible copy of this form can be found on page 272 in the appendix.]

PRIORITIZING THE STEPS FOR PACKING THE CAR

___Tent	___Sleeping bags	___Ground cloth	___Blankets
___Flashlights	___Toiletries	___Games	___Towels
___Water bottles	___Rain gear	___Camera	___Ice chest
___Rubber pads	___Cell phone	___Compass	___Sunblock
___Blankets	___Marshmallows	___Kindling	___Snacks

___Lanterns   ___Clothes   ___Matches   ___Food
___Backpacks   ___Hiking boots   ___Binoculars   ___Books

Discuss your child's rationale for numbering the list, and explain that in many situations priorities can be listed in either ascending or descending order of importance. There's no absolute sequence for this list, and your child may prefer to load the lanterns in the trunk before loading the kindling. The important concept that you want your child to grasp is that because such items as water bottles and snacks need to be accessible during the trip, they should be packed last and assigned the highest numbers. The tent would be among the items that are loaded first in the trunk and would have one of the lowest numbers. The objectives of the exercises are for your child to be able to express a logical rationale for her ordering system, to understand the concept of prioritizing, and to practice the ordering procedure.

The following explanation of the prioritizing procedure can be used with both older and younger children.

You: "As you can see, prioritizing the steps involved in a project can make complex jobs easier and more efficient. By prioritizing the required tasks or items, you'll know exactly what you need to do, and you won't spend valuable time going off in ten different directions. You can use this prioritizing method to create a practical and logical order for getting your schoolwork done. If you have to make tough choices about how to use your time, your priority list will make these choices less difficult. For example, you may have a math test tomorrow. If your priority is to get a good grade on the test, it will be easier to turn down an invitation to play basketball with your friends after school. The satisfaction of getting a good grade on the test is a higher priority than the immediate pleasure of playing another basketball game. You may be very tempted to play, but making the decision not to play is a no-brainer because you've prioritized getting a good grade over having fun for a few minutes. You can play at another time when you don't have to study for an important test.

"Because your teachers are continually giving you new assignments and projects to do, your school priority list will need to be adjusted more frequently than your nonschool priority list. You'll have to continually juggle how to use your time most effectively and productively. On Monday your science teacher may tell you that a unit test will be given on Friday. On the same day, your English teacher may tell you that an essay is due on Friday. You may have to write a history report that is due on Monday, and you may also have to study for a big math test that is scheduled for Thursday. Just having to think about all of these obligations can cause a migraine headache. To get everything done, it's obvious that you'll need to carefully coordinate your priorities with effective time management, assignment recording, and scheduling procedures. If you don't, you could easily become overwhelmed.

"I want to meet with you in two days and take a look at your current school priority list. If you need to add or modify specific long-term and short-term goals, make changes in the order, or add specific tasks or obligations to the list, we can discuss it. Once you get into the habit of establishing priorities and making appropriate changes, and do so consistently, I won't need to monitor and supervise you. You'll be able to do it on your own."

Now let's take a look at how the more democratic approach can be used to teach prioritizing procedures.

ESTABLISHING PRIORITIES

The More Democratic Approach

Guidelines

- Create a conducive context for interaction.
- Check out your child's perceptions (see checklist).
- Define the problem.
- Examine the evidence.
- Provide functional goal-setting procedures.
- Supervise implementation.
- Affirm your child for effort and progress.

Scenario: You are seated facing your child at the kitchen or dining room table.

You: "We recently spent time working together on establishing your personal short- and long-range goals. You realize that your short-term or interim goals are stepping-stones to attaining your long-term goals not only in school, but also outside of school. You went through a procedure of listing your daily and weekly school goals. I would now like us to take a look at the issue of priorities. This is the order in which you decide to do things. I'd like you to take a few minutes to complete the following checklist. [A reproducible copy of the checklist can be found on page 271 in the appendix.] After you finish, we'll discuss your responses to the statements."

Once your child has completed the checklist, you would begin examining her responses and sharing your own impressions. The tone should be less assertive and judgmental than the one modeled in the preceding autocratic approach. You would calmly discuss any discrepancies in your respective perceptions about the issues that are raised in the checklist.

You: "The ordering of short-term or interim goals is vital to your being able to attain your long-term school goals and out-of-school goals. The same is true about ordering your specific homework tasks when you have a great many short-term and long-term assignments that need to be completed. For example, you have your daily assignments that are due the next day, and you also have long-range assignments to do such as book reports, term papers, and studying for unit, mid-term, and final exams. To juggle all of these obligations successfully, you have to be able to create a practical sequence for completing the tasks in order of importance and urgency, and you need to develop a plan of action. You must decide when to begin reading the book for your book report and when to begin studying for the next exam. I'm sure you can see that goal setting, prioritizing, planning, and scheduling are directly linked to time management. All of these procedures must work together if you're to organize your life and complete your work efficiently. Okay. Let's apply these ordering principles to the long-term goals you previously indicated. Here's your list. I'd like you to number the list in order of importance to you." [You should discuss your child's rationale for ordering his goals and make the point that by ordering and sequencing the list, she has, in effect, created a priority list.]

"Now, I'd like you to go through the same process with your list of short-term or interim goals. Now that you have the hang of it, do the same ordering and sequencing procedure with your specific long-term school goals.

"To make sure that you have the hang of how to prioritize, I'd like you to do the following exercise in which you indicate the order for completing all of the steps involved in writing a term paper." (See steps described on page 117.)

Please note: If your child is younger and is not familiar with the steps involved in writing a term paper, have her do the alternative camping trip prioritizing exercise on page 272. Language for effectively introducing the exercise is found on pages 118–119. After she completes the activity, you would discuss the rationale for her ordering process.

You: "I'm sure you can see now that establishing priorities can make your life much easier. You'll be able to get to your targeted destination because you are proceeding sequentially from point A to point B to point C. If you practice establishing priorities whenever you're faced with a bunch of tasks or responsibilities, the procedure will become automatic. Before long, you'll probably be able to establish priorities in your head without necessarily having to write down the steps. For example, you might decide that you need to go to the drug store and then stop off at the dry cleaners before you head over to your friend's house. You may also conclude that you need to begin studying for the unit test before you begin doing your Spanish homework or before you begin writing your English essay. Organizing and planning your efforts will be much less challenging because you know how to set your priorities."

Learning how to prioritize is an easily learned and easily applied skill. This skill can have a profound impact on your child's efficiency and productivity in school and in the demanding world beyond school. With relatively little practice and guidance, your child can imprint sequencing and ordering procedures and make prioritizing an ingrained and automatic response whenever she's faced with multiple, time-urgent obligations. Taking the time to help her acquire this critically important capability represents one of the most astute and judicious investments you can make.

6

Handling Problems

Nicole felt that the walls were closing in on her. She hadn't cracked her earth science textbook for ten days. Not only had she not read the last two assigned chapters, but she had also fallen seriously behind in doing the lab write-ups. In fact, she hadn't submitted her lab notebook in more than three weeks, and the notebook, which was supposed to be submitted every Friday, would count for 30 percent of her grade in the course.

Before class began, Mr. Takeda asked Nicole where her lab book was. Thinking quickly, the tenth grader made up an excuse that she wanted to recopy the three most recent write-ups because they were sloppy. Nicole assured her clearly skeptical teacher that she would hand in the notebook on Monday. Mr. Takeda scowled. This was not the first time that Nicole had failed to meet deadlines in his class, and he was very aware of her propensity to make up creative excuses.

At home that evening, Nicole added up her grades on her earth science tests and homework assignments and figured that she was currently carrying a C in the course. This grade, of course, would be significantly reduced if Mr. Takeda gave her an F on her lab notebook for the semester. Even if he didn't give her an F, Nicole knew he would lower her grade on the three late write-ups when she finally submitted them. This assumed that she would actually get around to doing the write-ups. Nicole's problem was compounded by the fact that she also hadn't read the last two assigned textbook chapters. Unless she blocked out time to read and take notes on the chapters, Nicole was certain that she would flunk the next exam.

Nicole had fallen behind in school for a very fundamental reason—she was spending more than an hour and a half each evening talking on the phone to her boyfriend. She was also spending another forty-five minutes every night sending instant e-mail messages to her friends. Curtis had graduated high school the previous June, and he was taking a year off from school to work and earn money before enrolling in community college. As Curtis didn't have any homework, he would call Nicole three or four times a day, and they would talk for at least twenty-five minutes each time he called. Nicole realized that these conversations and the instant messaging were leaving her virtually no time to do her homework, but the sixteen-year-old hadn't been able to summon the necessary fortitude to tell Curtis that he had to limit his calls.

Despite her attempts to avoid thinking about her predicament, the consequences were staring Nicole in the face. She realized that she was at risk of not only failing earth science, but also several other courses. These Fs would pull her GPA down below 2.0, and she would have to go to summer school again if she wanted to graduate in two years with her class.

Nicole's most urgent predicament was her lab notebook. She estimated that it would take her a minimum of five hours to complete the three overdue write-ups, and she simply wasn't willing to forgo her nightly telephone conversations with Curtis or allocate time over the weekend to do the work. She had too many fun things planned. On Friday night she and Curtis would usually go to a movie or watch TV with friends. On Saturday and Sunday, they would hang out with their friends at the mall during the day, and there was always a party on Saturday night. On top of that, Nicole had her regular homework that was due on Monday. She usually left these assignments until ten P.M. on Sunday evening, and they were rarely if ever completed. "How am I supposed to find time to do everything?" Nicole thought bitterly.

Convinced that there was no way to extricate herself from the jam she was in, Nicole concluded her situation was hopeless, and she decided to let the chips fall where they may. If she flunked her science class, too bad. She would just have to go to summer school.

When Emily told Nicole that she had the perfect solution to the lab notebook problem, Nicole was eager to hear what her friend had to say. Emily had taken the earth science course from a different teacher during summer school and had gotten a B. Since she had done all the same dissections and lab experiments, she suggested that Nicole simply copy her lab book. As Mr. Takeda had never seen her lab book, Emily was certain that he would never figure out what was happening.

Nicole could see that the plan would solve her most immediate problem, and she decided to go ahead with it. Later that day, however, she began to have misgivings. She certainly didn't consider herself an angel, but she had never done anything like this before. Sure, she had occasionally glanced at a classmate's answers while taking a test, but what Emily was proposing would guarantee an F in the course if she were caught. She might even be suspended. What would happen if Mr. Takeda realized that she had copied another student's lab book? What would her parents say if she flunked because of cheating? One voice in her head said, "Do it! It's no big deal. You've cheated before, and there's no chance of getting caught." Another voice said, "This could be a major mistake. Mr. Takeda is going to catch on and nail you to the wall."

Nicole wrestled with what to do for the entire day. That night she tossed and turned and had trouble sleeping. At breakfast the next morning her father could see that she looked troubled and asked if anything was wrong. Nicole responded "No," and then she said something funny about her mom's runny scrambled eggs to throw him off the track.

When Emily told Nicole during first period that she had her lab book in her backpack, Nicole gritted her teeth and said, "I've decided not to do it." Emily looked at her friend as if she were crazy.

"That's really dumb, Nicole," Emily whispered.

"Yeah, I know. But I just can't do it."

"Then what are you going to do? You're gonna flunk the class for sure if you don't hand in your lab notebook."

"I don't know what to do. I just can't take the chance. If I got caught, I would be in really hot water, and my parents would go ballistic. I'd be grounded for life."

"Well, it's your call," Emily commented incredulously.

"What an awful mess!" Nicole replied.

SETTING THE STAGE FOR A DISASTER

Fact: *The ability to analyze situations, handle challenges, and solve problems is a requisite to achievement in every significant endeavor.* Children who fail to develop a functional system for extricating themselves from jams are at serious risk for not only experiencing a great deal of pain in life, but also for losing faith in themselves. Each time they confront a dilemma, they're vulnerable to making flawed choices and becoming over-whelmed and, perhaps, even dysfunctional.

Nicole's response to her situation underscores what happens when children lack adequate problem-solving skills. In the very first paragraph, one can see red danger flags flapping in the wind. Nicole's inability to analyze what's happening to her and her unwillingness to come to grips with her dilemma and make the necessary difficult choices are harbingers of an impending crisis. Her reactions to the predicament and the temptations, however, cannot be painted exclusively in black and white. Nicole has decided to prioritize her relationship with her boyfriend over her studies, and this flawed decision clearly places her in immediate academic peril. To her credit, the teenager does make the right choice about not copying her friend's lab notebook. Clearly, this decision is not motivated by ethical or moral considerations, but, rather, by the sixteen-year-old's justifiable concern about the consequences of getting caught. Nicole's awareness of basic cause-and-effect principles vis-à-vis cheating, however, is offset by her blatant disregard of the long-range consequences of allowing her romantic relationship with Curtis to interfere with her fulfilling her pressing academic obligations.

Unwilling to make the hard choices and sacrifices and to exert self-restraint vis-à-vis Curtis, Nicole elects not to deal with the boyfriend issue. Instead, she selects the path of least resistance and opts to maintain the status quo despite the certain grim academic repercussions. Fully aware of the implications of her decision, Nicole resigns herself to flunking her earth science class, going to summer school, and finishing high school with an abysmal G.P.A., assuming, of course, that she'll actually earn enough credits to graduate.

Most parents reading this case study would undoubtedly conclude that the solution to Nicole's dilemma is very simple. The sixteen-year-old must:

- Curtail the marathon school-night telephone conversations and instant messaging.
- Restrict her weekend social activities.
- Devote her free time to catching up academically.

On some level of consciousness, Nicole probably realizes what she needs to do about Curtis, but she's clearly averse to putting any restriction on the relationship. She's having too much fun. As most parents can attest, the heart and the mind of a romantically involved teenager do not always intersect, and when they don't, adolescents are prone to acting irrationally and making flawed choices. This dynamic is clearly operative in Nicole's case. She recognizes that her academic situation is deteriorating, but she persists in hurtling headlong down the track, even though she can see the wall looming at the end of the line. The handbrake is within reach, but Nicole refuses to pull on it.

Nicole's priorities are transparent. Her infatuation with Curtis and her preoccupation with having fun are clearly more important than passing her earth science course. This hierarchy of values plays the pivotal role in the pending disaster. Disinclined to suspending the immediate gratification in favor of the long-range gratification of getting good grades and having more options when she completes high school, Nicole singlemindedly pushes down on the accelerator.

The issue of Nicole's parents' role in the unfolding drama is not directly addressed, but one cannot help but wonder what they're doing while all this is transpiring. Why aren't they intervening when it's obvious that their daughter is acting irresponsibly and scuttling herself in school? Why aren't they asserting their prerogatives and putting a stop to the nightly telephone calls and instant messaging? Why aren't they restricting their daughter's weekend social activities until she can demonstrate that she's conscientiously applying herself in school?

Nicole's parents may not know all the specific details of their daughter's social escapades, but it's inconceivable that they aren't aware of what's happening. How can they justify their passivity in the face of an impending disaster? If their daughter lacks the necessary self-discipline to set limits, why aren't *they* setting the limits? Have they acquiesced to having no control over their daughter? Have they given up on her? The definitive answers to these critically important questions can not be found in the case study, and we can only infer that something is amiss in the family system.

Fact: *Parents have a compelling obligation to intervene assertively when faced with a child who is spinning out of control.* The starting point in the intervention process is for parents to communicate unequivocally and unambiguously to their child that her education is of vital importance to them and that they insist on effort, diligence, and academic responsibility. They must also explicitly communicate that they require their child to prioritize her schoolwork over her social life and that all privileges are contingent on demonstrable scholastic effort. Whether parents choose to broach these subjects democratically or autocratically, the issues must be addressed. Their child must understand that school is her primary job and takes precedence over everything else. They must unequivocally disabuse their child of any inclination to be academically irresponsible. The longer counterproductive and self-sabotaging attitudes and behavior persist, the more likely that this conduct will become an entrenched and hard-to-break habit. When a child is hurtling headlong down the track and unwilling to apply the brake, her parents must step on the brake for her. If they fail to do so, or wait too long, a derailment is inevitable.

In Nicole's case, imposing external control may provide an immediate fix for the current crisis, but this intervention is, at best, a stopgap and provides little assurance that the teenager will be able to handle similar situations down the road. In the long run, teaching Nicole how to identify key decision points in her life, analyze options, deal with predicaments, handle temptations, and anticipate immediate and long-range consequences of her behavior is a far more meaningful course of action. Nicole must acquire functional problem-solving skills. Her immediate predicament involves her earth science course. Handling this challenge, however, must also be viewed as a paradigm for Nicole being able to deal successfully with life's demands and enticements. Unless she's taught how to rationally analyze these types of situations and resolve these types of dilemmas, she's likely to remain vulnerable throughout her life.

Children who cannot solve their problems are at risk for becoming increasingly frustrated, demoralized, resistant, self-sabotaging, and dysfunctional. They are also at risk for evolving into adults who are unable to manage life's inevitable trials and tribulations.

SOLVING PROBLEMS

Fact: *Problems are an inescapable fact of life, and children who cannot constructively analyze and resolve their problems are at risk academically and psychologically.* When faced with a dilemma, children have a range of options. They can:

- Figure out how to fix or neutralize the problem.
- Run away from the problem.
- Deny the problem exists.
- Rationalize that the problem doesn't matter.
- Continue trying to handle the problem using methods that have already proven ineffectual.
- Become discouraged, demoralized, and, perhaps, dysfunctional.
- Conclude that effort is futile and give up.

All of the alternatives on the preceding list—with the obvious exception of the first alternative—are virtually guaranteed to produce unpleasant repercussions. Children who never learn how to come to grips with challenges and predicaments are destined to pay a steep price for their inadequately developed problem-solving skills.

Certainly, all children from time to time require help with handling some of the difficult dilemmas they encounter, but if they're to become self-confident and self-reliant, they must acquire their own immediately accessible problem-repair kit. Those who are immobilized by minor predicaments and who run for help whenever they encounter difficulty are prime candidates for becoming excessively dependent on their parents. These children are also at risk for remaining helpless, reliant, and codependent throughout life.

Fact: *Children must learn that major predicaments that aren't addressed and resolved rarely disappear of their own accord.* Children who stick their head in the sand and habitually run away from their problems are bound to discover that life isn't a fairy tale and that in the real world guardian angels aren't always hovering above them. This is a lesson that Nicole must learn if she's to get her academic life untracked. Her parents clearly have a compelling obligation to help her recognize the facts of life. They must figure out a way to guide Nicole to the realization that by allowing herself to be consumed by her relationship with her boyfriend, she's torpedoing herself academically. They must also help her recognize the implications of her choices. If Nicole refuses to admit that she has a problem in school, then she urgently requires a parents-instigated reality check. If, on the other hand, she's willing to accept that she does in fact have a problem, she must be taught how to solve the problem. It comes down to a question of priorities. It also comes down to Nicole's parents providing their daughter with essential guidance, support, rules, and limits.

Nicole has two basic choices. She can block out the requisite time to finish the overdue lab write-ups and do her studying, or she can continue on the current track while she hides her head in the sand and tries not to think about the impending disaster. One thing is certain: If the tenth grader chooses not to do the work, she'll have to pay the piper, and in this case, the piper is a science teacher named Mr. Takeda.

RUNNING AWAY FROM PROBLEMS

Fact: *The temptation to run from problems is especially appealing to academically discouraged children who feel inadequate and who lack self-confidence.* The unconscious "escape at all costs" mind-set of self-doubting children is driven by basic psychological survival instincts. This mind-set translates into "Why fight and get bloodied when you can run and avoid the battle?" The insecurities and apprehension of these vulnerable youngsters impel them to flee from dilemmas and challenges that could severely test and further undermine their already fragile emotional resources. Were they to confront problems head-on, strive to solve them, and then fail to do so, they would perceive these setbacks as additional tangible confirmations of their inadequacies. From the perspective of a demoralized and insecure child, it makes far more sense to simply pretend that the predicaments either don't exist or will somehow magically disappear from the radar screen.

Fact: *Achieving, self-confident children are generally more willing to confront and fix problems than are psychologically vulnerable children.* This can-do attitude, which stands in stark contrast to the mind-set of the academically discouraged child, can invariably be traced to having a positive problem-solving track record. Youngsters who've successfully handled dilemmas in the past have proven to themselves that they can handle just about anything that comes along. Ironically, many of these children may not actually be consciously aware of their problem-solving procedures. Despite this lack of conscious awareness, they nonetheless apply a highly functional and pragmatic problem-solving template whenever they're faced with a predicament. The methodology may vary slightly from child to child, but the basic procedure shares three key common denominators. Youngsters who successfully handle dilemmas:

- Identify the problem accurately (e.g., "I got a D on today's Spanish test.").
- Factor into their problem-solving deliberations past experiences with similar situations (e.g., "When Sean and I quizzed each other before last week's test, I got a 92.").
- Creatively brainstorm possible solutions.
- Select the most viable solution to try out (e.g., "I'll make sure that Sean and I sit together on the school bus so that we can quiz each other before the next test.").

In some cases, the solution to a problem may manifest spontaneously. In other cases, the solution is the end product of careful and deliberate analytical thinking and reflection. Children may wrestle with a predicament all day and go to bed still burdened. In the morning, they may wake up knowing the solution. Even while sleeping, their unconscious mind is mulling over the dilemma and sifting through the options. Of course, adults also avail themselves of this same unconscious sorting-out process when they're wrestling with their own dilemmas.

THE PARENTAL HOTLINE

Fact: *Some children will consult with their parents when faced with a major problem and will accept the help, advice, and counsel that's offered.* A child's willingness to consult with her parents about problems usually reflects three key factors: the child's personality, the nature of the rapport that has evolved over the years between the child and her parents, and the degree of trust that the child has in the parents' response style. If the child believes that her parents are empathetic, fair, and supportive, she is likely to seek and accept their advice and assistance. If, on the other hand, she concludes from past experience that her parents are intrusive, judgmental, punitive, and preachy, she's unlikely to solicit their advice or accept their assistance.

Fact: *Some children adamantly insist on handling their problems themselves, irrespective of the magnitude and seriousness of the situation.* This supreme, and perhaps headstrong, self-confidence and self-reliance may seem laudable on one level but, on another level, a child's resolve to go it alone when faced with serious problems and momentous choices can be risky, especially when the child lacks adequate life experience. Examples of serious dilemmas that could prove life-altering if handled improperly include:

- Should I agree to help my friend steal the final exam from the teacher's desk?
- Should I go to this party where I know that kids will be doing drugs?
- Should I agree to hide the package that belongs to my friend's brother even though she refuses to tell me what's inside?
- Should I take a shortcut through a gang area on the way to the concert?
- Should I buy a research paper from an online term paper company and submit it?
- Should I tell my teacher that a classmate is threatening to bring a gun to school?

Acute awareness of the potentially disastrous consequences that are likely to result if these questions are answered incorrectly is certain to strike fear and apprehension in parents. With the obvious exception of the last question, every parent desperately wants his or her child to respond to each question in the list with a resounding "No!" And every parent desperately wants his or her child to respond to the final question with a resounding "Yes!" The dread that parents feel in the pit of their stomach is triggered by their justifiable forboding about what could happen if their child confronts these situations and comes up with the wrong answers.

Fact: *Resistant, learning-aversive students are particularly prone to demonstrating stubborn go-it-alone attitude.* In many respects, the "don't interfere in my life" mind-set of resistant learners is designed to keep their parents at bay and to keep them from prying into situations that struggling students realize, either consciously or unconsciously, are being handled poorly. Entrenched defense and coping mechanisms prevent these children from acknowledging this mishandling. Certainly, Nicole would be the type of teenager who would be expected to aggressively resist any attempts on her parents' part to interfere with her relationship with her boyfriend or to ascertain its impact on her schoolwork. If her parents raised questions about the telephone calls, and were they to impose regulations and sanctions, Nicole would undoubtedly tell them in no uncertain terms to stop meddling in her affairs. Were her parents to heed this rebuke from a teenager who is clearly self-destructing academically, they would be forsaking one of their most critically important parental responsibilities.

Of course, not all of problems and challenges that children encounter are as momentous or heart-stopping as those described above. Nevertheless, even these less momentous dilemmas could still produce dire consequences if children seriously miscalculate. Examples include:

- Should I devote an extra hour to carefully proofreading my history term paper?
- Should I go straight onto college after graduating high school, or should I take a year off and look for a job?

- Should I party with my friends this weekend or spend the time studying for the history and the English midterm exams that I have to take on Monday?
- Should I spend extra time putting the important information in my class notes on index cards so that I easily study and review the key facts when preparing for the midterm?

Fact: *Parents must accept that, as children mature, their willingness to solicit and accept help with problems usually diminishes.* The desire for increasing autonomy and independence is a natural developmental phenomenon. Although parental feedback and guidance, when offered in moderation, can be invaluable resources when children are struggling with dilemmas, many youngsters, and particularly adolescents, often fail to appreciate the value of this well-meaning input. Their intense desire for independence and privacy often impels them to reject their parents' offers of assistance.

Aggressive and unsolicited parental intervention when children are confronted with predicaments can be a double-edged sword. In some situations, this intervention is absolutely imperative, especially when children are handling major challenges and problems poorly and are making obviously flawed choices that could produce calamitous repercussions. These urgent situations notwithstanding, there can be a significant potential downside when parents insist on becoming excessively involved in solving their child's problems. The involvement, however well-intentioned, could send a message to the child that her parents will always be there to rescue her and that they're prepared to take ownership of any and all predicaments that she encounters in life. The child may respond to this unconditional largesse by repeatedly dialing the parental 911 hotline whenever she finds herself in a jam, and the on-call rescue service could prevent the child from developing her own problem-solving skills and could foster a life-long codependency.

Fact: *Children who never learn how to solve problems on their own are at risk for becoming increasingly helpless, and their parents are at risk for becoming perennial enablers.* Clearly, the appropriateness and extent of parental involvement in helping children solve their problems requires an astute judgment call. This judgment call should be based on four key factors:

- The child's level of maturity.
- The risks involved in the presenting situation.
- The child's current problem-solving capabilities.
- The urgency of the problem.

Fact: *Self-confident children are usually convinced that they can handle most problems on their own.* Fortified by positive life experiences, these children view problems as annoying barriers that need to be knocked down, surmounted, or strategically circumvented. When confronted with one of these barriers, their attitude is, "Okay. I've got a problem here. What do I need to do to fix it?" Typical reactions include:

- "I'll figure out how to change the coach's attitude about my playing abilities."
- "I'll figure out how to do these geometry problems."
- "I'll figure out how to win the school election the next time."
- "I'll figure out how to pull up my grade in English."
- "I'll figure out how to convince my parents that I'm mature enough to get my learner's permit."

The common denominator in all of the preceding responses is self-assurance, and self-assurance is a function of success. Some children intuitively figure out how to handle problems. Some learn through trial and error. Some observe their parents, peers, and siblings solving problems and deliberately model their own problem-solving procedures on what they see. Other children lack these intuitive and observational capabilities and must be provided with a problem-solving template. Whether youngsters possess natural problem-solving skills or must be systematically taught these skills, the critical issue is that they learn how to deal successfully with life's challenges and dilemmas.

With effective instruction, virtually any child can master a practical step-by-step procedure for handling predicaments. Once they become convinced that they can fix what's gone wrong, their self-confidence, perceptions about themselves and the world, and willingness to confront dilemmas head-on will expand. The dynamics of this expansion are simple and straightforward: Problem-solving success produces self-confidence, and self-confidence, in turn, generates the conviction that life's problems are indeed soluble. As you can see, it's the basic achievement loop all over again (see page 12).

USING DIBS

In the preceding chapters, parents who selected the more democratic approach to modify their child's behaviors were asked to use a systematic problem-solving method called DIBS. (As previously indicated, the word DIBS is an acronym formed by the first letters of the four steps that comprise the procedure: *D*efine the problem; *I*dentify the causes; *B*rainstorm solutions; *S*elect a solution to try out.) This simple four-step method furnishes a powerful and easy-to-apply resource that children (and adults) can use to resolve virtually any problem.

If you've already successfully used the DIBS method with your child, you'll probably concur that children even as young as eight can quickly and easily master this powerful problem-solving procedure. With methodical instruction and sufficient encouragement, opportunities for practice, and affirmation for progress, the four steps will become an imprinted habit, and children will begin to routinely apply DIBS whenever they're facing a predicament. In many situations, children who have mastered the procedure will probably be able to run through the four steps in their mind without actually having to use pencil and paper. They'll automatically ask themselves:

- What's the problem?
- What's causing the problem?
- What are some creative solutions?
- Which of the brainstormed solutions seems best?

DIBS offers children an accessible and highly functional template that they can immediately superimpose on virtually any dilemma they're likely to encounter. Once they fully assimilate the procedures, they'll be far less vulnerable to becoming overwhelmed, frustrated, and demoralized by life's curveballs and sliders.

USING DIBS WITH NICOLE'S PROBLEM

If you haven't used the democratic approach in any of the preceding parent-child interactive exercises, it's recommended that you refer back to chapter 3 and reread pages 63–66 before you begin the following activity with your child. You'll find a detailed step-by-step description of how to use the procedure. Make a point of also looking at the list of Dos and Don'ts on pages 69–71. These suggestions can be instrumental in defusing resistance and avoiding showdowns and shoot-outs.

Whether your personal preference is to use the democratic or the autocratic approach when working with your child on altering counterproductive behavior, there are significant advantages to teaching your child the DIBS problem-solving procedure. This procedure can become an invaluable on-call resource that your child can use whenever she finds herself in a bind. To help her learn the method, it's recommended that you and your child use DIBS to analyze and resolve Nicole's predicament as described in the introductory case study. The procedure will furnish your child with an opportunity to apply DIBS in solving another teenager's real-world problem. For defended youngsters, this at-a-distance procedure can be far less threatening than having to immediately confront and deal with one of their own problems, and it usually triggers less knee-jerk resistance.

For children who have already used DIBS, applying the method to Nicole's predicament will serve as a review and reinforcement. For children who haven't yet been exposed to DIBS, some preliminaries are in order.

INTRODUCING DIBS TO CHILDREN WHO HAVEN'T YET USED THE PROCEDURE

Because your child is unfamiliar with DIBS, it's recommended, as stated above, that before you begin working with your child, you carefully examine how the method is applied in chapter 3 to address the issue of disorganization. To bring your child up to speed, you'll want to guide her through the problem-solving process described on pages 63–66.

To introduce this interactive problem-solving exercise, you might say, "I know that we've already dealt with the issue of disorganization, but I would like to revisit the subject and show you a neat procedure for dealing with problems. The method is called DIBS, and the word is an acronym for the four steps in the procedure. This is how it works." You would then explain the acronym as it was done in chapter 3, and you would use DIBS to solve the disorganization problem. To prevent overwhelming your child, be careful not to make the interactive session too long. This is especially relevant in the case of younger children. Your child will also need time to process and assimilate what she's learned. You may want to introduce DIBS and apply it to the disorganization problem and then schedule another session for you and your child to use DIBS to solve Nicole's predicament. A reproducible copy of the DIBS form can be found on page 265 of the appendix.

It's now time for children who have previously used DIBS and for those who have just learned the procedure to apply the method in solving Nicole's problem. You might say, "I want to read you a story about a tenth grader who finds herself in a bind in school." As it would probably be a turn-off for your child to see you reading the anecdote from a book entitled *The Resistant Learner,* a reproducible copy of the case study is provided on pages 273–276 the appendix. It's suggested that you read from one photocopy and that you give your child a second copy so that she can follow along.

You: "Now that we've read the anecdote, let me ask you a question. Do you believe that Nicole has a problem?"

At this juncture, your child may answer "yes" or "no." You want to examine her reasons without sounding critical or judgmental.

You might ask questions such as:

- "Do you think she's in danger of flunking the earth science course?"
- "What are the long-term consequences of what's happening?"
- "Are there steps she could take to fix the problem and avoid the consequences?"

You: "Okay. We agree that Nicole obviously has an important relationship with her boyfriend. We agree that she's spending a great deal of time talking on the phone with Curtis and sending instant messages to her friends. We agree that if she doesn't complete her lab write-ups she could end up flunking her earth science course. We also agree that Nicole does have a problem and that there will be consequences if she doesn't solve this problem. I'd like you to use DIBS to solve this problem. You can use this form. You'll begin with the D Step and accurately define Nicole's problem. I'm available to work with you if you would like me to, or you may prefer to do it on your own. It would actually be neat to work together on applying DIBS. It's your call."

As previously noted, one of the most initially challenging aspects of applying DIBS is for children to define the problem accurately. The definition (the *D*efine step) that you want your child to write down will ideally be: *Nicole is in danger of flunking her earth science course and perhaps other courses as well.*

Please note: It's Okay if your child's words differ slightly. The goal is for your child to sharpen her problem-defining skills, and your restrained and subtle guidance can be critically important in achieving this objective.

The causal factors (the *I*nvestigate step) you want your child to list will ideally include:

- Nicole is spending too much time talking on the phone to her boyfriend.
- Nicole is spending too much time sending instant messages to her friends.
- Nicole isn't leaving enough time to do her homework.
- Nicole isn't doing her lab write-ups.
- Nicole is unwilling to limit her weekend extracurricular activities.

Some of the solutions (the *B*rainstorming step) you want her to list will ideally include:

- She should limit her phone calls to her boyfriend.
- She should limit her instant messaging to no more than fifteen minutes every evening.
- She should set aside a big block of time each weekend to do homework and catch up.
- She should schedule two to three hours every night to do homework and catch up.
- She should make sure she writes up her lab reports right after doing the experiments.

You'll want to discuss with your child what she's written on the DIBS form. The tone of this discussion should be pleasant, and you should scrupulously avoid criticizing your child if you don't agree with the points that she has made. A far more effective strategy would be to respond to faulty logic or off-target ideas with thought-provoking points and questions.

You: "Sometimes it can be helpful to look at the issues from more than one perspective. It's obvious that having a boyfriend is very important to Nicole, and this undoubtedly would also be important to lots of girls in high school. Do you think it's possible to strike a balance between having a boyfriend, meeting your academic obligations, and getting decent grades? Would your brainstormed solution allow Nicole to achieve this balance? Based upon what you've read about her in the story, do you think she'd be willing to try your brainstormed idea? If not, why do you think she would reject the idea?

If your child is a resistant learner, there's a good chance that some of her behaviors parallel those of Nicole. The specifics may differ and your child may not be involved in a consuming romantic relationship, but her priorities may also be flawed and she, too, may be ignoring her academic obligations, procrastinating, running away from problems, and making defective decisions at critical junctures in her life.

The advantage of analyzing the modus operandi of another child with similar behaviors, attitudes, and issues is that it furnishes children with an opportunity to gain insight into their own maladaptive behaviors and attitudes. Examining this other person's conduct can be far less menacing to a highly defended child and far less likely to elicit knee-jerk resistance.

Providing your child with more than one effective problem-solving resource is certainly preferable to providing her with only one resource. Your child then has the option of choosing the method that works best for her. In some situations, she may prefer DIBS, and in other situations she may prefer to use the alternative method. It's now time to teach your child a second equally powerful problem-solving method.

USING GOALS TO SOLVE PROBLEMS

Fact: *Goal setting can be a highly effective tool for resolving or neutralizing problems.* Children who think strategically often discover that they can defuse problems by deliberately establishing specific and highly focused short- and long-term goals. For example, let's say that a ninth grader is distressed about her math grades. When she computes her test scores and homework grades, she finds that she's barely carrying a C– in the class. She realizes that she could get a D in the class if she receives low grades on the remaining weekly quizzes and does poorly on the next two unit tests and on the final exam. Because she plans to go to college, she realizes that getting a D in the course would be a major disaster. The D would also necessitate retaking the course during the summer, something she definitely doesn't want to do.

To solve this problem, the child could use DIBS. She might also use another problem-solving method called the Four-Step Goal-Setting System. If she uses this method, she would begin by describing the problem. In step two, she would target a realistic semester grade (for example, a B–) that would resolve the problem. This is her long-range goal. In step three, she would describe specific short-term goals that will allow her to attain her long-range goal. In step four, she would add additional details that improve the chances of the plan working. If the student were to use this method, her four-step plan would look like this:

Applying the Four-Step Goal-Setting System

Step 1
Describe Challenge/Problem: Improve my math grade.

Step 2
Long-Range Goal: Get a B– in math this semester.

Step 3
Short-Term Goals: Hand in homework assignments on time.
Carefully check over homework assignments
for mistakes.
Budget a minimum of forty minutes every
evening to study math and do math homework.
Carefully check over all test problems to find
careless errors.
Ask for help if I have difficulty understanding
the concepts and doing the problems.
Budget a minimum of two hours to study for
chapter tests.
Budget a minimum of six hours to study for
the math final.

Step 4
Specifics: Make certain that I carefully study the examples in the textbook before I begin doing the
assigned homework problems.
Carefully check over my work to find silly
mistakes.
Carefully go over all incorrect answers on
tests and homework assignments to make certain that I understand what I did wrong.
Don't leave studying for quizzes and tests until the last minute.
Study for tests with Heather (an A student).

If the student were to conscientiously apply the procedures described above during the remainder of the semester, her math problem would most likely be solved. The only potential obstacle that might stand in her way would entail her having difficulty comprehending the course content. If her friend Heather, the A student with whom she proposes to study, or her parents are unable to help her, she'd need to add another component to the *specifics section*, namely, getting help from a math tutor.

HELPING YOUR CHILD LEARN FSGSS

Fact: *Mastering any new skill requires deliberate application, adequate opportunities to practice, and skillful guidance and coaching.* A child's brain must imprint the individual components of each new skill before the skill will become automatic. Mastering the times tables and learning to type, spike a volleyball, put topspin on a tennis serve, or ride a skateboard are concrete examples of the axiom *practice makes perfect*.

To provide additional opportunities for your child to practice, it's recommended that you have your child use the Four-Step Goal-setting System as an alternative method for dealing with Nicole's earth science dilemma. Ask your child to quickly reread the case study. Using the form found in the appendix, have her systematically go through the steps. Your child may prefer to work with you on this exercise, or she may prefer to do it on her own. After your child has completed the procedure, you should discuss what she's written down, being careful to avoid expressing displeasure if you don't agree with some of her ideas. After this discussion, ask your child which method she prefers: DIBS or the Four-Step Goal-setting System. If she likes both procedures, you should discuss how one method might work best in certain situations and the alternative method might work best in other situations.

For further reinforcement, ask your child to select a problem that she's currently facing and have her use the goal-setting method to solve it. Irrespective of whether you personally prefer the democratic or autocratic approach, it's recommended that you use the democratic model when doing this activity with your child. The tone you establish should be one of working together so that your child can fully master a new and powerful resource. Make certain to provide encouragement and praise for progress. Children thrive on affirmation, even resistant children who have deliberately cultivated an "I couldn't care less" attitude.

To reinforce mastery of both DIBS and FPGSS, suggest to your child that she experiment using both procedures to solve school-related and nonschool-related problems over the next several weeks and that she keep you apprised of how the methods are working. Given that practice is a vital requisite to mastering any new skill, you want to encourage her to apply the two procedures until she's comfortable with them.

Be prepared to provide appropriate guidance while your child applies the methods. As she becomes more skilled, she'll probably insist on handling more and more problems on her own. This self-reliance clearly testifies to her enhanced problem-solving self-confidence. Nevertheless, you want her to know that you're available to help with thorny predicaments. The goal is for your child to assimilate the procedures and to consistently apply them on her own. You want DIBS and the Four-Step Goal-setting System to become automatic reflexes whenever your child runs into a problem.

USING GOALS TO HANDLE CHALLENGES AND SOLVE PROBLEMS

Step 1: Describe the problem or challenge.
Step 2: Identify a goal that would solve the problem.
Step 3: Set short-term goals.
Step 4: Identify specific actions that will make attaining short- and long-term goals possible.

The two problem-solving methods you've taught your child will serve her throughout life. As she becomes increasingly adept at handling problems, her self-assurance and self-esteem will expand commensurately. Once she firmly establishes the habit of using these powerful resources, she'll be able to handle whatever comes along.

7

Getting It Down on Paper and Getting It Done

A furtive glance at the clock confirmed that the nightmare would be over in less than five minutes. The ordeal couldn't end soon enough as far as Danielle was concerned. It had been an excruciating thirty-five minutes, and she was utterly bored as her teacher droned on and on about the French Revolution. "Who cares about King Louis XIV and the Third Estate? The dumb revolution happened more than two hundred years ago!" the fourteen-year-old thought bitterly.

As usual, Danielle hadn't participated in the class discussion because she was afraid she would say something stupid. The memory of the incident in third grade when her teacher embarrassed her in class because she kept losing her place when she read aloud still haunted her. That was six years ago, but the teacher's comment still reverberated in her mind: "Danielle, we would all be most appreciative if you would read the words that are actually on the page. Your version, young lady, is unfortunately nowhere near as good as the original." All the children laughed, and whenever Danielle recalled the incident she could still feel her shame and her burning cheeks. Despite her public humiliation, Danielle never told her parents about what happened that day.

Ever since, Danielle had refused to raise her hand to answer questions, volunteer information, or willingly participate in class discussions. Now as a ninth grader, she spoke only when a teacher called on her, and then with great reluctance. Usually her classmates would laugh at her off-the-wall answers and comments because it was obvious that she hadn't been paying attention and hadn't read the assigned pages in the textbook. Danielle would react to the laughter and her teacher's exasperation by looking perplexed. When the teacher turned her back, she would make silly faces and roll her eyes to the amusement of everyone in the class. Drawing pictures in her binder was far more interesting than trying to come up with answers to stupid questions about information she didn't understand and really didn't care about anyway, and the doodling helped pass the time and alleviate the boredom.

As Danielle absentmindedly drew cartoons on the cover of her binder, her teacher began to write the homework assignment on the chalkboard. "Thursday: history test, Chapter 3, Unit 1—Know important dates of the French Revolution and the social conditions that caused it." The teacher then began to discuss the unit test that would be given on Friday. She gave examples of the dates that students needed to memorize and briefly reviewed some of the social conditions that had caused the peasants to revolt and storm the Bastille in Paris. Realizing that the teacher was providing important clues about what would be covered on the test, most of Danielle's classmates furiously wrote down everything she said.

While the teacher was discussing the test, Danielle was reading the note that Stephanie had passed to her. Laughing audibly at Stephanie's description of an event at the party they had gone to on Saturday, Danielle suddenly realized that the teacher was glaring at her, and she immediately assumed her well-practiced innocent look. When the teacher turned her back to write additional information on the chalkboard, Danielle whispered something to Stephanie that caused her friend to smile broadly. In response, Danielle giggled, and this elicited another stern look from her irritated teacher. "Danielle, you'd better write down what I'm saying if you expect to pass this test," she admonished, deliberately punctuating the word "expect." Danielle reacted by looking contrite. On the top of her page of doodles, she hastily scribbled "history test." Then she began to read the second note that Stephanie passed to her. It was about the cute boy who had just transferred into their English class.

OMITTING THE CRUCIAL DETAILS

Fact: *Ineffectual learners are characteristically apathetic about important details that can make the difference between getting good grades or poor grades.* Irresponsibility and indifference are especially prevalent when resistant learners are faced with academic procedures that demand focused effort and self-discipline. To a child with a negative attitude about learning, having to meticulously record homework assignments every day can be an anathema. Vital information is frequently omitted or haphazardly slapped down on a sheet of binder paper or scrap paper. Key details such as which specific math problems have been assigned, what the directions are, when homework is due, when tests are scheduled, and what will be covered on tests are typically neglected. The predictable consequences of this failure to record homework assignments accurately include:

- Work that doesn't conform to explicit instructions.
- Missed deadlines.
- Incomplete assignments.
- Inadequate test preparation.
- Poor grades.

Even when teachers hand out a weekly assignment sheet, negligent students often proceed to lose the assignment sheet or disregard the vital information and instructions. By so doing, these students essentially negate their teachers' efforts to make certain that they know what their assignments are and when they're due.

Danielle's disdain for recording her assignments testifies to her "I couldn't care less" attitude. Although her class is studying one of the most fascinating events in European history, the ninth grader is uninterested and cerebrally detached. She's in class because she's required to be there. The course content has no meaning for her, and she has no desire to learn. While the other students diligently write down the teacher's hints about what will be covered on the chapter test, Danielle doodles in her binder and passes notes to her friend. She simply doesn't care enough to expend the necessary effort to record the clues, and in all likelihood this apathy applies not only in her history class, but in her other classes as well.

If Danielle was your daughter's best friend, and you were aware of her shenanigans, you might be tempted to admonish her for being foolish and irresponsible. Certainly, if you cared about Daniel and wanted to help her get her act together, this censure would be justifiable, as the teenager clearly seems intent on sabotaging herself academically. You might, however, want to consider a crucial mitigating factor: Danielle's self-defeating conduct is the unfortunate legacy of a teacher-instigated trauma. The behavior and attitudes she has adopted as a consequence of this trauma bear witness to the devastating emotional impact that an insensitive teacher can have on a young child whose self-concept is in its formative stages. For inexplicable reasons, this teacher felt impelled to publicly embarrass and belittle Danielle while she was struggling to read aloud, and the senseless disparagement caused a psychological wound that never fully healed. This humiliation in tandem with Danielle's obvious reading difficulties essentially destroyed the third grader's academic self-confidence.

Six years later, the damage caused by the teacher's caustic comment is painfully evident. Danielle is now a resistant, psychologically defeated teenager who is simply marking time in school until her educational ordeal is over. Firmly convinced that she's mentally incompetent, the fourteen-year-old appears compelled to confirm her inadequacies by acting witlessly in school. In much the same way that a child with deficient self-esteem might assume and cultivate the role of the class clown to make people laugh and to hide his insecurities, Danielle assumes and cultivates the role of the class dunce. Her behavior produces the desired effect, and she succeeds in convincing everyone that she is indeed functionally incompetent. Her self-deprecating actions are deliberate, but Danielle is probably oblivious to the unconscious psychological forces that drive her behavior. Although she can recall the distressing event, she is in all likelihood unaware of the actual extent of the emotional damage that was inflicted on her. Nor is she cognizant of how this seminal experience warped her sense of self, her perceptions, her associations with school and with learning, and her conduct.

That Danielle's deliberately cultivated self-deprecating demeanor mirrors her underlying feelings of inadequacy is self-evident. By acting in consonance with how she perceives herself and by assuming the role of the class dimwit, a dyslexic child fashions an identity for herself. With her off-the-wall comments and responses, an insecure and psychologically vulnerable fourteen-year-old proclaims, *This is who I am. This is how I act. It's okay to laugh at me.* Although this contrived persona further undermines her already diminished sense of self-worth, the manufactured identity also provides a comfort zone and a refuge.

Fact: *Successful students understand how the academic achievement game is played, and they realize that they can get better grades and reduce their stress by knowing precisely what their homework assignments are.* Achieving students are clear about what counts. They recognize that carefully recording their assignments is a requisite to creating a functional study schedule, developing an ordered flowchart of assigned tasks, and getting their work completed and submitted on time. They also realize that the payoffs attendant to getting good grades more than justify the effort and self-discipline required to write down their assignments.

The explanation for why children do a poor job of recording assignments varies. Some children have never been taught an effective homework-recording system. Others actually know how to record their assignments but lack the requisite willpower and self-discipline to make certain that they've included the essential information and details. And others such as Danielle, who are psychologically defended because of learning problems, no longer care enough about their academic performance to do what's clearly in their own self-interest.

FACTORS RESPONSIBLE FOR INADEQUATE HOMEWORK-RECORDING PROCEDURES

- deficient instruction
- inadequate supervision
- demoralization attributable to learning problems
- laziness
- poor motivation

- opposition to tasks requiring diligence
- habitual inattention to details
- delusions that key information can be recalled without needing to be recorded
- disregard of the consequences for failing to do assigned homework and for failing to submit the work on time
- concentration deficits that undermine self-discipline and attention to details

Children who fail to write down their assignments properly either don't fathom, or are in denial of, an immutable cause-and-effect principle that applies in school and in the world beyond school, namely, *you can't do the job properly if you don't know what the job entails.* Whatever the underlying motivation for their active or passive opposition to recording their homework assignments, these children are clearly on a collision course with the grading system.

HEY, I'LL REMEMBER . . .

Fact: *Children who are uncertain about their assignments are destined to work ineffectually.* The unwillingness of many resistant and underperforming students to record their assignments accurately and to include important details and specific directions can drive parents to despair. Acutely aware of the academic implications of their child's maladaptive behavior, these parents may recognize that intervention is vital, but they may be uncertain about how to intercede and about who should handle the intervention. Are they responsible for teaching their child effective homework-recording procedures and for monitoring their child to make certain he is consistently applying the procedures, or do these responsibilities rightfully belong to the teacher? This question is the equivalent of asking whether you should boil the tap water if the water supply becomes contaminated or whether you should wait for the water department to add more chlorine at the pumping plant. Clearly, in urgent situations, parents must count on themselves, and they must do whatever needs to done to make certain that their child handles the immediate crisis.

It would be ideal, of course, if all third-grade teachers systematically taught their students proper homework-recording methods. It would also be ideal if fourth- and fifth-grade teachers systematically reinforced these procedures and monitored students to make sure that they are consistently applying the methods. If such instruction and supervision are not provided, and a child is having difficulty recording oral or written assignments or properly utilizing teacher-prepared assignment sheets, then the child's parents have no choice but to teach the fundamentals and provide the necessary monitoring.

When teachers indicate on progress sheets and report cards that assignments aren't being completed properly or submitted on time, warning bells should go off. Scheduling a conference with the teachers in question is imperative. The child's specific homework-recording and homework-completion deficits must be identified, addressed, and corrected. Whether teachers or parents assume the instructional responsibility begs the issue. The problem needs to be solved, period.

If a child has been taught how to record assignments and refuses to do so, then the primary emphasis shifts from instruction to supervision. The child's parents (or tutor) must first confirm, however, that the child actually understands what needs to be written down. If they determine that the homework-recording problem isn't attributable to confusion, but rather to laziness and irresponsibility, they must methodically teach their child how to do the job, and they must unambiguously communicate that compliance with the homework-recording and homework-completion guidelines is obligatory. The next step is to keep a watchful eye on the child until she can unequivocally demonstrate that she's consistently doing what's required.

Fact: *Teachers' homework assignment procedures can vary widely.* Some teachers announce assignments orally at the end of class, and they require students to write down what they dictate. Some write the day's or the week's assignments on the chalkboard and require students to copy them. Others hand out prepared weekly or monthly homework sheets to sidestep the homework-recording dilemma and guarantee conformity. In fact, many school districts actually mandate that weekly teacher-prepared assignment sheets be provided for all students.

Whatever the homework assignment procedure, students must be able to go home at the end of the day knowing what their specific assignments are. If their teacher announces homework assignments orally, students must be capable of recording the verbally transmitted information accurately. If the teacher writes assignments on the chalkboard, they must be capable of meticulously copying the data on a designated assignment sheet in their binder. If the teacher furnishes weekly assignment sheets, students must preserve these sheets, refer to them when doing their homework, and make certain that they're completing their work as explicitly instructed.

Unfortunately, resistant learners such as Danielle often disavow the preceding common-sense procedure. More often than not, these children:

- scribble oral homework assignments haphazardly on scraps of paper.
- copy assignments written on the chalkboard imprecisely.
- stuff teacher-prepared assignment sheets into their backpack where they become another creased and disregarded piece of litter.

These propensities must be reoriented if underperforming children are to complete their work as instructed and succeed academically.

Fact: *Resistant learners generally regard homework as a diabolic torture that's unfairly imposed on them after they've already suffered through seven agonizing hours of school.* At the end of an excruciatingly unpleasant day, the last thing a struggling or learning-aversive child wants to confront is the prospect of having to do more schoolwork. The thought of being required to read twenty pages in a history textbook, do fifteen math problems, write a book report, learn twenty new Spanish vocabulary words and three irregular conjugations, and study for a science test typically triggers knee-jerk opposition. What the child really wants to do is forget about school. This means playing sports, listening to music, watching TV, playing video games, calling friends, or surfing the Internet. From the child's perspective, what kid would conceivably want to waste three precious hours doing homework and studying? That these students are disinclined to writing down and completing their assignments should come as no surprise. By not recording some or all of their assignments, they are able to delude themselves that everything is okay and perhaps temporarily deceive their parents that they don't really have any homework.

INEFFECTUAL LEARNING AND RECORDING
OF ASSIGNMENTS

Fact: *Children with learning and/or concentration problems are frequently confused about what's been assigned, when it's due, and what the explicit directions are.* Struggling learners with *auditory decoding* and *auditory memory* deficits are at a particular disadvantage when homework is announced orally. Because these students typically find it extremely challenging to listen, write, and recall at the same time, they are often overwhelmed by assignments that involve complex directions and contain a great deal of information. Their confusion, anxiety, and feelings of incompetence magnify their homework recording difficulties, and they often go into shutdown when their teachers announce their homework assignments. Believing in miracles, they simply trust that they'll somehow figure out what they're supposed to do when they get home.

Students with *visual processing difficulties* also have difficulty handling homework assignments. These children characteristically struggle to understand and assimilate written information, irrespective of whether assignments are written on the chalkboard or handed out on teacher-prepared weekly assignment sheets. ADHD can, of course, further compound the homework recording difficulties of students who have auditory or visual processing deficits.

Whereas efficient learners can usually figure out on their own how to create an effective homework-recording system, ineffectual learners often lack this intuitive capability. These students require formal, methodical instruction in how to record assignments and effectively utilize assignment handouts. Unfortunately, for inexplicable reasons many elementary schools do not provide this systematic instruction.

Fact: *Once children are taught how to record their assignments, they must practice until the procedures are imprinted.* Resistant learners require a practical, functional, easy-to-learn, and easy-to-apply homework-recording system. The procedures must then be consistently applied until they're fully assimilated and become automatic. When teachers announce assignments or discuss homework handouts, children must be trained to immediately open their binder to a designated section where assignments are written and where teacher-prepared weekly assignment sheets are inserted. Once they've been taught how to record the key information and how to use homework handouts effectively, they must be monitored until they can demonstrate that they can get the job done properly. In the interim, parents will need to verify the legibility, accuracy, and completeness of their child's recorded assignments, and they'll need to provide feedback, encouragement, and affirmation for improvement. (See pages 52–53). They'll also need to verify their child is completing and submitting her assignments on time. (Methods for achieving these objectives are described later in this chapter.)

THE NUTS AND BOLTS OF RECORDING ASSIGNMENTS

Fact: *Teachers are intolerant of conduct that they consider irresponsible, and this intolerance becomes especially evident in middle school and high school.* With obvious justification, teachers require that homework be completed according to their instructions. They also require that assignments be submitted on time. For example, a Spanish teacher might instruct students to write their name on the top line adjacent to the red right-hand margin and to write the date on the second line adjacent to the red margin. She may indicate that she wants students to use a pencil and to skip a line between their answers. She may also instruct students to circle the vocabulary word that they've used, underline each regular verb once, and underline each irregular verb twice. Realizing that the teacher will lower their grade if they fail to comply with her explicit directions, successful students will make certain that they meticulously follow these directions.

Resistant students have a very different attitude about following directions. Even if they actually do record their teacher's instructions, these children often then proceed to disregard the directions. Their obliviousness and, in some instances, willful heedlessness is consonant with the indifference to requirements and details that is characteristic of ineffectual learners.

Teachers look very unfavorably on students who ignore their instructions, and they penalize those who are cavalier about meeting deadlines, negligent about details, and unwilling to proofread their work for careless mistakes. These teachers are also disinclined to accept excuses unless there's a compelling justification. Successful students recognize that they must adjust to their teachers' assignment style, and they must comply with their teachers' demands. This expedient pragmatism is the benchmark of strategic thinking, and strategic thinking is one of the key factors that differentiates achieving students from underachieving students.

To make the foregoing discussion more concrete, imagine that the following English assignment is written on the chalkboard or is included in a teacher-prepared homework sheet.

ENGLISH ASSIGNMENT
DATE: 10/21

Exercises at the end of Unit 2, page 29. Answer odd-numbered questions (1, 3, 5, 7, 9, and 11). Number each answer and use complete sentences. Underline transitive verbs once and intransitive verbs twice. Skip a line between each answer. Write your name on the top line, right-hand side. Write the date below. Due tomorrow—10/22.

As you can see, the teacher's instructions are precise and easy to understand. A child who is convinced that she can recall the information by simply reading it once on the chalkboard may not bother to record the assignment, or she may simply write: "Unit 1, chapter 2. Do exercises." Having omitted key details, the student is likely to submit work that doesn't conform to the teacher's clearly stated directions. Unless she has a photographic memory, she's likely to forget something. Even if the preceding assignment were recorded on a teacher-prepared weekly homework assignment sheet, the child who casually glances at the instructions without carefully making note of the specific instructions is likely to overlook key details.

Fact: *To assume that your child's school will address homework-recording difficulties could prove to be a serious miscalculation.* If your child is in elementary school, her teacher may agree to verify at the end of the day that she has written down her assignments correctly and has completed and submitted the previous day's homework. It's unlikely, however, that middle school and high school teachers would be willing to do so, especially in view of the fact that they may be teaching as many as 150 students every day. Many teachers in the upper grades would maintain that it's not their job to play "nursemaid" to irresponsible students. They would also contend that their students should be solely accountable for recording their assignments. These teachers are likely to construe the failure to record assignments or follow the instructions on homework handouts as indicative of an attitude problem. They don't want to hear excuses about why a student is having difficulty recording or understanding her assignments, and they would vigorously assert that their job is to teach and not to mollycoddle neglectful students.

Even if a teacher were to consent to monitor a child's homework-recording methods, this is at best a stopgap measure. There's always a major potential downside to continual and excessive supervision: The child could become dependent on her teacher to provide this ongoing monitoring service. Certainly, teacher supervision is invaluable during the short-term, but unless children learn how to get the information down on paper, the homework-recording problem is likely to recur when the supervision is withdrawn. For this reason, it's imperative that the parents of a negligent student provide their child with practical homework-recording procedures and that they insist that she consistently use these procedures. At the onset, parents will need to supply ongoing supervision, encouragement, feedback, and affirmation for progress. Once the child masters the system and experiences the benefits, she'll be more predisposed to use the system consistently.

A PROCEDURAL BLUEPRINT: TEACHING THE ABCs OF RECORDING ASSIGNMENTS

Fact: *Highly functional homework-recording and homework-completion procedures can be quickly taught and easily assimilated.* A concomitant to teaching your child an effective homework-recording system is to communicate unequivocally to your child that she's expected to use the system every day. She must realize that you're going to monitor her until you're certain that she's writing down precisely what needs to be written down and that she's completing the assigned work and submitting it when it's due.

Even if your child's teacher provides a homework handout at the beginning of the week, your child should still be taught how to record orally conveyed assignments and assignments that are written on the chalkboard. Next year's teachers may not hand out prepared assignment sheets. Teachers also frequently expand in class on the information recorded on homework handouts. They may offer clues about how to do math problems, provide hints about what will be covered on the next Spanish test, make suggestions about how to do research for an assigned term paper, and explain a complex procedure described in a chemistry textbook. Your child must be able to record this information.

You can choose either the autocratic or the democratic approach to teach your child effective homework-recording procedures. Select the method that's most congruent with your parenting style and the method that you believe can be used most productively with your child.

Let's first examine an autocratic method. If you recall, certain specific guidelines can make this approach more effective.

RECORDING ASSIGNMENTS
The Autocratic Approach

Guidelines

- Create a conducive context for interaction.
- Check out your child's perceptions (see checklist).
- Define the problem.
- Examine the evidence.
- Provide functional assignment-recording procedures.
- Supervise implementation.
- Acknowledge effort and affirm progress.

Let's now see how the more autocratic approach might be applied to teach your child homework-recording skills.

Scenario: (*Please note: The interactive context you initiate parallels the one you created in dealing with disorganization.*) You ask your child to come into the kitchen or the dining room. You are calm. Siblings in the area should be instructed to leave. You ask your child to sit in a chair facing you so that you can establish and maintain eye contact. Your tone of voice is friendly and nonthreatening, but, at the same time, firm and decisive.

You: "As you recall, I was concerned about your disorganization, and we've addressed this concern. I have another concern. Let me tell you what it is. I'm distressed that you aren't accurately recording your assignments. I can tell from your teachers' comments on report cards and progress reports that you're not handing in your work on time and that the assignments you do hand in are often incomplete and don't follow the teachers' specific instructions. I don't want to get into an argument about this with you now. I believe that you do, in fact, have a problem with recording your assignments, and I want you to solve this problem. Before we examine the problem, I want you to take a few minutes to complete another checklist. Be honest in filling it out, and don't try to respond the way you think I want you to respond. Here's the checklist. Take as much time as you need to complete it."

Give your child a few moments to complete the inventory. If she has significant reading problems, you may need to help her read the statements on the checklist. Depending on her age and learning difficulties, you may also need to explain how to use the code. If you do help your child with the checklist, remember not to express—verbally or with facial expressions—a positive or negative reaction to her responses as she completes the inventory. (A reproducible copy of this inventory can be found on page 278 in the appendix.)

ASSIGNMENT-RECORDING CHECKLIST

CODE: 1 = Never 2 = Rarely 3 = Sometimes 4 = Often 5 = Always

I know what my assignments are in every subject. ___

I write down important details such as page numbers,
assigned problems, and specific directions. ___

I make certain that I know when my assignments are due. ___

I record all of the clues that my teachers provide about
what will be covered on tests. ___

I use abbreviations that I can understand. ___

I note the due date for long-range projects such as
book reports and term papers. ___

I write down the announced dates of all tests and exams. ___

I carefully read and carefully follow instructions on
teacher-prepared assignment sheets. ___

I check off my completed assignments on my assignment sheet. ___

I make certain that I bring my completed assignments to school. ___

I make certain that I submit my assignments on time. ___

I keep my assignment sheet in a specific location in my binder. ___

Scenario: After giving your child sufficient time to complete the checklist, you return to the kitchen or dining room. You pull up a chair and ask your child to sit next to you.

You: "Let's take a look at your responses to the statements on the checklist. Before beginning, I want to say once more that you are entitled to your opinions, and I am entitled to mine. If there are differences, we need to discuss them calmly. Okay. You've indicated that you know what your assignments are in every subject. My impressions are very different. In fact, let's take a look at your assignment sheet now. I'd like you to get your binder."

Scenario: You have your child's assignment sheet in front of you. (If her teacher distributes a teacher-prepared assignment sheet, you'll need to modify the following interaction. You would go through the handout and show her how to identify and use highlighters to indicate important information such as problem numbers and explicit directions for doing specific assignments. This instructional procedure is summarized on page 174. Even if your child's teacher provides homework handouts, it would still be advisable to do the following activity with her, as she will at some point need to know how to record assignments on her own.)

You: "What I see is information scribbled haphazardly on pages in your binder. There's no apparent system. You've recorded very little information and very few, if any, details about your teachers' specific instructions. I also don't see your English or science assignments recorded on the sheet. If I were filling out the checklist for you, I'd have to mark a 5 about your knowing what your assignments are in every subject. Do you think it would be unreasonable for me to give you a 5? If so, tell me why."

Allow your child to express her feelings, even if her position contradicts the evidence, but to avoid an argument or showdown, refer back to this evidence when you respond to her contentions.

You would then go through the entire checklist while being careful not to be demeaning. Examine the concrete and observable evidence with your child. Reemphasize that you don't want to argue but, rather, that you want compare responses based upon the facts. When you and your child have completed this procedure (it should take no more than ten minutes), it's time to move onto the next step. (Please note: Don't be deterred if your child tells you that her teachers have already shown her how to record assignments. If she's not writing down her homework, she obviously needs additional instruction, practice, and reinforcement. You want her to realize unequivocally that you want the homework-recording procedure to become an automatic habit.)

You: "Okay. I'm convinced that you have difficulty recording your assignments properly. There's no need for us to argue about this. The evidence is in your binder. If you reject this evidence and refuse to

acknowledge that you have a problem, things get more complicated. You're simply going to have to trust me that you aren't writing down your homework assignments accurately and completely.
This cannot help but have a negative effect on your grades. You're
going to have to bow to my wishes and solve this problem before
you torpedo yourself in school."

Allow your child to respond, but make it clear—without expressing
frustration or anger—that you fully expect her to resolve the issue.

You: "You're going to begin solving the problem now. Take a look at
this model homework assignment sheet [see page 166]. As you can
see, it provides space for writing down an entire week's assignments. Subjects are listed vertically on the left and the days of the
week are listed horizontally across the top. This model is a sample
of a student's assignment sheet. You can see that the student is using abbreviations to save time and space. Let's take a few moments
to examine a list of common abbreviations that you can use to
record your assignments [see page 164]. To familiarize you with
the abbreviations, I'd like you to read the Monday and Tuesday
sample assignments for each subject. The more practice you have
using the abbreviations, the better. Before long they will become
second nature and using them will become automatic. [Be prepared
to help your child decode unfamiliar abbreviations such as t.p.
(term paper).] Notice that there's also a place to mark when each
assignment has been completed. To help you learn the system, I'll
pretend to be your teacher in each of your academic subjects, and
I'll give you a make-believe assignment [dictate the assignments
found on page 165]. I want you to write down the assignments just
as you would in school."

Blank reproducible copies of both assignment sheets can be found
on pages 280–281 in the appendix. As your child may make mistakes
and may want to start over, it is recommended that you photocopy several copies of the practice assignment sheet.

You: "You can use the sample assignment sheet as a guide and incorporate as many abbreviations as possible, but make sure that you can read your own abbreviations. When I read the assignment aloud, I'll speak slowly and clearly. If your teacher speaks more rapidly, you'll have to force yourself to write quickly when you're in class. As you become more skilled in recording oral assignments and using abbreviations, you'll find that your writing speed will increase. Later you'll practice recording a different assignment that we'll pretend has been written on the chalkboard. Obviously, this assignment will actually have to be written on a piece of paper, as we don't have a chalkboard. You'll copy the key information onto a second blank assignment sheet. Then you'll examine an example of a teacher-prepared assignment handout. You'll learn how to use it, and you'll get into the habit of reading the information carefully and using different highlighters to indicate important details such as assigned problems, due dates, test dates, and important directions."

(Please note: These interactive sessions should last no more than twenty to thirty minutes and should be geared to your child's maturity and attention span. Overkill will make the interactive sessions painful for both you and your child and will trigger counterproductive resistance and resentment. Your child will probably require two or three sessions to complete this homework-recording activity. Stop when you observe that your child has reached the saturation point and announce, "We'll finish up tomorrow.")

Common Abbreviations:

ans = answer	exp = explain	prac = practice	r.w. = rewrite
b.r. = book report	fin = finish	prob = problems	sec = section
ch = chapter	F = final exam	prfrd = proofread	sen = sentence
comp = complete	form = formula	Q = quiz	sk = skip
crct = correct	h.i. = hand in	ques = question	sp = spell
d = due	hmw = homework	rd = read	st = study
df = define	h/o = handout	r.d. = rough draft	s.w. = show work
	imp = important	rp = repeat	T = test
E = exam	l = learn	rpt = report	T.P. = term paper
ess = essay	m/t = midterm exam	rr = reread	u = unit
ex = example	o/b = open book	rvs = revise	vocab = vocabulary
exer = exercise	p = page	rvw = review	wkbk = workbook

Symbols:

¶ = paragraph	+ = plus	− = minus	> = greater than
< = less than	# = number	@ = at	% = percent
$ = money	& = and	* = important	{} = combine
>> = leading to	≤ = less than or equal to	≥ = more than or equal to	≠ = not equal to
± = plus or minus	÷ = divide	× = multiply	? = question

Sample Assignment Sheet

SUBJECTS	MONDAY	TUESDAY	WEDNESDAY	THURSDAY	FRIDAY
Math	p 127–28 probs. 10–20 s.w. I form p 120 *completed: X*	rvw p 125–27 p 128–29 probs. 1–15 sw *completed: X*	*completed:*	*completed:*	*completed:*
Social Studies	ch 5 rd p 92–99 ans ques p 102 1–8 comp sen *completed: X*	begin research T.P. Fr. Revol. rd ch 5 p 131–40 ans ques p. 142 1–7 comp. sen *completed: X*	*completed:*	*completed:*	*completed:*
English	rd story p. 81–89 ans ques p 94 st vocab wrds p 95 *completed: X*	write 10 sen. voc. wrds. p. 61 prfrd. b.r. *completed: X*	*completed:*	*completed:*	*completed:*
Science	u 4 p 80–89 I forms p 87 *completed: X*	rd 74–80 ans ques 1–8 p. 81 *completed: X*	*completed:*	*completed:*	*completed:*
Tests & Reports	math Q. Friday 10/17 u. 3 Eng. b.r. Mon. 10/20 *completed:* *completed:*	voc Q Thurs. 10/16 *completed:* *completed:*	*completed:* *completed:*	*completed:* *completed:*	*completed:* *completed:*

Practice Assignment Sheet

SUBJECTS	MONDAY	TUESDAY	WEDNESDAY	THURSDAY	FRIDAY
Math	completed:	completed:	completed:	completed:	completed:
Social Studies	completed:	completed:	completed:	completed:	completed:
English	completed:	completed:	completed:	completed:	completed:
Science	completed:	completed:	completed:	completed:	completed:
Tests & Reports	completed: completed:	completed: completed:	completed: completed:	completed: completed:	completed: completed:

PRACTICE ORAL HOMEWORK ASSIGNMENT

Please note: Abbreviations have not been used below. Your child, however, should use them when recording these practice assignments on the assignment sheet.

Social Studies:	Due Tues.
	Read pages 72–80
	Answer questions 1–7 pg. 81
	Complete sentences. Skip line between answers.
	Test on chapter 2 Friday
Science:	Due Wed.
	Read pages 82–91
	Know definitions of six words on page 93
Math:	Due Tues.
	page 52 problems 1–9
	page 53 problems 1–6
	show your work (not just the answers)
English:	Due Tues.
	Learn vocabulary words page 76
	Use each word in a sentence that shows you understand the meaning. Underline the vocabulary word.

As you dictate the assignment, look over your child's shoulder and provide guidance and encouragement. Remember that this is a focused skill development and practice session, and not a "test." Your approach may be autocratic in that you're insisting that your child methodically apply specific homework recording procedures, but the tone you establish should be friendly. You want to create a positive context, but at the same time you want to communicate unequivocally that it's time for the assignment-recording problem to be resolved.

Scenario: You're now going to focus on making certain that your child knows how to use teacher-prepared assignment sheets. You and your child are sitting at a table with a facsimile homework assignment handout that focuses on two subjects—math and science.

You: "Let's look at this sample assignment handout and pretend that a teacher has handed it out at the beginning of the week. As you can see, I've provided four highlight pens. You're going to practice reading the handout carefully and using the highlighter to indicate key details. You're also going to learn to check off each assignment on the handout after you've completed it."

SAMPLE TEACHER-PREPARED MATH AND SCIENCE ASSIGNMENT SHEETS

Math:
Due Tues.
page 17
problems 1–8 (show work)
Due Wed.
page 20 problems 1–12 (show work)
Due Thurs.
page 25
problems 1–12 (show work)
Due Fri.
page 29
problems 1–7 (show work)

Science:
Due Tues.
Exercises page 60 1–8
Test Wed.
Due Wed.
Read pages 61–66
Exercises page 67 1–5
Due Thurs.
Pages 67–73
Exercises page 76 1–6
Due Fri.
Test

You: "You're going to use these four highlighters. Choose one color to highlight specific pages, exercises and problem numbers, the second color to indicate *due dates* for assignments, the third color to highlight scheduled tests and quizzes and reports and papers that are due later, and the fourth color to highlight specific instruction. On a separate piece of paper in your binder, I want you to write down a code that indicates what the colors represent. You'll consistently use these same colors from this point on whenever you're given a teacher-prepared assignment sheet. The last step in the procedure is to check off each assignment when it's completed. Okay. You've learned the system. For the next two weeks I'll monitor you to make certain you're using the system consistently. When you can demonstrate that you're recording your assignments properly, I'll no longer need to continue monitoring you. There are, however, four additional steps that you'll need to take:

- Make sure that you're following your teacher's directions carefully. If she wants you to skip a line after each answer, make certain that you do so.
- Check over your work for careless mistakes.
- Make certain that you submit your completed assignments when they're due.
- Insert your assignment sheet in the front of your binder so that you can always find it.

Once the system becomes a habit, you'll use it automatically."

Let's now examine how the more democratic approach can be used to solve the homework-recording problem.

RECORDING ASSIGNMENTS
The Democratic Approach

Guidelines

- Create a conducive context for interaction.
- Check out your child's perceptions (see checklist).
- Define the problem.
- Examine the evidence.
- Provide functional homework-recording procedures.
- Supervise implementation.
- Acknowledge effort and affirm progress.

Scenario: *The first two steps of this method are the same as the one used in the autocratic approach.* The primary difference is one of tone. You inform your child that you're concerned about how she's recording her assignments. She completes the checklist (see page 160). You ask her to show you her assignment sheet. You review her responses on the checklist, examine the "evidence" in her binder, and communicate your observations. You're now sitting at the kitchen or dining room table. Your child is sitting next to you.

You: "Okay. From our discussion about your responses on the checklist, you can tell that I have a problem about how you're recording your assignments. I want to work with you on solving this problem. We'll use DIBS, the method we used to deal with the disorganization problem. If you recall, DIBS is an acronym made from the first letter of the four steps in this problem-solving system. Let's review the four steps by writing them again on a piece of paper."

DIBS

Define the Problem: _____

Investigate the Causes of the Problem: _____

_____

_____

_____

_____

Brainstorm Solutions to the Problem: _____

_____

_____

Select a Solution to Try Out: _____

You: "I'll start out by defining my problem."

Define: I* don't want to receive any more notes from your teacher telling me that you're not completing your assignments properly and submitting them on time.

Investigate: I can see that you're continually confused about your homework assignments.

I hear you calling your friends to find out what's been assigned.

---

*Remember to use "I" messages as opposed to "you" messages (e.g., "I get upset when you don't record your assignments properly." versus "You make me upset when you don't record your assignments properly.") As previously stated, this less accusatory communication strategy is less likely to elicit resistance and resentment.

I'm convinced your incomplete and late assignments are having a negative effect on the quality of our schoolwork and your grades.

I experience a lot of stress because I believe that you're torpedoing yourself in school.

Brainstorm: I could accept that you aren't going to record your assignments properly.

I could let you sink or swim on your own in school.

I could teach you an effective system for recording your assignments.

Solution: I could teach you an effective system for recording your assignments.

You: "I hope you can see that the first two brainstormed solutions are unacceptable because I have a responsibility to make certain that you make your best effort in school. The only realistic choice I have is to help you develop a procedure for doing a better job of recording your assignments and to make certain you use this procedure consistently.

"Now that I've solved my problem, let's use DIBS to help you solve your problem. If you don't agree that you're having difficulty recording assignments, so be it. Based upon the evidence that we examined, I'm convinced that there's a problem."

(Please note: As this juncture, you may want to reason with your child and patiently discuss the "evidence" and why this evidence indicates a homework-recording problem. Ideally, your child will acknowledge the difficulty and be receptive to developing a better homework-recording system. If your child resists acknowledging the problem, tell her that you still want her to use DIBS.)

You: "Okay, let's use this DIBS form to define the problem accurately."

Using the form with the DIBS steps that you've previously photocopied, you would guide your child through the four-step process.

You might want to refer to chapter 6 to review what you've taught your child about using DIBS. The problem should be defined accurately and precisely, e.g., "I'm not recording my assignments properly." One of the possible causes that your child lists in the Investigate section could be: "I've developed some bad habits." Make suggestions, but resist the temptation to do the DIBS exercise for your child. To do so would discourage her from developing her own thinking skills and would dissuade her from active involvement in the problem-solving process. Allow your child to include heartfelt reasons that you might consider illogical, such as: "I don't write down my assignments because I hate school." These reasons should be acknowledged, listed, and discussed. Permit your child to list brainstormed solutions that you believe are unreasonable or impractical. These should be examined with sensitivity. Make certain by means of discussion and suggestion that she also includes on her brainstorming list words to the effect: "I need to develop a homework-recording system." Guiding her to include this solution may require finesse on your part. You might then suggest that she select this solution as the first one to try out. Once she makes this selection, have her list the steps that she must take to achieve the objective. During this problem-solving process, you can make suggestions and provide guidance but avoid being heavy-handed and autocratically imposing solutions on your child. The objective is for your child to formulate, ideally on her own, specific steps that can solve her problem, such as using an assignment sheet on which she can list each subject and write down directions, page numbers, specific exercises, problem numbers, and due dates. You must remind yourself that one of your important goals is to help your child master a problem-solving methodology that she'll be able to use not only in this particular situation, but also in a range of other challenging situations that will present themselves throughout her life. It's important to acknowledge and affirm your child's insights. At this juncture, you should say: "Let's look at this sample assignment sheet [page 280] and this list of abbreviations. Then let's see if you can read the abbreviations used on the sample sheet. I'm going to give you a practice assignment and you'll write it down in the assignment sheet."

Use the instructional procedures described in the Autocratic Approach section (page 158).

REVIEWING THE STEPS FOR RECORDING AND COMPLETING ASSIGNMENTS

#1 Make certain that you record key details and directions (page numbers, problem or exercise numbers, due dates, and specific instructions.)

#2 Use abbreviations that you understand.

#3 Use different colored highlighters to indicate assigned problems, due dates, and long-range projects on teacher-prepared assignment sheets.

#4 Pay special attention to the teacher's hints about what will be covered on quizzes and tests.

#5 Check off each completed assignment.

#6 Make certain you submit your completed assignments on time.

Rest assured that virtually every child can assimilate the homework-recording procedures described in this chapter. With sufficient practice, supervision, and encouragement, these procedures will become an automatic habit.

8

Dealing with the Clock

As usual, Curtis ran out of time and didn't complete his history report by the Friday deadline. A consummate procrastinator, the eleven-year-old had long ago placed homework at the top of his "put off for as long as possible" list. The fact that he hadn't finished the report on time didn't surprise his mother at all. Assignments left until the very last minute and incomplete homework were standard operating procedure.

The after-school routine was predictable. Curtis would arrive home from school at 3:15 and immediately head to his room where he would go online. After about thirty minutes of visiting his favorite Web sites, he would switch to playing video games on his Game Boy and would do so until dinnertime at six. Although his mother had established clear-cut guidelines about when the fifth grader was to start his homework, enforcing the regulations was another story.

According to the rules, Curtis was free after school for an hour and a half to do whatever he wanted. At five he was to start his homework and work until dinner. After dinner he was supposed to study without distractions and with minimal study breaks until his homework was finished. This meant no TV, video games, telephone calls, or Internet. When he completed his studying, he could watch TV, telephone friends, play games, or go online until bedtime at nine thirty.

In practice, these rules had little effect on the eleven-year-old. Curtis would find a million excuses not to begin his homework at five. He would fool around in his room, surf the Internet, or begin shooting baskets using a toy basketball and a small basketball hoop that he had affixed to the back of the door to his room. Time would slip away, and

Curtis rarely cracked a book before his mother called him downstairs for dinner. This invariably led to tension and recriminations at the table. His mother would ask if he had begun his homework, and Curtis would respond with obvious exasperation, "Don't worry. I'll do it after dinner." For emphasis, he would make a point of carefully enunciating each word.

After dinner, Curtis would come up with more excuses for not studying. At about thirty minutes before bedtime, he would switch on the homework afterburner, but this burst of effort was invariably too little and too late to make a difference. He always ran out of time, and his assignments were usually incomplete and replete with careless spelling and math mistakes. Sometimes Curtis would submit his homework late, and sometimes he wouldn't even bother to submit it at all.

Studying for tests was also invariably left to the last minute, although Curtis could usually manage to pass tests with minimal studying because he was very bright. The marginal grades he received seemed to satisfy him, but it was obvious to everyone that the eleven-year-old was capable of much more.

Curtis's teacher was resigned to his irresponsibility and regularly "rewarded" his lack of effort, shoddy work, incomplete assignments, and missed deadlines with Ds and occasional Fs. When the teacher averaged Curtis's test scores and homework grades, Curtis usually had barely a passing grade in each subject. Mr. Carter's comments on progress sheets and report cards regularly included, "Curtis is not working up to his full potential," and "Curtis is not studying or handing in his homework."

The nightly after-dinner confrontations were scripted. Curtis's mother would poke her head into his room and see him sprawled on the floor playing a game, shooting baskets, or tossing a ball in the air. She would then remind him about his homework. If he were still goofing off the second time she looked in on him, she would sternly admonish him. The third time, she would have a fit. Curtis would scream "Leave me alone! I'm doing my homework." And his mother would yell back, "Do you call lying on the floor and tossing a ball through a hoop doing your homework? I want you to get down to work, now! And I want all of your homework done by bedtime. I'm sick and tired of getting nasty notes from your teacher." Curtis would then retort, "Stop hassling me! I'll get it done." But, of course, this rarely happened.

Curtis's mother detested the nightly battles. In exasperation, she would shake her head and storm out of the room, slamming the door on the way out. When she was feeling particularly tired and stressed from work, she wouldn't even bother to enter Curtis's room. On these days, she simply didn't have the strength to confront her son. But she also realized that unless she continually prodded him, he would run out of time and arrive at school the next morning virtually empty-handed. The confrontations had become a recurring nightmare, and Curtis's mother regretted that her son's father lived two thousand miles away and that he saw Curtis only on alternating major holidays and for one month during the summer. The halfhearted reproaches he directed at Curtis about doing his homework when the two spoke on the telephone every week were essentially ineffectual. Curtis's mother had to accept the reality of the situation. She was for all intents and purposes a single parent, and as such she had no one to help her with the daily discipline chores. Whenever she thought about the fact that her son was only in fifth grade and that she was facing the prospect of having to deal with seven more years of nightly showdowns, she would usually get a pounding migraine. There didn't appear to be any solution, and the seeming futility of the situation made her feel depressed, vulnerable, and resentful.

CHURNING OUT STRESS AND TENSION

Fact: *Successful time management and academic achievement are inextricably linked.* Children who fail to acquire efficient planning, scheduling, and clock-handling skills are invariably in a crisis mode. At the last minute, they're usually in a frenzy to complete their assignments, write their essays and book reports, and study for impending tests, assuming, of course, that they're actually willing to do the assigned work. Seemingly indifferent or oblivious to the predictable consequences of their conduct, they chronically procrastinate and then use every possible excuse to justify their behavior. Despite irrefutable proof that their poor planning and disjointed studying are damaging their grades, they continue to mismanage time. Despite the red pencil marks on their assignments and tests and the stress that their procrastination produces for everyone in the family, they insist on doing it "their way."

In cases of chronic procrastination, the potential for resentment increases significantly. This resentment is a two-way street. Despairing parents may begin to perceive their child as a relentless and devious foe who is intent on making their lives miserable. In turn, the child may perceive his parents as judgmental and unremitting enemies who delight in continually nagging, lecturing, threatening, and meting out punishments, and who are intent on making his life unbearable. Bitterness, tension, and resistance are the all-too-common derivatives of this continual state of war.

Curtis clearly exemplifies the "I couldn't care less" and "put it off for as long as possible" mind-set. Despite his superior intelligence, the eleven-year-old seems perfectly content to coast through school doing the absolute minimum possible. Having placed academics at the bottom of his priority list, he defiantly resists his mother's efforts to prod him to do his work, and instead precipitates repeated confrontations that turn her life into a living hell. The script is well rehearsed. The dialogue is carefully crafted. The stage is blocked. The actors know their lines by heart, and the curtain goes up at five P.M. every school night. Unfortunately, the play is grueling and tedious, and unless the script is revised, the show will be canceled long before it reaches the bright lights of Broadway.

You may be wondering why Curtis's mom doesn't simply take away his TV, basketball, and Game Boy until he conforms to the homework rules and demonstrates improved motivation and grades. This is certainly a legitimate question. That Curtis's mother is emotionally drained by the continual struggle to get her son to do his work is painfully clear. Exhausted at the end of day, she probably lacks the fortitude to initiate additional unpleasant confrontations. She may also be hoping that Curtis's time-management problem will somehow correct itself and that he'll somehow get his act together and begin to achieve at a level commensurate with his ability. This is the equivalent of expecting to win the lottery. Without assertive intervention, Curtis's resistance and time-*mis*management problem are likely to persist with potentially disastrous academic consequences.

The situation is reminiscent of an old TV ad promoting an oil filter. In the background, viewers can see a car with its hood up and steam billowing from the engine. In the foreground, a grizzled mechanic looks at the camera, turns his head to view the car, stares again at the camera, and says matter-of-factly, "You can pay me now, or you can pay me later." The message is unequivocal: You take care of your car and service it regularly, or down the road you'll pay a much steeper price for your neglect. This admonition about fixing problems in a timely way also clearly applies to Curtis. Unless the eleven-year-old's mother figures out how to intercede constructively and get his time-management problem fixed, her son's self-sabotaging behavior could end up causing both of them inestimable grief.

After reading the description of Curtis's behavior and his mother's responses, you may be inclined to fault her for not enforcing firm and consistent homework rules. It's important, however, to acknowledge the monumental challenges that this single working parent of a willful underachiever confronts everyday. Handling the resistance and maladaptive conduct of any pre-adolescent can test the resolve of even the most dedicated parents. When one parent must shoulder all of the child-rearing responsibilities alone, her parenting decisions, methods, and style of discipline may not always appear perfectly logical, consistent, and codified to the objective outside observer. Having to actually fight the battle is a very different experience than watching the battle unfold on TV.

Despite the recalcitrance that Curtis's mother faces, it's clear that the time has come for firm and proactive intervention, even if this intervention is certain to produce unpleasant confrontations and recriminations. The homework rules obviously aren't working, and she has all but lost control of the situation. Curtis is on the cusp of becoming an entrenched and perhaps lifelong underachiever. The window of opportunity is closing, and unless Curtis is quickly disabused of his "get off my case" attitude and his "I'll do what I want" behavior, the prognosis for his success in school and in the workplace is poor. The sooner the eleven-year-old realizes that his conduct is unequivocally unacceptable, the better. The engine is smoking and the problem must be fixed. (Methods for achieving this objective are presented later in the chapter.)

COMMON INDICATORS OF TIME MISMANAGEMENT

- Resistance to studying and doing homework
- Deficient motivation and effort
- Irresponsibility
- Difficulty planing ahead
- Difficulty defining long-term and interim goals
- Difficulty establishing priorities
- Procrastination
- Incomplete assignments
- Disorganization
- Missed deadlines
- Shoddy work attributable to not allocating sufficient time to proof-read assignments and correct careless mistakes
- Continual stress attributable to feeling overwhelmed by homework
- Repeated excuses for marginal performance
- Constant family tension attributable to continual last-minute crises

THE "I DON'T CARE" MIND-SET

Fact: *Children for whom academic achievement has no personal meaning are often cavalier about fulfilling academic responsibilities, managing time, scheduling tasks, and meeting deadlines.* It's unrealistic to expect children to be diligent when achievement doesn't matter to them and when they have no personally significant short- and long-term academic goals. Having little incentive to act responsibly, study conscientiously, meet commitments, apply self-discipline, and complete their work, many of these indifferent learners do little more than go through the motions in school. Deadlines, timetables, and schedules are irrelevant to them. Once this "I couldn't care less" mind-set becomes embedded, the fate of the academically apathetic child is all but sealed. By the age of eleven, the child may have already become a determined underachiever. Certainly, Curtis could serve as the poster boy for this unfortunate turn of events.

A fundamental irony is evident. Children perform marginally, mismanage time, and work inefficiently because school doesn't matter to them. And school doesn't matter to them in part because they perform marginally, mismanage time, and work inefficiently. Clearly, this dynamic must be altered, and the most effective means for doing so is to make certain that resistant, procrastinating children acquire the necessary academic, planning, and scheduling skills to achieve academically. Once these children conclude that they can do better in school by managing their time more effectively, and once they begin to experience the sense of accomplishment and pride attendant to academic achievement, their aversion to establishing a study schedule will usually diminish. A new dynamic can be established, and the daily stress and conflict about studying and doing homework will dissipate.

THE "IDENTIFIED PATIENT"

Fact: *The self-sabotaging behavior of children who continually mismanage time can become a dominating feature in the family interaction.* If you have a Curtis at home, you know from firsthand experience that his "I'll do it tomorrow" behavior can turn every school night into a nightmare. As you watch your child dally and delay, you can feel your frustration mounting. The lame excuses and transparent rationalization only serve to stoke the fire. Finally, you reach the boiling point in much the same way as Curtis's mom did, and you begin to rant and rave about procrastination, incomplete assignments, missed deadlines, and shoddy work. In response, your child rants and raves about your being unfair, or he simple tunes out your criticism and reproaches and slams the door to his room. Over time, this interaction will devolve into a predictable daily routine. You push, and your child resists. "Get down to work!" you exclaim. "Leave me alone! I'll get my homework done," your child retorts. The more you push, the more he resists. You become the heavy, the critical parent, and the enforcer, and worst of all, you realize your attempts to alter your child's behavior are essentially ineffectual. Despite your admonitions and threats, he continues to procrastinate. Your child has become in psychological parlance the "identified patient." If only he would straighten up and fly right, everyone in the family would be happy. In reality, the situation is far more complex and involves overlapping issues that include establishing consistent rules, communicating clearly and unequivocally your values vis-à-vis effort and diligence, teaching your child the fundamentals of how to successfully manage time, and providing coherent and unswerving guidance and supervision. Your child's resistance, procrastination, and counterproductive attitudes and behaviors are, in fact, shared family problems. If the issues are to be resolved, you and your child must examine your respective roles in the dynamics of these problems.

The phenomenon of shared responsibility is especially evident in the case study. There's no question that Curtis appears intent on sabotaging himself in school, but it's also clear that Curtis's mother is unwittingly contributing to the problem by responding inadequately to her son's misconduct. That Curtis needs to be reeled in is self-evident. That his mother needs to learn how to operate the reel is also self-evident.

Before recurring malfunctions can be fixed, the nature of the problem must be carefully examined. The child may be the one who is malfunctioning, but his parents must be willing to take an objective look at their own responses to the recurring breakdowns, and they must decide if their parenting behaviors need to be modified. For example, do they constantly nag and lecture? Do they continually deliver sermons? Do they repeatedly threaten their child and then not follow through? Do they inconsistently enforce the rules they've established? Do they deliberately orchestrate opportunities for their child to succeed? Do they praise their child for progress and successes? Do they make certain that their child has the necessary academic tools to do what's being asked? If parents conclude that their strategy for dealing with problems is faulty, they must figure out what's not working and make the necessary repairs.

Fact: *Students who plan and schedule time ineffectually must be guided to the realization that efficient time management can make their life easier.*

Ironically, the cause-and-effect connection between effective time management and achievement is often lost on those children most in need of recognizing this link. The other obvious cause-and-effect link between handling the clock effectually and creating more free time also usually doesn't register. On either a conscious or unconscious level, time-oblivious children ascribe to the Swahili code popularized in *The Lion King*—*acuna matata*. No problem—don't worry. Over time this out-of-synch-with-reality way of thinking is likely to become embedded, and the associated maladaptive habits could persist into adulthood.

Fact: *Children who chronically mismanage time often resort to contrived excuses and rationalizations to justify their inadequate effort and diligence.* For apathetic students who lack effective clock-management skills, making excuses is frequently standard operating procedure. Despite the fact that their assurances, rationalizations, justifications, and distortions of truth are transparent and fool no one, these children nonetheless continue to float them.

TYPICAL EXCUSES, RATIONALIZATIONS, AND JUSTIFICATIONS FOR CHRONIC TIME MISMANAGEMENT

- "It's not my fault that I didn't complete the assignment. The teacher gave us too much homework, and I didn't have enough time to finish it."
- "I don't have any homework. I did it in school."
- "I'll get it done."
- "I can finish my homework tomorrow before class."
- "I still have plenty of time. The book report isn't due until sometime next week."

By blaming, concocting excuses, denying responsibility, and contending that everything is okay when it clearly isn't, time-challenged children try to convince themselves and others that they don't have problems with planning and scheduling. The self-deceptions crumble when report cards are sent home. The evidence of their time mismanagement is recorded in black and white and corroborated by teachers' pointed comments. Unfortunately, even this tangible proof may not be sufficient to convince headstrong, in-denial children that they need to alter their maladaptive modus operandi.

Fact: *Difficulty scheduling, planning, and managing time does not necessarily indicate that a child is unmotivated or irresponsible.* Many students who have poor time-management skills are conscientious and actually want to complete their homework and meet deadlines, but they don't know how to efficiently sequence their academic obligations. Despite good intentions, they may spend prodigious amounts of time spinning their wheels. Forced by their poor planning and scheduling into a continual crisis mode, these youngsters often become increasingly frustrated, discouraged, and demoralized. To cope with seemingly impossible-to-meet demands and deadlines, they frequently resort to complaining about injustices, requesting sympathy, and continually soliciting help. Examples of the typical plaintive litany include:

- "Can you *please* help me? I'll never get my book report done on time!"
- "The science test is tomorrow, and I don't understand anything! You've got to help me!"
- "This is too hard, and I can't do it on my own."
- "I can't figure out what we're supposed to do."
- "The teacher never explained how to do this."

These laments are, of course, more understandable and justifiable when children have learning problems and lack essential skills. Completing homework and developing a realistic study schedule can obviously pose major challenges for struggling students, and these youngsters often legitimately require extra support, monitoring, and assistance with planning and scheduling.

Mournful pleas for help, whether legitimate or manipulative, can put parents in a double bind. If they deny assistance to their child, they could inadvertently cause him to become discouraged, demoralized, and academically incapacitated. If they respond unconditionally to the requests, they could unwittingly encourage him to become excessively dependent. Despite their good intentions, parents may discover that by acquiescing to their child's "please throw me a life preserver" appeals, they've turned themselves into perennial enablers and rescuers. The child may misconstrue his parents' intentions and may misinterpret their offers of help as permission, or even encouragement, to remain helpless. Parents who find themselves in a perpetual rescuing and enabling mode must be prepared to objectively examine their own agenda to determine if they have an underlying psychological need to assume the role of eternal savior.

Perceiving a child's frustration, a parent may say innocuously, "I'll help you with those math problems." If this is a recurring script, the child may register:

- "Don't worry. You can always count on my being here to save you."
- "You don't have to take responsibility for doing anything on your own."
- "I'm content if you just make the minimal effort."

The obvious solution to the *help or not help conundrum* is for parents to selectively ration their assistance and to base the rationing system on justifiable need. In order to make these astute judgments, parents must dispassionately analyze each request and determine which are legitimate and which are manipulative. In some situations, they may respond, "Sure, I can help you with that." In other situations, they may need to respond, "Hey, I know that you know how to do that problem. You need to figure it out on your own." Unless parents are deliberately discriminating, they may find themselves fostering a codependency that could seriously damage their child's self-concept. This codependency might endure well beyond high school and could produce disastrous consequences.

Children who do not intuitively figure out how to handle time effectively must be systematically taught practical procedures for sequencing tasks, making realistic time estimates, and creating a functional flowchart that will allow them to meet their in-school and out-of-school obligations. They must not only understand the principles of managing time, but they must also translate these principles into functional operational procedures. They must be capable of making realistic estimates of the amount of time required to complete specific assignments, and they must be willing to exert the necessary effort and self-discipline to finish the job on time. In effect, these children must acquire an internal clock that is synchronized with the external clock that regulates their world. When their chemistry teacher tells them that their lab book covering the first three experiments is due on November 29, they had better be able to devise a functional procedure for completing the experiments, writing them up, and getting their lab book submitted in time to meet the deadline. Children who fail to acquire these scheduling, planning, and time-management skills are destined to be woefully ill-prepared to meet the demands they'll inevitably encounter in life.

THE KEY COMPONENTS OF EFFECTIVE TIME MANAGEMENT

Children must be able to:

- estimate accurately how much time is required to complete each assignment.
- estimate accurately how much time is required to prepare for tests.
- break down multifaceted assignments into specific manageable components.
- establish a logical sequence for completing tasks.
- develop a plan for completing long-range obligations such as reports and term papers.
- incorporate study requirements into a functional study schedule.
- create a task flowchart.
- meet deadlines.

TIME AWARENESS

Fact: *The process of acquiring self-discipline, cultivating a work ethic, and developing time awareness begins in kindergarten.* From day one of school, children learn that there are rules and procedures that they're expected to follow and time constraints to which they're expected to conform. Kindergartners are required to settle down on command, raise their hand to be recognized, pay attention, work conscientiously for sustained periods of time, and finish projects within a specified, albeit somewhat flexible time frame. As they progress through kindergarten, teachers' requirements for blocks of sustained effort by students expand incrementally. By the end of this first year of school, children are expected to be capable of sitting at a desk or table and completing assigned tasks with relative independence and without disturbing other children.

In first grade, time-awareness indoctrination expands in earnest. Children are confronted with multiple in-class assignments that their teachers expect them to finish within defined time constraints. When homework is assigned—a practice that is becoming increasingly common even in first grade—children are required to complete their work and submit it when it's due. These time constraints become even more demanding in second and third grade. Children who can estimate how much time their homework assignments require, develop, with or without parental assistance, a functional study schedule, and get their work completed on time have a distinct advantage over those whose efforts are scattered, sporadic, inefficient, and crisis-driven.

Fact: *Time management demands expand significantly when children enter middle school and expand again when they enter high school.* Instead of one teacher, children in the upper grades must now deal with many teachers. Each teacher assigns homework without being aware of what other teachers have assigned, and children may periodically find themselves overloaded with work. Nonetheless, they are expected to get the work done. To successfully manage these competing demands on their time, students must become consummate jugglers.

Middle and high school students must not only be able to budget adequate time to complete their daily homework assignments and study for tomorrow's quiz, but they must also be able to allocate adequate time for long-range obligations. The obligations include preparing for midterm and final exams, writing book reports, and completing term papers. These planning and scheduling skills are requisites not only to scholastic achievement, but also to vocational achievement.

Success in virtually every endeavor hinges on the ability to handle the clock, meet deadlines, plan ahead, and sequence responsibilities.

IS TIME-AWARENESS INNATE?

Fact: *Some children intuitively figure out how to handle time demands and time constraints.* Time-conscious children rarely have to be prodded to do their homework. They make note of how long it takes to do a particular task, store the data in their on-board cerebral computer, and use this data as a frame of reference when they are faced with similar tasks.

As children progress from grade to grade, their database expands, and they're able to make accurate and virtually instantaneous estimates about how much time they must allocate to fulfill each of their academic obligations. Based on their past experiences, they realize that doing a seventh-grade math homework assignment typically requires approximately twenty-five minutes and that reading and taking notes on the assigned pages in their science textbook typically requires approximately forty-five minutes. They realize that they must allocate approximately three hours to study effectively for the next social studies chapter test. They also know that they can avoid a crisis if they allot approximately three weeks to read a book for their monthly book report and if they set aside a total of four hours for writing the report. When computing the required time, they factor into the equation the relevant tasks such as the number of pages in the book they're reading and how challenging the book is to read and understand. They also factor into the equation their reading and writing skills and the amount of time they'll probably need to write a first draft, make revisions, edit, polish, proofread, and prepare the final draft. Depending on the size of the book, they may decide to schedule thirty minutes of reading each evening for three weeks and four separate one-hour blocks of time to write the report. Or they may schedule seven or eight more lengthy blocks of time to read the book and two sustained blocks of time to write the report. The implementation of their strategy and the outcome will directly reflect the efficiency and effectiveness of their time management, planning, organization, and effort.

Fact: *Children who don't learn from their past positive and negative* *clock-management experiences are likely to make inaccurate time-requirement estimates.* Despite previous planning and scheduling fiascoes, many underperforming children continue to misjudge how much time they need to do their work. For example, they may set aside fifteen minutes of study time every evening to do their science homework when they should realize from past experience that their teacher's typical assignment cannot possibly be completed in less than thirty minutes. Their faulty estimate may be attributable to their simply not wanting to spend the thirty minutes doing science homework, or to a conscious or unconscious self-deception about how much time they require to complete and carefully check over their work. Certainly, a pattern of Ds and Fs on late, incomplete, and error-ridden assignments should alert them that their time estimates are inaccurate, but many underperforming children refuse to acknowledge even this incontrovertible evidence and insist on repeating their miscalculations.

Some underperforming youngsters actually set aside adequate time to do their homework, but then proceed to work inefficiently. Because they become distracted and take breaks every few minutes, they may stretch a thirty-minute assignment into one requiring an hour or more to complete. Their inefficient work habits, which may be attributable to ADHD, often necessitate their having to study late into the evening. Even if these children burn the midnight oil, they may still run out of time. Of course, there's another negative repercussion when children compensate for time-management difficulties by working late at night. Sleep-deprived children are often mentally and physically exhausted the following day, and this exhaustion cannot help but have an impact on their learning efficiency.

Whether substandard academic performance is attributable to poor decoding skills, reading comprehension deficits, deficient study habits, ADHD, or inadequate time management, the consequences can be profound and lasting. Chronically poor grades are virtually guaranteed to take a toll on a child's self-concept, and the child receiving those poor grades is at risk for perceiving himself as unintelligent and inadequate. As the child's academic performance nosedives, so, too, will his motivation, effort, expectations, and aspirations.

LEARNING PROBLEMS AND TIME MANAGEMENT

Fact: *Planning and time management are especially problematic for children who are struggling with learning problems.* Managing the clock is rarely a high priority for children who must battle every day to master fundamental skills and comprehend and assimilate information. The primary preoccupation of many of these children is to handle basic demands, such as deciphering words accurately, understanding and retaining information, spelling correctly, solving math problems, writing legibly, following written and verbal instructions, writing comprehensible sentences and essays, and proofreading their work for careless mistakes. When academic survival hinges on the ability to cope with a seemingly never-ending series of challenges and crises, meticulous planning is a luxury. The deficient academic skills of these students can obviously undermine any attempt on their part to plan ahead, make realistic time estimates, and develop a functional study schedule.

The justifiable preoccupation with academic survival notwithstanding, students who learn ineffectually must be taught how to allocate their study time and sequence their assignments. This translates into their learning how to gauge their study requirements based on their past experiences and current skills and how to use these estimates to create a functional schedule that allows them to meet both their immediate and their long-range obligations.

Struggling students who don't figure out how to manage time on their own are at risk for becoming dependent on their parents to prod and shepherd them through school. Clearly, the key objectives of any effective remedial strategy are to help ineffectual learners improve their academic skills and to furnish them with the essential planning and scheduling tools they need to fulfill their scholastic obligations. Teaching them how to manage the clock is central to the development of these vital planning and scheduling capabilities.

TIME-MANAGEMENT DIFFICULTIES AND ADHD

Fact: *Children with ADHD are especially vulnerable to becoming overpowered by their homework obligations.* The pressure on children with focusing problems to complete their work can be unrelenting. Their distractibility, impulsiveness, and inattentiveness to details can erect major task-completion barriers and can hamper their ability to manage time and develop a functional study schedule. Creating and using a study schedule requires self-discipline, and self-discipline is an attribute that children with ADHD sorely lack.

For chronically inattentive, impulsive, and easily distracted students, just staying on task consumes much if not all of their physical and mental energy. The most pressing concern of these children is to get their work done as quickly and painlessly as possible. Making careful predictions about time requirements and planning and scheduling long-range, multifaceted projects typically eclipse their self-regulation capabilities. Having to manage the time requirements for writing a term paper or a book report can produce monumental clock-management and task-completion woes for ADHD students. Procrastination and slipshod work are the all-too-common responses to these hardships.

Fact: *As ADHD children with poor time-management skills progress into middle school and high school, the challenge of having to complete assignments in five different subjects can be overpowering.* ADHD students who can't handle time constraints are at risk for becoming increasingly academically dysfunctional as they progress into the upper grades and the scholastic demands expand. These children are also at risk for becoming progressively more frustrated, demoralized, and resistant to learning. Faced with responsibilities they cannot meet, some will choose the path of least resistance and simply shut down in school. Others may compensate by becoming increasingly dependent on their parents to supervise them and help them complete their work. This dependency often assumes a love/hate form. Whereas many ADHD students need their parents to prod and monitor them, these children may also paradoxically resent the intrusions and the constant control that their parents exert over their life. Other ADHD children, however, may respond quite differently and may become addicted to the codependency and the safety net that their parents provide.

REACTIVE BEHAVIOR

Fact: *Difficulty managing time may be linked to children's reactions to their parents' own clock-handling behavior.* Some parents of "time-challenged" children may themselves be nonchalant about time demands and constraints, and their children may model their own time-management style on their parents' seemingly cavalier modus operandi. Other parents may be at the opposite end of the time-awareness continuum and may be excessively time-driven, insisting that everything be scheduled minutely down to the last second. They're never, ever late for an appointment, and in fact often arrive early. More often than not, they insist on equal time diligence from everyone in the family. In reaction, their children may rebel against this perceived time obsession by consciously or unconsciously rejecting what they consider to be weird, stress-producing behavior.

Whatever the underlying reasons for their time-management difficulties, reactive children often fail to imprint a key fact of life: *You must get the job done on time.* The deadlines may involve finishing a school assignment or applying for a college scholarship by a cut-off date, and later in life may involve submitting a tax return on time and completing projects at work.

Ironically, children with the greatest need to improve their clock-handling skills are often the most resistant to doing so. Some are oblivious to the obvious consequences of their time mismanagement. Others are in denial about the implications of their maladaptive behavior.

TEACHING YOUR CHILD HOW TO MANAGE TIME

Fact: *Every child of normal intelligence can be systematically taught practical, easy-to-learn and easy-to-use methods for improving clock-handling and scheduling skills.* By providing effective and systematic instruction, sufficient opportunities to practice, adequate supervision, and affirmation for progress, you can significantly enhance your child's time-management abilities. Your objective is to achieve cognitive behavioral change. This translates into methodically altering your child's negative behavior by teaching and reinforcing positive behavior and by helping your child acquire greater insight. (See pages 52–53 to review cognitive behavioral change principles.)

You will want to guide your child to the realization that effective time management and careful planning can produce four desirable payoffs, namely:

- Improved grades
- More free time
- Reduced stress and family conflict
- Fewer clashes with teachers

Fact: *It's unrealistic to expect children with poor time-management skills to welcome with open arms suggestions that require them to alter entrenched behaviors.* As is the case with adults, children are creatures of habit and are often resistant to relinquishing behaviors to which they've become accustomed, however self-defeating these behaviors may be. Effecting meaningful changes in a child's embedded conduct requires a well-conceived instructional procedure and a great deal of patience and fortitude. Your child must realize that you're unequivocally committed to teaching him how to handle time more effectively and to making certain that he alters counterproductive conduct.

The Keys to Teaching Time-Management Skills

- Urge your child to target specific academic goals.
- Teach your child how to establish priorities.
- Help your child identify his specific academic obligations.
- Show your child how to logically sequence tasks.
- Help your child create a study schedule that will permit him to attain his objectives.
- Insist that your child adhere to the schedule despite temptations to do otherwise.
- Encourage a periodic evaluation of the schedule's effectiveness.
- Demonstrate how to make scheduling adjustments when appropriate.

HELPING YOUR CHILD DESIGN A STUDY SCHEDULE

Fact: *The antidote for time mismanagement is to provide children with a functional scheduling template.* The first step in the process of teaching children how to budget time is to show them how to analyze their study requirements. Your child begins this process by realistically estimating the average amount of time he must devote to homework and studying every evening in each subject. His estimates should factor three critically important elements into the analysis:

- The nature and difficulty of specific assignments (e.g., being required to read fifteen pages in his social studies textbook and write answers to ten questions about the content).
- His current skills (e.g., his facility with reading comprehension and visual recall).
- His past experiences with similar tasks (e.g., the advisability of allocating extra time to reread the assigned pages before answering the questions).

Once your child completes this assessment, he then transfers the projected time requirements onto a daily study schedule. (See below.)

If your child normally requires extra time to complete assignments, it's important that you encourage him to build a realistic buffer into his schedule. Should his time predictions prove faulty, you should be prepared to teach him how to analyze what went wrong and to show him how to make adjustments so that he can avoid repeating the same time miscalculations. For example, you might say, "It looks like your science homework took about twenty minutes longer to finish than you anticipated. The questions were probably more difficult than you expected, and I noticed that you had to continually refer back to the chapter to answer them. I think it would be smart to budget extra time in your schedule for doing your science assignments."

A six-step procedure for creating a study schedule is described on pages 200–205. If your child struggles with any of the steps, you should be prepared to provide additional guidance and support. It's recommended that you make extra copies of "My Weekly Study Schedule" and "My Weekend Study Schedule." These could come in handy if your child chooses to use different colored felt markers instead of words to indicate blocks of study time. Should he make mistakes in coloring and coding the schedule, you can simply hand him a clean copy. (Reproducible copies of the forms used below can be found on pages 287–288 in the appendix.)

As is the case with all of the topics examined in this book, you can select the autocratic or democratic approach when working with your child. Your choice of methods will be influenced by the parenting style with which you feel most comfortable and by the methodology that is most likely to be effective, given your child's personality, attitudes, and behavior.

The following modeled interactive scripts are quite lengthy. By no means should you attempt to memorize them! Read through the script. Form an idea of what your objectives are, what you need to communicate, and what techniques are being used. You might even want to jot down the key points you want to address on an index card. Get a sense of the procedures. *Then use your own words.* Feel free to make your explanations more succinct or more expansive so that they fit with your communication style, your child's age, and your child's ability to assimilate instructions. If you find that the autocratic approach is too forceful, make the appropriate style and tone adjustments. If you find the democratic approach is not forceful enough, again make whatever changes you deem appropriate. You know your child better than anyone. Just remember to convey clarity of purpose, firmness, and positive expectations. You want your child to recognize that you're his ally, and not his mortal enemy.

Let's first examine the autocratic approach for dealing with a time-management problem. To reiterate advice given in preceding chapters, the following guidelines are recommended:

TIME MANAGEMENT SKILLS
The Autocratic Approach

Guidelines

- Create a conducive context for interaction.
- Check your child's perceptions (see checklist).
- Define the problem.
- Examine the evidence.
- Provide functional time-management procedures.
- Supervise implementation.
- Affirm your child for effort and progress.

Let's see how the autocratic approach might be applied. Remember that the objective is to modify your child's counterproductive behavior and to provide a hands-on method for handling time more efficiently. You want your child to realize that you mean business and that you are determined that he change his modus operandi. Your tone of voice should be firm and decisive but at the same time friendly and nonmenacing. If you use the autocratic approach with younger children who are not yet highly resistant, you would certainly want to be very gentle. In the case of younger children, you'll also need to modify some of the instructions, forms, and suggested study-time allocations. You might also want to consider using the more democratic approach with younger children.

Scenario: You ask your child to come into the kitchen or the dining room. You are calm. Any siblings in the area should be instructed to leave. You ask your child to sit in a chair facing you so that you can establish and maintain eye contact.

You: "I have a problem. I frankly don't like the way you're doing your homework. I don't like having to nag you about starting and completing your studying. Before we examine my problem and find a solution, I want you to take a few minutes to complete this checklist. It's similar to other checklists you have filled out. Be honest and don't try to say what you think I want to hear. Here's the checklist. I'll leave the room while you complete it. Let me know when you're done." [A re-producible copy of this checklist can be found on page 284 in the appendix.]

If your child has reading problems, you may need to help him read the checklist statements. Depending on your child's age and learning difficulties, you may also need to explain in greater detail how to use the color code. If you help your child with the checklist, be careful not to express any positive or negative reactions—verbally or with facial expressions—to his responses to the statements.

TIME-MANAGEMENT CHECKLIST

CODE: 1 = Never 2 = Rarely 3 = Sometimes 4 = Often 5 = Always

I begin my homework at a specified time every school night. ____

I don't need to be reminded by my parents to begin my homework. ____

I have a good idea about how long it will take me to do each assignment. ____

I set aside sufficient time to do my homework and study for tests. ____

I set aside sufficient time to check over my work for errors
and silly mistakes. ____

I complete my assignments. ____

I hand in my work on time. ____

I allow enough time to proofread my written assignments
and check my math homework for careless mistakes. ____

I schedule sufficient time to complete long-range
assignments such as book reports and term papers. ____

I avoid crises by planning ahead. ____

I budget sufficient time to study for midterm and final exams. ____

I begin studying for exams several days before. ____

I study for at least twenty-five minutes at a stretch before
taking a short break. ____

I resist becoming distracted when I study and do homework. ____

I interrupt my studying every few minutes. ____

I make reasonable adjustments in my study schedule based
on past experience (for example, a bad grade on a test
or a bad grade on a math homework assignment). ____

Scenario: After giving your child sufficient time to complete the checklist, you return to the kitchen or dining room. You pull up a chair and sit next to your child.

You: "Let's take a look at your responses on the checklist. Before beginning, I want to repeat something that I've said before: You're entitled to your opinions, and I'm entitled to mine. If we disagree, we need to discuss the differences calmly. Okay. Let's take a look at the checklist and go through your responses. I'll tell you if I disagree, but I don't want to get into an argument. I'll simply point out areas where we don't see eye to eye."

Review your child's responses to the statements and indicate where you disagree with a particular response. Children often latch onto self-protecting rationalizations for their maladaptive behavior, and their responses may appear disingenuous. You should react to these fabrications matter-of-factly. For example, you might say:

- "I have a very different impression. I see you leaving your studying to the last minute, and I see you procrastinating."
- "I've received notes from your teacher indicating that your homework isn't being completed and isn't being handed in on time. Would you like to read those notes?"
- "I often see you fooling around in your room when you're supposed to be studying."
- "I observe that you're taking study breaks every few minutes."
- "I see red marks on your corrected assignments that indicate you haven't proofread your essays or checked over your math for careless mistakes."
- "I see you putting off studying and then cramming for tests at the last minute."

You: "Let's take a look at some of last week's corrected math and English homework. I'd like you to get the returned homework assignments from last week. Okay. What I see are lots of red marks indicating careless mistakes with the basics—adding, subtracting,

and dividing. I know that you know how to do these math problems. [This statement would obviously need to be modified if your
child does, in fact, have a math problem or learning disability.] I also
see lots of careless spelling and grammar mistakes on the essay you
submitted. I can only conclude that you either didn't want to take
the time to check over your work or that you ran out of time and
didn't have a chance to do the checking. If I were filling out the
checklist, I would have to mark a 5 after the statement 'I allow
enough time to proofread my written assignments and check my
math homework for careless mistakes.' Do you think it would be
unreasonable for me to give you a 5? If so, tell me why."

Allow your child to express his feelings, even if his position contradicts
the evidence. As you examine your child's responses to the statements on
the checklist, be careful to avoid being accusatory or demeaning. Refer to
report cards, notes from teachers, corrected assignments, and your own
observations. The analysis should require no more than ten minutes. It's
time to proceed to the next step—creating a study schedule.

You: "As I previously said, I have a problem with having to continually nag you to get your work done. It's clear that you also have a
problem involving planning and scheduling your homework obligations. There's no need for us to argue about this. The evidence is
on the table. I can also show you notes and progress reports that I
received from your teachers and comments on your report cards. If
you choose to reject this evidence and not admit that you have a
time-management problem, then you're going to have to take my
word for it. I want you to solve this problem before you completely
torpedo yourself in school."

Allow your child to respond, but make it clear—without expressing
frustration or anger—that he must solve the time management problem whether or not he concurs with your conclusions.

You: "I'm going to help you design a study schedule. The first step
is for you to estimate the approximate amount of daily study

time required in each of your subjects. This estimate should be based on past experience. For example, you know approximately how many math problems your teacher typically assigns, and you know approximately how much time it takes to finish the assignment. You might estimate that on average you need thirty minutes every evening to do math. On some nights you may need less time. On other nights, and especially when you're preparing for a test, you may need more. Okay. Let's plug in the numbers." [Reproducible copies of the following forms can be found on pages 285–288 in the appendix.]

SIX-STEP TIME-MANAGEMENT METHOD

Step 1: *List all academic subjects and approximate amount of daily time required to complete the assigned work.*

Academic Obligations

APPROXIMATE PROJECTED DAILY STUDY TIME REQUIRED TO DO A FIRST-RATE JOB OF STUDYING

My Courses   Study Time Required

_____   _____

_____   _____

_____   _____

_____   _____

_____   _____

_____   _____

Total Daily Study Time: _____

You: "I've asked your teachers how much time on average they expect eighth-grade students to spend doing homework in each subject. If your estimates do not agree with their guidelines, then we'll need to set up conferences with your teachers. As the semester progresses, you can make adjustments in your time projections based upon your experiences. You may find that you can complete the work in less time than you estimated, or you may find that you need additional study time. Now you're ready to do the next step."

Point out that students who have reading, comprehension, math, vocabulary, and writing difficulties should be prepared to do more homework than students who have no problems in these areas.

Step 2: *Write down when you want to do your homework.*

You: "Let's say you estimate that you need to study approximately 2.5 hours every evening. You decide that you want to do your homework between five P.M. and six P.M. and between seven thirty P.M. and nine P.M.). Okay. Insert the times when you plan to study below."

Monday: _____

Tuesday: _____

Wednesday: _____

Thursday: _____

Friday: _____

Saturday: _____

Sunday: _____

Step 3: Use words or colored felt pens or pencils to indicate on your schedule the times when you plan to study. Let's first look at this sample schedule.

SAMPLE WEEKLY STUDY SCHEDULE

TIME:	MON.	TUES.	WED.	THURS.	FRI.
7:20 A.M.–7:45 A.M.	Breakfast	Breakfast	Breakfast	Breakfast	Breakfast
7:50–8:20	School bus	School bus	School bus	School bus	School bus
8:25–2:50	School	School	School	School	School
3:00–3:30	School bus	School bus	School bus	School bus	School bus
3:30–5:00	Free	Free	Free	Free	Free
5:00–5:30	Biology	Biology	Biology	Biology	Free
5:40–6:10	Spanish	Spanish	Spanish	Spanish	Free
6:15–6:45	Dinner	Dinner	Dinner	Dinner	Dinner
6:50–7:30	English	English	English	English	Free
7:40–8:10	Math	Math	Math	Math	Free
8:25–9:00	History	History	History	History	Free
9:00–10:00	Free	Free	Free	Free	Free

You: "As you can see, this student has breakfast between 7:20 and 7:45 A.M. and is on the school bus between 7:50 A.M. and 8:20 A.M. He gets home at 3:30 P.M. and then has one and a half hours of free time. He begins doing his homework at five and completes his biology and Spanish homework before dinner.

"I want you to use this sample as a guide and create your own schedule. I have felt markers if you would like to use colors instead of words to indicate how blocks of time are assigned on the schedule. If you decide to use colors, you'll need a code that explains the meaning of each color. For instance, blue could indicate dinnertime, and red might indicate math."

MY WEEKLY STUDY SCHEDULE

TIME:	MON.	TUES.	WED.	THURS.	FRI.

Optional color code if felt markers or crayons are used to indicate blocks of time:

[ ]_____   [ ]_____   [ ]_____   [ ]_____   [ ]_____   [ ]_____

Step 4: *Use the same procedure (Step 3) to complete a weekend study schedule.*

My Weekend Study Schedule

TIME:	Saturday	Sunday

Optional color code if felt markers or crayons are used to indicate blocks of time:

[ ]_____   [ ]_____   [ ]_____   [ ]_____   [ ]_____   [ ]_____

You: "I'll make two photocopies of your weekday and weekend schedules tomorrow. I want you to put one copy of each schedule in plastic sleeves and insert them in the front of your binder. I want you to tape the second copy on the wall near your desk. I'll expect you to use your new schedules consistently for the next two weeks before we discuss making adjustments. Changes will be based on whether or not your grades improve. We both share the same goal—to create a schedule that works for you and makes your life easier."

Step 5: *Maintain your schedule for two weeks without having to be reminded or prodded.*

You: "Observe how your schedule is working for you. After a two-week trial period, you may want to fine tune the schedule. This means making changes that will improve the schedule and make it work even better. Remember, your schedule should be your friend, and not your enemy!"

Step 6: *Record your grades in every subject* (tests, homework assignments, reports, etc.).

You: "You can use the following form to keep track of your test and homework grades for the next two weeks. You can leave the form at home or insert it in your binder. This recording process will allow you to track your performance and fine tune your schedule. For example, if your English grade doesn't improve, you'll need to set aside more time to study English."

"There are two ways to keep track of your grades. You can record your grades on the following form, or you can record them on a grade-tracking graph (see page 210). You choose the method that you like best."

(Reproducible copies of the following forms can be found on pages 289–293 in the appendix.)

TWO WEEK GRADE-TRACKING EXPERIMENT
Method 1: Grade Recording Form

COURSE: _____

Homework:

Date____ Grade____ Date____ Grade____ Date____ Grade____ Date____ Grade____

Date____ Grade____ Date____ Grade____ Date____ Grade____ Date____ Grade____

Date____ Grade____ Date____ Grade____ Date____ Grade____ Date____ Grade____

Quizzes/Tests/Exams/Papers:

Date____ Grade____ Date____ Grade____ Date____ Grade____ Date____ Grade____

Date____ Grade____ Date____ Grade____ Date____ Grade____ Date____ Grade____

COURSE: _____

Homework:

Date____ Grade____   Date____ Grade____   Date____ Grade____   Date____ Grade____

Date____ Grade____   Date____ Grade____   Date____ Grade____   Date____ Grade____

Date____ Grade____   Date____ Grade____   Date____ Grade____   Date____ Grade____

Quizzes/Tests/Exams/Papers:

Date____ Grade____   Date____ Grade____   Date____ Grade____   Date____ Grade____

Date____ Grade____   Date____ Grade____   Date____ Grade____   Date____ Grade____

COURSE: _____

Homework:

Date____ Grade____   Date____ Grade____   Date____ Grade____   Date____ Grade____

Date____ Grade____   Date____ Grade____   Date____ Grade____   Date____ Grade____

Date____ Grade____   Date____ Grade____   Date____ Grade____   Date____ Grade____

Quizzes/Tests/Exams/Papers:

Date_____ Grade_____ Date_____ Grade_____ Date_____ Grade_____ Date_____ Grade_____

Date_____ Grade_____ Date_____ Grade_____ Date_____ Grade_____ Date_____ Grade_____

COURSE:_____

Homework:

Date_____ Grade_____ Date_____ Grade_____ Date_____ Grade_____ Date_____ Grade_____

Date_____ Grade_____ Date_____ Grade_____ Date_____ Grade_____ Date_____ Grade_____

Date_____ Grade_____ Date_____ Grade_____ Date_____ Grade_____ Date_____ Grade_____

Quizzes/Tests/Exams/Papers:

Date_____ Grade_____ Date_____ Grade_____ Date_____ Grade_____ Date_____ Grade_____

Date_____ Grade_____ Date_____ Grade_____ Date_____ Grade_____ Date_____ Grade_____

COURSE: _____

Homework:

Date___ Grade___ Date___ Grade___ Date___ Grade___ Date___ Grade___

Date___ Grade___ Date___ Grade___ Date___ Grade___ Date___ Grade___

Date___ Grade___ Date___ Grade___ Date___ Grade___ Date___ Grade___

Quizzes/Tests/Exams/Papers:

Date___ Grade___ Date___ Grade___ Date___ Grade___ Date___ Grade___

Date___ Grade___ Date___ Grade___ Date___ Grade___ Date___ Grade___

You: "Let's take a look at the following sample graphs. The first graph keeps track of grades on homework assignments. The second keeps track of your grades on tests. The advantage of the graph system is that you can determine if you're making progress with a quick glance at the performance line that you plot based upon the grades you receive. If the performance line moves up during the first two weeks of the experiment, you can reasonably conclude that your enhanced time management methods are working. If the performance line isn't moving up, then other steps need to be taken. These might include further enhancements in areas that we've already covered, such as improving organization in your study areas, accurate recording of assignments, establishing goals, setting priorities, etc."

METHOD 2: GRADE-TRACKING GRAPH

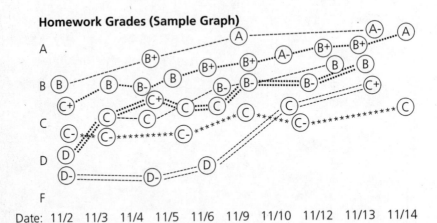

Homework Grades (Sample Graph)

Date: 11/2 11/3 11/4 11/5 11/6 11/9 11/10 11/12 11/13 11/14

Code: English------   Spanish ....   Biology *********   Math :::::::   Gov't ------

Test Grades (Sample Graph)

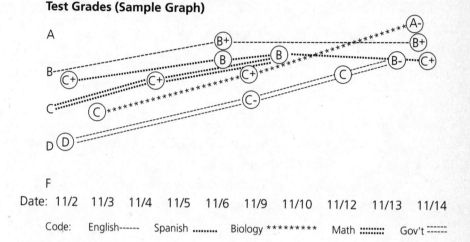

Date: 11/2 11/3 11/4 11/5 11/6 11/9 11/10 11/12 11/13 11/14

Code: English------ Spanish .... Biology ******** Math :::::::: Gov't -----

You: "OK. You now have a weekday and weekend study schedule and a system for keeping track of your grades. I'll monitor you for a while to make sure that you're using the schedules. When I'm convinced you're consistently using them, I'll stop. I want you to work for a minimum of twenty-five minutes without taking a study break (See the Recommended Study Break Formula below.) You can then take a five-minute break. If you're able to work for longer periods, that's great. Fewer breaks will allow you to finish your homework more quickly. The sooner you complete your work and check it over for mistakes, the more free time you'll have. This is important: When I come into your room, I don't want to find you fooling around. I want to see you studying. Understood? If you wish, you can use an egg timer to keep track of how long you study. You can set the time for twenty-five minutes, and when the bell sounds, you can take a short break. I'm certain that you can make your study schedule work, and I'm certain that your grades will improve if you maintain the schedule and discipline yourself to work conscientiously. By so doing, you'll be able to fulfill your homework obligations and meet your teachers' deadlines for submitting your work.

RECOMMENDED FORMULA FOR STUDY BREAKS

4th–6th Grade: Study and work conscientiously for a minimum of **twenty minutes** before taking a *five-minute break*.

7th–8th Grade: Study and work conscientiously for a minimum of **twenty-five minutes** before taking a *five-minute break*.

9th–12th Grade: Study or work conscientiously for a minimum of **thirty minutes** before taking a *five-minute break*.

Now let's examine how the more democratic approach might be applied. Please note that the democratic approach may not be successful with highly defended or highly resistant children. These youngsters may not be willing to participate in a "let's work together on solving this problem" context and may respond best to the more autocratic approach in which you clearly spell out firm and unequivocal expectations, guidelines, and performance standards.

TIME-MANAGEMENT SKILLS

The Democratic Approach

Guidelines

- Create a conducive context for interaction.
- Check your child's perceptions (see checklist).
- Model the problem-solving procedure (DIBS).
- Have child apply DIBS.
- Provide functional time-management procedures.
- Supervise implementation.
- Affirm your child for effort and progress.

Scenario: You're sitting with your child at the kitchen or dining room table. You've already asked him to complete the time-management checklist, and you've asked him to get his graded homework assignments and tests from the last three weeks. The initial lead-in is the same as the one described in the more autocratic approach.

You: "Let's take a look at some of your most recent corrected math and English homework assignments. What I'm seeing on these papers is lots of red marks that indicate careless mistakes with adding, subtracting, and dividing. I'm sure that you know how to do these math problems. [This statement would need to be modified if your child has a math problem or a learning disability.] I can only conclude that you either didn't want to take the time to check over your work or that you ran out of time and didn't correct the mistakes. If I were to fill out the checklist, I'd have to mark a 5 after the statement 'I allow enough time to proofread my written assignments and check my math homework for careless mistakes.' Do you think it would be unreasonable for me to give you a 5? If so, tell me why."

Allow your child to express his feelings, even if his position contradicts the obvious evidence. In this case, you might simply say "What you're saying doesn't seem to fit with what I observe on your corrected assignments. Based upon the evidence, I believe that you do have a problem with managing your study time." (As you run down your child's responses to the checklist statements, be careful to avoid being accusatory or demeaning. Refer to report cards, notes from teachers, corrected assignments, and your own observations. When you've completed this examination, which should take no more than ten minutes, it's time to proceed to the next step.)

You: "I have a problem with how you're handling your study time. Because I care about how you do in school, I need to solve this problem. I'm going to use the DIBS to do so. As you know, the word DIBS is an acronym made from the first letter of the four steps in the method. If we list the letters that make up the acronym vertically, it will look like this:"

DIBS

Define the Problem: _____

Investigate the Causes of the Problem: _____

                                                     _____

                                                     _____

                                                     _____

Brainstorm Solutions to the Problem: _____

                                                     _____

                                                     _____

                                                     _____

Select a Solution to Try Out: _____

You: "I'll start out by defining my problem."

> **Define:**   I* don't want to have to nag you continually about
>   doing your homework.
>   Now I'm going to investigate what's causing my
>   problem.
>
> **Investigate:** I get upset when I see you procrastinating and fool-
>   ing around when you're supposed to be studying.
>   I get upset when I know you haven't completed
>   your homework because you've run out of time.

---

*Remember to use "I" messages as opposed to "you" messages (e.g., "I get upset when you procrastinate" versus "You drive me crazy when you procrastinate.)

I get upset when you become stressed because you don't have time to finish your work.

I get upset when you receive bad grades on your homework and on tests because you didn't budget enough time to study properly.

Brainstorm: I could accept your procrastination and fooling around when you're supposed to be studying.

I could accept your lowered grades.

I could let you sink or swim on your own in school.

I could accept the stress and tension at home.

I could help you learn how to manage time better.

Solution: I could help you learn how to manage time better.

You: "I hope that you can see that the first four brainstormed solutions are unacceptable for the following reasons:

- I wouldn't be doing my job as a parent if I allowed you to be irresponsible.
- I can't permit you to do poorly in school because you aren't budgeting enough time to complete your assignments.
- I can't allow you to develop bad habits that cause stress and tension in the family and that could cause problems for you throughout your life.

"The only realistic choice that I have is to help you figure out how to manage your study time more effectively. I want you to use the DIBS method to help you solve your problem. The first step is for you to define the problem accurately."

You can either write the DIBS steps on a piece of paper or photocopy the form on page 294 in the appendix and then guide your child through the problem-solving procedure. Encourage him to define the problem accurately. As previously stated, this first step can be challenging, and your child may require guidance.

You want to lead your child to the following definition of the problem: "I'm having difficulty managing my study time." Alternative definitions might include: "I am not doing as well as I should in school because I run out of time when I do my homework," or simply "I don't have enough time to finish my homework." One of the possible causes of the problem that your child might list is: "I fool around when I should be studying."

DIBS can be tricky at first for some children. You should discuss your child's answers with him and make suggestions, but you should resist the temptation to fill in the blanks for him. To do so would discourage your child from developing his own analytical thinking skills and would dissuade him from becoming actively involved in the problem-solving process.

Allow your child to include heartfelt reasons in the Investigate section such as: "I procrastinate because I hate school." These reasons should be acknowledged, discussed, and included. (Please note: Your child may still resist acknowledging that he has a problem. In this case, you'll need to assume a more active role in helping him complete the DIBS procedure.)

Permit your child to list brainstormed solutions that you may consider unreasonable or impractical. These should be examined with sensitivity. Make certain through discussion and by means of suggestion that he also includes on his brainstorming list words to the effect: "I need to develop a system for handling my study time," or "I need to learn how to plan better." Suggest that he select one of these solutions as the first one to try out. Once he makes this selection, have him list the steps that he must take to achieve the objective.

Again, it's certainly okay to diplomatically make suggestions and to provide guidance. The goal is for your child to come up with specific steps that can solve the problem. These might include: *estimate my study requirements accurately; budget enough time to do my homework; start my homework at an agreed-upon time.* Acknowledge and affirm your child's insights about how to deal with the problem.

At this juncture, you should say: "I'm going to teach you a really good system for handling the clock." You're now ready to begin teaching your child the Six-Step Time Management Method described on pages 200–205. The major difference between the more autocratic approach versus the more democratic approach primarily involves the tone and texture of your interaction. In the autocratic approach, your primary objective is to modify maladaptive behavior expediently. It's a no-nonsense method, and the message you're communicating is, "This issue needs to be resolved now. End of discussion." In the democratic approach you want to create an engaging, dynamic, and cooperative problem-solving context. The procedure is akin to an exploration. As you interact with your child using this approach, you want to make encouraging statements such as:

- "Estimating the time you need for homework in each subject is like doing a math problem."
- "Using felt markers to indicate how you use your study time is the fun part. What color would you like to use to indicate homework time for science?"

You: "Well, you now have a weekday schedule and a weekend schedule. Once your study schedule starts working for you, you'll probably discover that you have a lot more free time. Having a schedule is like training every day in a sport such as gymnastics or track. The secret to making the schedule work is to keep to it, even if it requires making some sacrifices. This means coming in and starting your homework when you agreed to without having to be reminded. It also means studying even if there is something else you would rather be doing. At times, this can be challenging. For example, you might be playing a computer game at five o'clock, the time when you agreed to begin your homework. Quitting the game and saying to yourself, I have to start my homework, can be difficult, but you must remind yourself that this is the agreement you made with yourself and with me. It boils down to a question of self-discipline.

"It's also important that you study without distractions and interruptions for a reasonable period of time without taking a break. Kids of your age should be able to work without interruptions for twenty-five minutes at a time. Some kids who can concentrate for longer periods of time may prefer to study for forty-five minutes before taking a rest. If you can't work for twenty-five minutes, you can build your study endurance by creating a personal study training program and using an egg timer. The first day, you could set the timer for twelve minutes. When the buzzer goes off, you can take a two-minute break. You could get up and walk around or "shoot baskets" with crumpled paper. Then back to work. The next day you set the timer at thirteen minutes. Each day you add one minute to the time you study before taking your break. Before you know it, you will be able to study for twenty-five minutes at a time! Training your brain is like training your body to play a sport. To develop top-notch skills, strength, endurance, and self-confidence, you must be prepared to practice."

A PERSONAL STUDY-SCHEDULE AGREEMENT

Irrespective of whether you've used the more autocratic or more democratic method, it's recommended that you have your child sign a "contract." This contract encourages the ongoing use of the schedule and commits him to using the schedule for two weeks before making adjustments. The overall objective is that the habit of managing time effectively be firmly imprinted. You want efficient time management to become an automatic reflex. (A reproducible copy of this form can be found on page 295 in the appendix.)

A STUDY-SCHEDULE AGREEMENT

I, _____, agree to use the study schedule I created for a two-week trial period. I will keep track of my grades on homework and tests during this period. If after using the schedule for two weeks I decide that my schedule should be changed or fine-tuned, I'll discuss the changes with my parents. I understand that if I'm preparing for a test, I may need to set aside more time for studying before the test. If I do make adjustments in my day-to-day schedule, I'll use the revised schedule for a minimum of *four weeks*. During this period I'll continue to keep track of my grades. If I'm pleased with the results and my grades improve, I'll continue to use the schedule for the rest of the school year. I may make further adjustments every *four weeks* after discussing the proposed changes with my parents. Finally, I agree to keep to my study schedule without having to be prodded or reminded.

Signed: _____

Date: _____

Witness: _____

As your child applies time-management principles, his skills will improve. He'll begin to schedule and sequence tasks automatically. Once he gets into the habit, his productivity and efficiency will improve dramatically. Time mismanagement will no longer be a problem.

9

Figuring Out How to Win the Study Game

Kelly's apprehension was fast approaching critical mass. Faced with the prospect of having to take a chapter test in her government class the following day, the knot of anxiety that gripped her stomach and the trembling in her hands presaged her standard day-before-the-test meltdown. The eighth grader spent much of the day ruminating about the impending exam, and by the afternoon her foreboding became so consuming that she could barely pay attention in her classes. Kelly's anxiety was exacerbated by her realization that if she did as poorly as she expected on the looming test and on the final exam that she had to take in two weeks, she was certain to get an F in the course. This would add another disaster to an already lengthy list of academic debacles dating back to third grade. An F would also cause her GPA to drop below 1.9, a watershed event that Kelly had been desperately trying to avoid.

By the time Kelly entered fourth grade, she was already fully resigned to doing poorly on tests. It didn't matter what the subject was. The results were the same. Occasionally, she might get lucky and squeak by with a C- or even a C, but these were rare events. Kelly's calamitous expectations intensified when she entered middle school, and by eighth grade she was fully convinced that she was hopelessly retarded.

The test-taking scenario was scripted. The teacher would hand out the test, and invariably one of the very first questions would confuse the fourteen-year-old. Alarms would immediately go off in her head. Her mind would start racing, and she would begin bombarding herself with reproaches. "This doesn't make any sense. I must have studied the wrong pages!" "We were never taught how to solve these problems!" "The teacher is trying to trick me!" "I'm going to choose the wrong answer for sure!" As her panic intensified, she would forget everything she had ostensibly studied. Her mind would shut down, and she would begin to hyperventilate. The remaining questions on the test would become a blur. It was as if she were being asked about information she had never seen before. By the time she handed in the test, the strain had escalated to the point where Kelly felt like sobbing aloud.

Convinced in advance that studying was a waste of time and poor grades were inevitable, Kelly's studying was, at best, perfunctory. Her standard operating procedure was to study on her bed with her elbows resting on the comforter, her chin propped in the palms of her hands, and her textbook positioned in front of her. Staring with glassy eyes at the textbook, she would mindlessly turn the pages. From time to time, she would glance over at her class notes, but what little information she had recorded was essentially useless. The incoherent scribbling bore witness to the fact that she had understood virtually nothing of what had been covered in class.

"What's the sense of studying if I'm going to fail anyway?" Kelly would lament to her parents. When her frustration erupted, her mother and father could do little to console her. They would offer words of encouragement and logical reasons why she should keep on trying but, although they wouldn't admit it, they, too, had arrived at the same conclusion as their daughter. Studying seemed to be an exercise in futility.

Kelly could decode the words in her textbooks without difficulty, but understanding what the words actually meant was another matter. Despite her obvious difficulty grasping the content in her textbooks, the fourteen-year-old's scores on standardized achievement tests actually indicated that her reading comprehension was hovering near grade level.

When Kelly entered fifth grade, her parents had become so alarmed by their daughter's academic deterioration and emotional outbursts that they insisted she be diagnostically tested. They were undeterred by the fact that the child-study team and the school psychologist didn't consider Kelly to be a legitimate candidate for a resource program. In response to their persistence, the psychologist grudgingly agreed to administer the evaluation. The results of this assessment confirmed that Kelly had no specific perceptual processing deficits. The tests also confirmed that her reading comprehension was two months below grade level and her math was several months above grade level. Based on these scores, the psychologist asserted that Kelly did not qualify for the RSP (Resource Specialist Program). Although he acknowledged that Kelly was struggling academically, he explained that the school was not mandated to provide specialized instruction when there are no measurable indications of a specific learning disability. His perfunctory manner clearly communicated that he considered the matter closed.

To verify the test results, Kelly's parents had their daughter evaluated by a private psychologist. This assessment confirmed what the school psychologist had told them. There were no underlying decoding deficits. Kelly's IQ was in the average range, and given her near-grade-level reading scores, Kelly should, in theory, have been capable of assimilating the content of her courses and of passing tests in school. In practice, this obviously wasn't happening. Kelly was assimilating virtually nothing when she studied, and she was failing virtually every test she took.

To rule out ADHD as a possible explanation for Kelly's difficulties, the psychologist asked Kelly's parents and two of her core subject teachers to complete a comprehensive behavioral inventory. The completed inventories indicated that Kelly did not have ADHD. When the clearly puzzled psychologist then recommended more extensive testing. Kelly's parents declined. They had already spent more than twelve hundred dollars on the evaluation, and they were unwilling to invest more money in a process that seemed fruitless. When Kelly's mother and father left the psychologist's office, they were as confused as they were when they first entered.

Left to her own devices, Kelly continued to suffer from chronic apprehension and test anxiety, and she continued to perform dismally. When her graded tests were returned, she would hide them from her friends by immediately shoving the papers into her backpack. If by chance a classmate happened to glimpse at one of the grades before she could hide it, Kelly would explain her poor performance by telling the classmate that she hadn't studied for the test. Then she would quickly change the subject.

Although Kelly's frustration and anger rarely boiled over in school, emotional outbursts were nightly occurrences at home. As she tried to do her homework, Kelly would become confused and frustrated. Unable to contain her exasperation, she would start pounding her fists on her desk and rail against the teacher. At these moments, all Kelly's distraught parents could do was to try to calm her down.

Kelly's mother and father ultimately abandoned their efforts to get help for their child in school. Years of battling with unsympathetic school administrators had left them embittered, resentful, and resigned. The dismissive comment of a visibly annoyed vice principal at Kelly's middle school was the straw that broke the camel's back. "I'm sorry, but there are no appropriate programs at our school for Kelly. You may just have to accept the fact that your daughter will never be a good student," he informed them with a condescending tone. With his facial expression and body language, the vice principal plainly communicated that he was tired of dealing with the matter. He reiterated that Kelly didn't meet the qualifying criteria for being provided with remedial learning assistance. There was nothing more that he could do.

This newest rebuff only deepened Kelly's parents' despair. They could see that their daughter was being psychologically damaged but felt powerless to provide for her educational needs. As time progressed, they became increasingly resigned to the futility of trying to procure help for their daughter.

After a typical nightly tantrum about how dumb she, the textbook, and the teacher were, Kelly's anger would usually subside. The emotional catharsis would temporarily break the logjam, and despite her conviction that her answers to the questions on the impending test would be wrong, Kelly would reluctantly start to study again using her customary robotic study procedures. "So what!" she would mutter through clenched teeth. "I don't care! I'm just stupid, and there's nothing I can do about it."

WHEN CHILDREN DON'T QUALIFY FOR HELP

Fact: *School special education programs are designed to address children's perceptual processing and academic skills deficits and to provide a safety net while students are acquiring the requisite skills to catch up and keep up with their classes.* Sometimes a struggling child's learning difficulties fit neatly in the diagnostic/treatment box. The child manifests the classic symptoms of a specific learning disability, and diagnosis by the school psychologist is routine. If the assessment indicates that the child's symptoms conform to state- and school-district-mandated eligibility criteria, the child is identified as a candidate for a learning assistance program, or, in cases of a severe dysfunction, in a full-time special day class. An I.E.P. (Individual Educational Plan) meeting is then scheduled. At this meeting, the child's parents and school personnel define specific skill-improvement objectives and develop a focused remedial strategy that will ideally help the child attain these objectives. If the child's parents concur with and endorse the plan, the strategy is then implemented with the child typically taking part in a daily forty- to forty-five-minute individual or small group resource program supervised by a specially trained resource specialist.

    Fact: *School districts apply rigid eligibility standards to determine which children are provided with help.* Only 3 to 4 percent of underperforming students are generally eligible for resource programs and full-time special day class programs. Many children with less severe, enigmatic, intermittent, or atypical learning difficulties are never furnished formal assistance. As Kelly's parents learned, a student's academic difficulties must be directly attributable to specific identifiable perceptual processing deficits, and there must be a significant discrepancy between the child's ability and performance as measured by standardized achievement tests and in-class functioning. In many districts, children must test a minimum of two years below grade level to be considered for a special education program. In effect, legions of underperforming children such as Kelly whose learning difficulties do not meet the special education qualification criteria are essentially abandoned by the educational system.

    Kelly's learning problems clearly do not fit neatly into the standard diagnostic/treatment cubbyhole, and her academic difficulties appear to be punctuated with contradictions. She struggles to assimilate the content of her textbooks but has no trouble decoding the words. Two other factors are even more puzzling: Kelly's reading comprehension skills are near grade level, and her IQ is in average range. Given these scores, she should possess the requisite skills and intelligence to understand and recall what she's studying and get passing grades on tests. Why then is she doing so poorly on these tests?

In view of her repeated setbacks in school, Kelly's test phobia, test anxiety, catastrophic expectations are certainly understandable. Her failures exact a disastrous psychological toll and shred her self-confidence. Having no evidence to the contrary, Kelly simply concludes that she's mentally defective and functions accordingly.

Despite her difficulty assimilating and retaining information, and her abysmal grades, Kelly is left to sink or swim on her own, even though it's apparent that she doesn't know how to swim or even tread water. She's flailing in the surf and being pulled away from shore, but no one at her school is prepared to rescue her, much less throw her a floatation device. Each successive test-taking fiasco leaves another indelible negative imprint on her psyche, and these disasters inexorably warp her perceptions about herself and her capabilities.

The rationale for excluding Kelly from a learning program essentially boils down to the economic principle of supply and demand. Inasmuch as vast numbers of children underperform academically, the school district's primary concern, and by extension the state and federal government's primary concern, is that without rigid eligibility criteria, enrollment in learning assistance programs would quickly eclipse available funding and personnel resources. As no alternative assistance program is offered Kelly, one can only infer that her school doesn't provide teacher-supervised tutoring or a peer tutoring program for struggling students who fail to qualify for special education.

Two revealing sentences pop out in the case study: "They could see that Kelly was being psychologically damaged, but they felt powerless to provide for their daughter's educational needs. As time progressed, however, they became increasingly resigned to the futility of trying to procure help for their daughter." Perhaps you found yourself wondering why Kelly's parents became resigned? Yes, it's true that they were repeatedly rebuffed when they tried to get help for their daughter at school, but why didn't they consider hiring a qualified private tutor to help Kelly? This would seem such a logical course of action, and it's inconceivable that the idea had never occurred to them. It's also inconceivable that the private psychologist who evaluated Kelly didn't recommend tutoring or educational therapy. Perhaps he did, but Kelly's parents may have disregarded the recommendation. Was it the expense or faulty judgment that deterred them from seeking private learning assistance? As these issues are not addressed in the case study, we can only speculate about what transpired.

To their credit, Kelly's parents sought a second opinion and took their daughter to be evaluated by the private psychologist. The results only added to their bewilderment. How could Kelly's average intelligence and near-average reading scores be reconciled with the fact that she was receiving Ds and Fs on virtually every test she took? The explanations for this seeming contradiction are found in the case study.

- **Statement:** "Kelly's studying was at best perfunctory."
  Interpretation: Kelly learns passively, and her mind is disengaged when she's studying.
- **Statement:** "Staring with glassy eyes at the textbook, she would mindlessly turn the pages."
  Interpretation: Kelly lacks effective study skills and doesn't know how to identify and assimilate key information.
- **Statement:** "The incoherent scribbling bore witness to the fact that she had understood virtually nothing of what had been covered in class."
  Interpretation: Kelly doesn't know how to take lecture notes, nor does she know how to use notes when she studies.
- **Statement:** "As her panic intensified, she would forget everything she had ostensibly studied."
  Interpretation: Kelly's test phobia and test anxiety are causing her to become dysfunctional when she takes exams.
- **Statement:** "It was as if she were being asked about information she had never seen before."

Interpretation: Kelly's doesn't know how to identify and memorize important information when she studies.

- **Statement:** "Studying seemed an exercise in futility."
  Interpretation: Kelly's negative associations with learning are causing her to become demoralized and incapacitated.
- **Statement:** "Kelly was assimilating virtually nothing when she studied."
  Interpretation: Kelly's reading comprehension skills are inadequate, despite her test scores, and her comprehension deficits are impeding her ability to master the content of her textbooks.
- **Statement:** "As she tried to do her homework, Kelly would invariably become confused and frustrated. Unable to contain her exasperation, she would start pounding her fists on her desk and rail against the teacher."
  Interpretation: Kelly's psychological stress is overwhelming her coping mechanisms and is rendering her academically dysfunctional.

DISREGARDING THE SIGNALS

Fact: *Parents cannot afford to remain passive when their child is clearly malfunctioning in school.* Parental resignation when a child is learning ineffectually, falling further and further behind, and becoming increasingly frustrated and discouraged is not a viable option. The sooner effective remedial support is provided, the better. Had this help been provided for Kelly in first, second, or third grade, it's likely that she wouldn't have ended up defeated, demoralized, and learning-aversive in eighth grade.

The danger flags indicating that Kelly had a reading comprehension and information assimilation problem were undoubtedly flapping throughout elementary school. (In high-achieving schools, reading at or near grade level may be insufficient to assure decent grades.) The school's refusal to intervene did not absolve Kelly's parents from exhausting every available option for procuring help for their daughter. In fact, the school's intransigence should have been the primary catalyst for actively seeking help in the private sector.

Mistakes were obviously made, and it serves no purpose to excoriate

Kelly's parents. At this juncture, the immediate challenge is to fix the problem. To do so, four specific remedial steps must be taken:

- Enhance Kelly's reading comprehension.
- Teach Kelly how to learn actively and study productively.
- Reduce Kelly's test-taking anxiety.
- Improve Kelly's test-taking skills.

To simply commiserate with a child such as Kelly and urge her to keep on trying is clearly insufficient. Defeated learners are seldom receptive to hearing that they should disregard their failing grades and continue to work conscientiously, and most will simply ignore the pep talks and admonitions. If given the choice of fight or flight, the vast majority of academically demoralized children will try to run away from their problems and frustrations, and they will usually do so by giving up and shutting down. To persist in the face of seemingly certain defeat requires extraordinary grit and determination, and most defeated learners lack these qualities. That Kelly continued to do her work at all was actually quite remarkable, given her woefully inadequate skills and her recurrent failures in school.

TO TEST OR NOT TO TEST

Fact: *Private diagnostic testing can be used to substantiate or refute the results of in-school evaluations and to furnish additional information that may prove beneficial when designing an individualized remedial program.* As a general rule, the more data parents, resource specialists, tutors, and educational therapists have about a child's learning difficulties, the better. By employing a method called *differential diagnosis*, a psychologist can systematically rule out what's not causing the problem, and through this process of elimination ultimately identify what is causing the problem. Extensive private diagnostic testing, however, can be an expensive indulgence and may be unwarranted, especially if the testing is superfluous and replicates testing that's already been done in school.

The four primary benefits of additional comprehensive testing include:

- substantiating or refuting previous test results that may be in doubt.
- pinpointing with greater precision the factors responsible for a child's learning difficulties.
- providing insight into a child's learning style, intelligence type, and preferred learning modality.
- shaping the remedial program so that it addresses the child's learning deficits, teaches her how to successfully compensate for these deficits, and shows her how to capitalize on her learning strengths.

For example, a psychologist might determine that a child's comprehension and retention deficits are attributable to problems processing information quickly and forming visual pictures in her mind when she studies. The tests might also establish that the child's comprehension deficiencies are linked to difficulty drawing inferences and applying information that she reads, or they might indicate that the child isn't using the most productive learning modality when she attempts to assimilate information in her textbooks. This data could then be used to design a more effective learning assistance strategy. (See chapter 2 to review information about identifying intelligence types, learning strengths, and preferred learning modalities.)

At issue in Kelly's case is whether comprehensive testing by a psychologist charging approximately $150.00 an hour is necessary. Could the information about her reading problems and about her learning strengths and preferences be obtained without having to pay a psychologist to administer additional tests, write a report, and have another conference with Kelly's parents? The answer to this question is a qualified "yes." Certainly, in puzzling cases and in instances in which the parent and the school cannot agree about the nature of a child's learning difficulties, a comprehensive specialized evaluation by an independent clinical or educational psychologist, or a neuropsychologist, is appropriate. In other instances, there are less expensive options for deriving the core information that's needed to design an effective remedial strategy. Remember, the basic testing has already been done in Kelly's case. In fact, it's been done twice, once by the school psychologist and once by the private psychologist.

A qualified tutor or educational therapist who is working with Kelly could probably take over any further testing duties. He or she could administer another reading test and could employ a relatively simple procedure called *item analysis* to identify the specific types of comprehension errors Kelly is making. The tutor could use readily available inventories to identify Kelly's intelligence type, learning strengths, and preferred learning modalities and could utilize specialized teaching materials to improve Kelly's skills in the identified deficit areas. The tutor could also use a diagnostic inventory to analyze Kelly's study skills deficits and could employ specialized teaching materials to correct these deficits. (See the Learning Preference Inventory on pages 34–37 and the Study Skills Inventory on pages 247–248.)

Many parents have limited financial resources, and they must make judicious decisions about how to best allocate their resources. They must decide if money that might be spent on comprehensive diagnostic testing could be better spent on providing remedial help. When do parents reach the point of diminishing returns vis-à-vis diagnostic testing? When do they have enough information to switch from a testing track to a treatment track? When is it time to bring a child such as Kelly into the "shop" and have a top-notch mechanic do some basic diagnostics and make the repairs?

Kelly's reading-comprehension and test-taking problems are solvable. An experienced educator using good teaching materials could unquestionably develop a remedial program that will improve her reading comprehension. This person could also unquestionably teach her how to study more productively as opposed to mechanically.

Kelly is long overdue for a major tune-up. The warning lights on the dashboard are blinking, and the engine is overheating.

PASSIVE LEARNING VERSUS ACTIVE LEARNING

Fact: *Passive learning and ineffectual learning are interlaced.* Children who are intellectually disengaged when they learn cannot possibly perform at a level commensurate with the full abilities. Those who study in a robotic manner may believe that they're working conscientiously and meeting their academic obligations, but they're clearly deluding themselves. Oblivious to the cause-and-effect connection between their subpar achievement and their failure to actively involve their brain when they study, these children operate on automatic pilot and are unaware that their plane is flying upside down.

For Kelly, studying translates into lying on her bed in a mental stupor and mindlessly flipping the pages in her textbook. She doesn't know how to take notes, and she doesn't know how to identify and assimilate key information. Given her ineffectual study procedures and passive learning style, Kelly's abysmal test performance should surprise no one.

Fact: *Chronically frustrated and demoralized children often cope with their feelings of inadequacy and sense of futility by shutting down mentally.* Many struggling learners aren't aware that they're learning passively and that their brain is disengaged when they study. When queried about their study procedures, they are likely to justify their disinterest and passivity by arguing that the material they're being required to learn is boring and irrelevant. A classic chicken-or-egg conundrum becomes apparent, namely does substandard performance cause passive learning, or does passive learning cause substandard performance? The answer is "yes" to both questions. Chronic learning difficulties can cause children to defend themselves psychologically by becoming passive and ineffectual learners, and passive and ineffectual learning can, in turn, cause chronic academic difficulties. Whatever the origins, etiology, and dynamics of the ineffectual/passive learning phenomenon, the effects are usually disastrous and typically include maladaptive behavior, reduced functionality, and diminished self-confidence.

Fact: *Academic achievement requires a fully engaged mind, functional academic skills, and an effective, individualized learning strategy.* Successful students intuitively recognize the need for active mental involvement in the learning process. These children:

- think about the significance of what they're studying.
- identify important information.
- pinpoint information that their teachers are likely to consider significant and would want them to understand and recall.

- anticipate the questions their teachers are likely to ask on tests in order to determine if the course content has been mastered.

Having targeted what's important, successful students deliberately and methodically develop a pragmatic and individualized strategy for assimilating the key information. They're goal-directed. They want to achieve and excel. They want to experience the sense of accomplishment and feelings of pride attendant to getting good grades. These children don't consider being required to learn new information and skills to be distasteful or a cruel plot on the part of their teachers to make their lives miserable. They're excited about learning how to solve challenging algebra problems. They want to learn how to speak Spanish. They want to learn about global warming, the Civil War, and photosynthesis. Certainly there are times when they would rather be doing something other than studying, but more often than not they're amenable to doing their work and they're prepared to work conscientiously. This active learning modus operandi starkly contrasts to the characteristic "put it off for as long as possible and then get it finished as quickly as possible" mind-set of resistant children who learn passively.

Yes, it's likely that many of these enthusiastic and actively engaged learners never had to struggle with dyslexia, ADHD, and reading comprehension problems. It's also likely that learning has been easy for them. Given the psychological impact of children's previous negative associations with learning, you may be wondering whether it's possible and realistic for chronically underperforming youngsters to become enthusiastic and actively engaged learners. The answer is yes. Intervene early and effectively, furnish underachieving children with the essential reading, math, time-management, organizational, goal-setting, and study tools they need to win in school, engineer opportunities for them to experience success, and provide support, encouragement, and affirmation for their effort and progress, and a turnaround is unequivocally attainable. Passive, ineffectual, and resistant learners can, in fact, transform themselves into ardent, actively engaged learners.

QUESTIONS AND ANSWERS ABOUT "NONQUALIFYING" LEARNING DIFFICULTIES

Question: If diagnostic testing indicates that a child of average intelligence doesn't have an authenticated learning disability, why would the child have trouble identifying, assimilating, and recalling information and why would she consistently fail tests?

Answer: Nonlearning disabled children may have difficulty mastering the content of their courses and may test poorly for seven basic reasons:

- They don't know how to capitalize on their natural talents and learning strengths.
- Their reading comprehension skills, even if determined to be at approximate grade level, are insufficient to assure decent grades in challenging middle and high school courses.
- They have concentration difficulties.
- They don't know how to study productively.
- They are unmotivated to learn.
- They have subtle, intermittent, or atypical processing and/or memory deficits that impede their ability to learn efficiently and retain important information.
- They are emotionally and mentally immobilized by excessive test phobia and test-taking anxiety.

Question: Can the comprehension, retention, and test-taking skills of underperforming students who learn atypically and who don't fit neatly into the diagnostic/treatment box be improved?

Answer: In virtually every case, the reading comprehension, retention, and test-taking skills of underperforming students can be significantly improved if they're provided with effective remedial instruction.

Question: Can children overcome chronic test phobias and test-taking anxiety?

Answer: Children can be taught specific effective techniques for reducing their debilitating test phobia and test-taking anxiety. As their academic performance and self-confidence improve, their apprehensions are likely to diminish.

Question: Can a struggling child's study efficiency be significantly enhanced?

Answer: A competent tutor or educational therapist using an effective instructional program can play an instrumental role in helping children acquire more productive study skills.

TUTORING AND EDUCATIONAL THERAPY

Fact: *Parents who understand the issues that are impeding their child's learning can evaluate their child's needs more astutely, weigh their learning-assistance options more judiciously, and monitor progress more incisively.* As previously noted, there are two basic options when seeking private learning assistance for a struggling child—tutoring or educational therapy.

Tutors who work with younger children are typically college students, college graduates, or classroom teachers. Many of the latter are either retired or are working as tutors to supplement their income. Tutors at the elementary school level are typically generalists who do not necessarily have training in the field of special education. Tutors at the middle and high school level are typically content-area specialists. Although many of these tutors have no background in special education, they have usually taught, or are currently teaching, the particular subject in high school or middle school and usually have an advanced degree in a specific content area. One tutor may specialize in English while another may specialize in math.

Educational therapists, on the other hand, are generally not content-area specialists. They have an advanced degree in special education and in most instances are certified resource specialists with extensive postgraduate training in special education. This advanced training and their hands-on experience as resource specialists equips them to deal not only with general homework and test-taking issues, but also to identify and remediate underlying learning deficits. (Certification by the National Association of Educational Therapists requires that resource specialists demonstrate advanced competencies in assessing and remediating learning dysfunctions.)

The instructional procedures used by tutors and educational therapists often differ. For example, a child may be struggling in history and may be at risk of failing the midterm exam. Using the child's textbook, a tutor would typically explain content-area issues that are causing confusion and would help the child with her homework and with preparing for the exam.

An educational therapist would most likely take a different tack. After assessing the student, the educational therapist may conclude that the child doesn't know how to identify important information, take textbook and lecture notes, memorize key facts, and anticipate multiple choice, short answer, true-false, and essay questions that the teacher is likely to ask on the midterm. As is the case with a tutor, the educational therapist would use the student's textbook to help the child understand the content and complete her homework, but he or she would also methodically identify and address the causal factors responsible for the child's poor performance. The objective would be to help the student pass the midterm while also addressing any underlying visual-memory and study-skills deficits. Most educational therapists would also undoubtedly focus on showing the child how to capitalize on her natural learning strengths and preferred learning modality or modalities and on teaching the child productive learning skills that are applicable in all content areas. (See the sections on learning styles and multiple intelligences on pages 33–44.) To achieve these objectives, the therapist would utilize specialized teaching materials that the typical tutor may not be trained to use.

Regardless of whether a child is working with a tutor or an educational therapist, the immediate priority is to help the child with the homework assignments she finds confusing and to help her prepare for tests. In some respects, the distinction between remedial strategies is analogous to treating the symptoms of bacterial pneumonia with an antibiotic versus treating the symptoms and then inoculating the child to prevent future incidents.

Fact: *The challenges tutors and educational therapists face are compounded when children are having difficulty in several subjects and are overwhelmed by their daily homework assignments.* Children who learn ineffectually often fall behind in more than one subject. This all-too-common phenomenon offers a compelling argument for helping struggling children come to grips with the specific underlying learning deficits that are undermining their performance. If a child is in crisis, and there isn't enough time to address the causal factors during the school year, these issues may need to be addressed during summer vacation when there are no impinging daily homework demands. This, of course, assumes that the student is not attending summer school.

The issue of deferring on addressing the underlying factors and focusing instead on immediate urgent problems should be discussed with the tutor or educational therapist at an early stage in the learning-assistance process. The priorities, thrust, and content of the tutoring program should then be periodically revisited to make certain that the program is on target and is responsive to the child's current needs.

PARENTAL TUTORING VERSUS PROFESSIONAL TUTORING

Fact: *Becoming your child's tutor can be tricky and risky.* In previous chapters, you were urged to take an aggressive and proactive role in the process of effecting positive cognitive behavioral changes in your child's academic modus operandi. Be forewarned that you may not be able to assume this same assertive role in helping your child overcome her specific academic deficiencies. To tutor your own child requires a special rapport and a great deal of patience, teaching competence, and sustained effort. This is especially true in the case of older students who have a long history of academic difficulties and who are actively or passively resistant to help. You must gauge the challenges objectively. If your intuition tells you that it would be a mistake to become your child's tutor, trust your intuition. In some respects the situation is analogous to changing the oil in your car. Some people who are mechanically oriented enjoy rolling up their sleeves and doing the work themselves. Others are more than happy to pay someone else to do the job.

There are certain basic requirements for successfully tutoring your own child. Primary among them is that you be comfortable with and capable of implementing an instructional program. You must also be relatively knowledgeable about the content area in which you are tutoring. The types of issues you should consider before you step into the ring include:

- Can you tutor your child in geometry if you haven't solved a geometry problem in more than twenty years?
- Can you help your child with Spanish grammar if you took German or French in high school or if you yourself were not a particularly good foreign language student?
- Can you explain chemistry principles when you've forgotten virtually everything you learned in high school about chemistry?
- Can you help your child take notes, identify and memorize key data, and prepare for a final exam when you haven't prepared for exams in more than two decades?

These obstacles are surmountable if you are sufficiently motivated, possess natural teaching skills, and can successfully relate to your child in an instructional mode. You should, however, consider another potential roadblock: The curriculum may have changed greatly since you were in high school. An example of this shift is in the way math is now taught in many schools. In some schools, algebraic-type equations are being introduced to students in second grade, and this instructional methodology affects how prealgebra and algebra are taught at the middle and high school levels. You may have been taught math very differently. You must decide whether you can learn the new instructional methods and teach the content in a way that doesn't further confuse your child and add to her likely already negative associations with math.

Finally, there's one more significant downside risk when parents elect to become their child's tutor. Parents, and especially those who were themselves good students, may lose their patience when working with a struggling child, and if they express their exasperation, they could do more harm than good. The relationship between a parent and a child is complex and multifaceted, and emotional issues that are part and parcel of all family relationships can complicate and undermine your efforts to tutor your child. Even highly competent teachers are often hesitant to work with their own child for the same reason that physicians are unwilling to treat their own family members. They realize that it's extremely difficult to remain objective and that this lack of objectivity could cloud their judgment and cause them to respond inappropriately.

When parents become their child's tutor, traditional roles and boundaries are altered, and this shift may cause children to become confused, uncomfortable, resentful, defended, and/or resistant. Many children don't want their parents to be their academic tutors, the phenomenon of home schooling notwithstanding. Parents who nonetheless insist on becoming their child's tutor often discover that productive tutoring is untenable in a negatively charged atmosphere.

After considering the foregoing, you may conclude that it would be wiser to farm out the tutoring job to a qualified professional who has extensive experience in assessing children's learning needs and in designing and implementing an effective learning-assistance strategy. If you do decide to seek professional help, there are still critically important support functions that you should be prepared to assume. These include:

- Explaining to your child the reasons why tutoring or educational therapy is necessary.
- Communicating clearly and unequivocally that you value education and that you're committed to doing everything possible to ensure that your child succeeds in school.
- Defusing resistance.
- Supporting the tutor's efforts.
- Encouraging your child's sustained diligence.
- Providing emotional backing, affirmation, and praise for progress.
- Making certain that you and the tutor are on the same page, that the remediation plan is on target, and that all of the necessary bases will be covered.

Your understanding of the issues and periodic updates from the tutor will enable you to mentor and monitor your child more effectively during the tutoring process. You should not hesitate to request informal progress reports. This input will keep you apprised of progress and will alert you to any obstacles that are encountered.

A note of caution about interfacing with the tutor is in order. Your legitimate desire to be informed about what's transpiring during the tutoring sessions shouldn't be construed as a license to be intrusive. Once you select a skilled person whom you believe can teach your child effectively, you should allow this person leeway to do the job. You should also allow a reasonable amount of time for the tutor to achieve the agreed-upon objectives. Yes, the meter is running, and the cab is expensive, but you must be realistic about how long it takes to get across town.

If you and your child begin to lose confidence in the tutor, discuss your concerns with the tutor. If your misgivings cannot be allayed, find another tutor. Be vigilant, however, about allowing yourself to be manipulated by your child, especially if she's resistant to the idea of receiving learning assistance. Your child may claim that the tutor is doing a poor job in order to convince you to discontinue the process. You'll need to carefully analyze the data and make an informed judgment. Don't hesitate to factor your intuition into the decision-making process.

Fact: *Urgency is a primary consideration in determining immediate tutoring objectives and priorities.* Children who are confused and overwhelmed by their homework, have fallen far behind in several classes, and are at risk of failing one or more courses are clearly in a crisis mode and are vulnerable to becoming demoralized and shutting down academically. Helping these youngsters keep up with the class, complete their assignments, and study for impending tests is the most immediate priority and may require all of the tutor's efforts. The amount of time budgeted each week for tutoring must obviously be factored into the learning-assistance strategy. If a child's academic needs are extensive and if only one or two hours can be allotted each week for tutoring, it may be difficult for the tutor to cover all the bases. As previously suggested, addressing the underlying deficits may need to be deferred until summer.

The following questions are designed to help you select the appropriate educator to work with your child and to improve the likelihood that you and this person are on the same page.

ISSUES TO DISCUSS WITH THE TUTOR OR EDUCATIONAL THERAPIST

- What is your educational background and tutoring experience?
- What are the specific deficits you plan on addressing in the tutoring sessions?
- What are your specific objectives?
- Can you give me an idea of your proposed instructional strategy?
- Do you plan to focus primarily on correcting underlying deficiencies, or on helping my child do her immediate homework and study for tests?
- Can urgent problems and underlying deficits be addressed concurrently?
- How do you assess improvement?
- Do you expect my child to do additional homework to supplement the tutoring sessions?
- Will you solicit information and feedback about progress from my child's teachers?
- What is the minimum amount of tutoring time each week that you would need to attain the targeted academic objectives?
- What is the optimal amount of time each week that you would want to work with my child?
- Is there a particular sequence in which you propose to address the identified problems (e.g., will you focus on reading-comprehension deficiencies before you focus on study-skills deficiencies, or will you work in both areas concurrently)?
- How can I best support your efforts?
- Is there anything you expect me to do at home to supplement the tutoring?
- If appropriate, will you help my child make adjustments in her study schedule?
- Can you make a ballpark estimate as to how many hours will be required to achieve the objectives you've defined?

IMPROVING READING COMPREHENSION

Fact: *To read with good comprehension, children require a range of interrelated skills.* On the most basic reading level, children must be able to decipher and make sense out of words. Students who have been taught to read using the sight method must be capable of recognizing previously introduced words. Those who have been taught to read using the phonics method must be capable of sounding out unfamiliar words.

Once children progress beyond the basic decoding, they face additional challenges. They must also be able to understand, recall, and apply what they read. Unfortunately, this shift from deciphering words to comprehending information can prove extremely difficult for some children.

Fact: *There are three levels of reading comprehension.* The most basic level—the literal level—requires that children be able to retain information. This level is emphasized in the lower grades in conjunction with teaching children decoding skills. For example, a child might read the following in a science textbook: "Lasers can produce intense heat and can be use to weld tiny electronic circuits and perform surgery. Other lasers do not produce heat and are used to store computer data, read bar codes on items at the checkout counter in a store, record music, aim weapons, and track satellites." On a subsequent test, the student might then be asked the following literal question: "What are seven ways in which lasers can be used?"

As students progress into the upper grades, they must also be able to comprehend on the inferential level (i.e., drawing conclusions from what they read) and on an applicative level (i.e., using information that they read). For example, a student who reads the preceding statement about lasers might be asked to discuss the impact of lasers on modern society. This would involve drawing inferences from the statement. The student might also be asked to describe four specific ways she might use lasers to treat patients if she were a doctor. This would require her to recall and logically apply what she read in the statement. To respond to these types of inferential and applicative questions, the student must be capable of more than simply remembering facts. She must think carefully and consider the information and its implications. Stated differently, she must train her mind to think actively when she reads.

THE THREE LEVELS OF READING COMPREHENSION

Level 1:   *Literal Comprehension*—Being able to recall written information.

Example: Mt. Everest is located in the Himalayas between Nepal and Tibet and it is the highest mountain in the world.

Example of a literal test question: What is the highest mountain in the world and where is it located?

Level 2:   *Inferential Comprehension*—Being able to understand and draw logical conclusions and inferences from information that is implied but not directly stated.

Example: Even experienced climbers can underestimate the challenging winds and sudden climate changes on mountains such as Mt. Everest, and these meteorological miscalculations could prove deadly.

Example of an inferential test question: What advantages do today's mountain climbers have over those who were first to climb Mt. Everest?

Level 3:   *Applicative Comprehension*—Being able to apply information.

Example: Survival in extreme mountain-climbing conditions often hinges on careful preparation and methodically reducing the risks.

Example of an applicative test question: If you were climbing Mt. Everest, what specific logical steps could you take to improve your chances of survival during the climb?

Most middle school and high school teachers expect students to be capable of answering test questions that probe their literal, inferential, and applicative comprehension. Simply being able to read words and memorize information, while certainly important, does not necessarily guarantee good grades in high school classes. This is especially true in college prep and advance placement courses where teachers require that students be able to demonstrate that they have achieved insight and can apply what they've learned. Students who are in the habit of studying with the cerebral lights out are usually in for a nasty surprise when they take tests in these advanced classes.

Fact: *When provided with effective instruction and sufficient opportunities to practice, most children can acquire a full range of reading comprehension skills.* Certainly, the perceptual-processing deficits associated with dyslexia or the behaviors associated with ADHD can compound the challenge of being able to read with good comprehension. Absent a debilitating learning disability, information-assimilation skills encompassing all three levels of understanding can be taught to virtually any child of normal intelligence. Qualified tutors and educational therapists can train students to ask themselves incisive question when they read, so that their brain is actively engaged in the process of assimilating the information. They can teach students how to identify important information and differentiate main ideas from details, and they can teach students how to "chew up" data so that they can understand, recall, and use the data.

THE NUTS AND BOLTS OF GOOD READING COMPREHENSION

Students must be capable of:

- Identifying important information.
- Distinguishing main ideas from details.
- Understanding key issues and concepts.
- Recalling relevant data.
- Drawing logical inferences and conclusions from what they're reading.
- Utilizing the information that they read.
- Applying analytical and critical thinking skills.
- Organizing and classifying data.
- Linking what's currently being learned with what's already been learned.

Recommendation: *If your child is struggling with reading comprehension and is receiving tutorial assistance, verify that the tutor or educational therapist has identified the specific deficits and has a plan in place for correcting these deficiencies.* Unless time for focused remedial instruction is integrated into the tutoring strategy, the tutoring will be little more than a Band-Aid, and the reading comprehension deficits will persist and continue to undermine your child's academic performance.

Specialized teaching materials can be used that focus on systematically developing all three levels of reading comprehension. Most experienced tutors probably already have these materials or can procure them at a teacher supply store or online.

If you are tutoring your child, ask someone with experience to help you with an item analysis of your child's reading errors. In this procedure, your child's incorrect answers on a reading test are analyzed and identified as representing literal, inferential, or applicative errors. Even though your child may not be enrolled in a special education program, the school resource specialist may be willing to do the analysis for you. Also ask the resource specialist and your child's teacher for recommendations about instructional materials that you can use with your child once the specific deficits have been identified. Check out your local teacher supply store. Usually the salespeople at such stores have been or are currently teachers. You can also go online and research reading instruction materials designed for home schooling and for remedial instruction. In addition, you may want to contact organizations and parent support groups that can provide you with direction and invaluable information. These organizations can be researched online by keying in search words such as: learning differences, dyslexia, and reading problems.

LEARNING HOW TO STUDY

Fact: *Good study skills are essential to academic achievement.* Teaching students how to study is not an especially high priority in most American schools. Many middle and high school teachers assume that students will either acquire effective study skills naturally or that these skills will be taught in elementary school. Conversely, many elementary school teachers assume these "advanced" skills will be taught in middle school and high school. Certainly, some students do, in fact, figure out how to study efficiently without formal and methodical instruction, but countless other potentially capable students never get the hang of it. Using only a fraction of their abilities, these students muddle through school and chronically underachieve.

Children who have learning problems are especially at risk for never learning how to study productively. Even students enrolled in RSP may never be taught essential study skills, as learning assistance is typically devoted to helping children complete their class work and homework and to helping them resolve their perceptual-processing deficits. Although time may be allocated to helping students prepare for tests in their mainstream classes, rarely is sufficient time actually devoted to teaching these struggling learners methodical study procedures. As a consequence, many learning-disabled students do not develop an effective, individualized learning strategy, and they lurch from academic crisis to academic crisis without knowing how to identify, understand, and assimilate important information.

INDICATORS OF DEFICIENT STUDY SKILLS

Students have difficulty:
- Recording assignments accurately.
- Managing time efficiently.
- Planning ahead.
- Meeting deadlines.
- Organizing their materials.
- Identifying important information when they study.
- Differentiating main ideas and concepts from details and facts.
- Reading with good comprehension.
- Taking effective lecture and textbook notes.
- Memorizing important information.
- Anticipating questions that are likely to be asked on tests.
- Proofreading carefully and checking for errors.
- Developing a comprehensive test-preparation procedure.

As you scan this list, you'll recognize that several of the basic components of effective study skills have already been addressed. A succinct description and discussion of the remaining components follows. Understanding the nuts and bolts of effective study skills, while unquestionably important, is one thing, but actually teaching children how to take notes and prepare for exams is another. If you or your child's tutor decide to implement a study-skills-enhancement program, you would want to review materials specifically designed to help students study more productively. You can check out what's available in your local bookstore, teacher-supply store, and online. (Also see the bibliography for specific program suggestions.)

A brief description of the study skills components that have not yet been addressed is found below. You'll also find succinct teaching suggestions for tutoring your own child.

PRESENTING THE IDEA OF STUDY-SKILLS INSTRUCTION

Fact: *Willing participation in a learning-assistance program is preferable to forced participation.* You want your child to understand the reasons why you're insisting that she work on improving her study skills. You also want her to realize that these skills will make her life easier and improve her academic performance. If she refuses to acknowledge the reasonableness of your desire to help her study more productively and is resistant to the idea of receiving help, you must nonetheless pursue your plan to make certain she possesses the requisite skills to achieve academically. In effect, you're going to have to tell her, "I know we don't agree, but you're going to have to trust me on this one. You can choose to resist, or you can choose to accept the help that's offered. I must be convinced that I've done everything possible to provide you with the tools you need to do well in school."

Before your child begins to work with you or with a tutor on improving her study skills, it's important that she complete the following inventory. This inventory will help you and your child identify the specific study skills–deficit areas that are impeding her academic achievement. As you have done in previous chapters, you would use her responses to the statement in the inventory as a springboard for a discussion about study skills. You would compare your impressions with your child's impressions about the specific issues covered in the inventory. Then, using either the autocratic or the democratic approach that was modeled in the preceding chapters, you would clearly communicate that the identified study-skills deficits must be corrected if she's to function in school at a level equivalent with her true abilities.

STUDY SKILLS INVENTORY

Please note: This inventory does not address organizational, time-management, goal-setting, prioritizing, and study-environment issues that are also key components in effective studying. These issues have been comprehensively addressed in the preceding chapters. A reproducible copy of this inventory can be found on page 296 in the appendix.

Code: 1 = Never 2 = Rarely 3 = Sometimes 4 = Often 5 = Always
- I understand what I read in my textbooks.   ____
- I can recall information I read in textbooks.   ____
- I can recall information I hear in class.   ____
- I can follow written instructions.   ____
- I become confused when I study.   ____
- I become bored when I study.   ____
- I can identify important information when I study.   ____
- I can recall key information when I take tests.   ____
- I know how to take good notes in class.   ____
- I know how to take good notes from textbooks.   ____
- I can figure out what questions my teachers are likely to ask on tests.   ____
- I can correctly answer multiple-choice test questions.   ____
- I can correctly answer short-answer test questions.   ____
- I can correctly answer true-false test questions   ____
- I can correctly answer essay test questions.   ____
- I can correctly answer fill-in-the-blank test questions.   ____
- I have confidence in my test-taking skills.   ____

Interpretation: A pattern of 1, 2, and 3 responses to the preceding statements indicates that your child would benefit from systematic study skills instruction. Depending on your child's responses to the statements in the inventory and your own observations of her study procedures, you may decide to emphasize the following component skills.

Please Note: The following brief discussion of specific study-skills deficits and teaching suggestions are intended for parents who are taking on the role of tutoring their own child. Professional tutors and educational therapists will undoubtedly have their own strategies and techniques for addressing your child's deficits.

IDENTIFYING IMPORTANT INFORMATION

When children study they must be able to recognize what's important. They must also be able to identify main ideas, concepts, facts, and details. For example, a high school student might read the following section in a history chapter.

"The French Revolution lasted from 1789 until 1799. The revolution produced lasting radical changes in French society and government. The rule of French kings ended and the rights of the middle class (merchants, lawyers, and government officials) were strengthened. The social conditions of the peasants (small farm owners and farm workers) improved and democratic ideals were incorporated into a constitution."

The student reading these sentences must be prepared to identify and memorize key details such as the dates of the French Revolution. She must also recognize the important main ideas, namely, that the revolution radically changed French society, ended the monarchy, expanded the rights of the middle class, improved the living conditions of the peasants, and incorporated democracy into a formal constitution. Assimilating the significance of this information requires more than simple recall. It requires active, engaged thinking. Children who want to do well in school must train themselves to ask questions as they study, such as: Why was the French Revolution so significant? When did it happen? What caused it to happen? Didn't the American Revolution occur around this time? Which came first? Did the American Revolution and the U.S. Bill of Rights and the U.S. Constitution have an impact on the people of France? This questioning procedure is integral with active thinking and active learning.

Teaching children to ask probing questions when they read and study is instrumental in transforming passive and perfunctory learners into mentally engaged and inquisitive learners. When a child's active thinking switch is turned on, reading comprehension and retention cannot help but improve. Teaching children to methodically identify and differentiate key concepts and details when they study not only stimulates engaged thinking, it is also a precursor to taking effective textbook notes. (Note-taking is examined in the next section.)

TEACHING SUGGESTION FOR PARENTS TUTORING THEIR OWN CHILD:

- Examine assigned units in your child's history or science textbook and have her use one highlighter to indicate key facts and details and a second highlighter in another color to indicate key concepts and main ideas. (Be prepared to pay for the textbook, as schools rigorously discourage marking up school-owned books. The benefits of your child learning how to highlight effectively far outweigh the cost of the book.)
- Keep the sessions relatively short.
- Discuss your child's reasons for classifying information as a main idea or a detail.

TAKING TEXTBOOK NOTES

A highly effective technique for taking notes and stimulating active thinking is for students to turn each chapter section heading into a main idea question. The facts and details listed in note-taking form under the section question in effect answer the question. For example:

Subtitle:	**The Civil War in Rome in 32 B.C.**
Main idea question:	**Why was there a civil war in Rome in 32 B.C.?**
Alternatives:	**What caused the civil war in Rome in 32 B.C.?**
	How did the civil war in Rome in 32 B.C. occur?

Students would then proceed using a standard note-taking format to provide details about the civil war and its causes. These details would be taken from the assigned textbook pages. For example:

Why was there a civil war in Rome in 32 B.C.?

- Octavian ruled Rome while Marc Antony away
- Octvn tried to seize pwer
- M.A. & Octvn becme enemies → civil war to cntrl empire
- Octvn defted fleet of M.A. & Cleopatra → Battle of Actium 31 B.C.

Please note: These notes are intended to serve as a model. Abbreviations are intentionally used.)

TEACHING SUGGESTIONS FOR PARENTS TUTORING THEIR OWN CHILD

Go through several sections of your child's history or science textbook and have her underline or highlight key facts and data. Discuss her reasons for considering certain information important. Using abbreviations and speedwriting whenever possible (see list on page 164), have her record this data in the note-taking format modeled above. These procedures should be practiced until they are assimilated, but the session should be short so that resistance is avoided.

TAKING LECTURE NOTES

Trying to listen, understand, and write at the same time can be extremely challenging for struggling students. Some students feel secure only when they write down everything the teacher says in a lecture. Some have difficulty figuring out what's important. Others may want to think about what's being said and find that taking notes is distracting and interferes with their ability to think. Irrespective of children's confusion or preferences, they must be able to record the key information that the teacher considers important for future reference when studying. Providing children with "tricks of the trade" and furnishing them with opportunities to practice taking notes is the most expedient way to enhance their note-taking skills.

PROCEDURES FOR ENHANCING LECTURE NOTE-TAKING SKILLS

Locate: Sit next to a good student in class, and when this student writes down information, do the same.

Focus: Deliberately push nonrelevant thoughts from your mind, use relaxation techniques (see pages 255–256) to become more centered, sit in the first row to minimize visual and auditory distractions (especially important for students with ADHD).

Be Alert: Look for "signals" or "flags" that teachers use to indicate important information. These may include repeating certain facts, or statements such as "in conclusion," writing information on the chalkboard, changing verbal tone and intonation, and punctuating key information with a particular hand gesture. Pay close attention to the teacher's summation and recap of the main points during the last few minutes of class.

Abbreviate: Use comprehensible abbreviations so that you can write more quickly.

Speed-think: Don't spend excessive time trying to digest everything the teacher is saying when you take notes. Think about the content after class.

Speed-write: Train yourself to write down information quickly by abbreviating and leaving out unnecessary letters and words.

Evaluate: Assess your teacher's lecture style and tendencies. If your teacher asks questions while lecturing, make note that the teacher expects students to think about the lecture as it's presented and not simply record everything that's said. After assessing the teacher's lecture style and preferences, adjust your note-taking procedures accordingly.

Question: Ask teachers to clarify information at appropriate points during the lecture if you're confused.

Compare: Compare your notes with those of a classmate who is doing well in the course, especially if your note-taking skills are weak.

Practice: Practice note-taking by having a friend or a parent give a "minilecture." Use these practice sessions to make sure that you've recorded the necessary information and to improve your skills and self-confidence.

Pretend: Use your class and lecture notes to practice giving your own "pretend" lectures covering the material you're studying. This will help you better understand the content.

Organize: Organize key information from lectures, and reorganize, revise, amplify, and/or recopy any sections of your notes that are confusing.

TEACHING SUGGESTIONS FOR PARENTS TUTORING THEIR OWN CHILD:

The most effective means for helping your child improve her note-taking skills is to provide opportunities for her to practice. Consider preparing and giving a minilecture using content from one of her textbooks. By so doing, you would, in effect, be assuming the role of a teacher. Stop every few minutes to review what your child has recorded, and discuss why she included certain information that seemed important and omitted other information that seemed unimportant. If there's disagreement, discuss your differing perspectives.

TEACHING ANALYTICAL AND CRITICAL THINKING

Teaching your child how to probe beneath surface appearances and to question statements and suppositions is a key stimulus for active, cerebrally engaged learning. For example, let's say that you're helping your child in an American history course. Your child reads in her textbook that nuclear power plants spew fewer pollutants into the environment than fossil fuel plants and that the electricity produced by nuclear plants is cheaper and less vulnerable to spikes in oil prices. You would want your child to get into the habit of asking probing questions about these types of statements. These questions might include:

What are the potential risks to becoming reliant on nuclear energy? Can the spent radioactive fuel rods be disposed of safely? What are the chances of a meltdown such as that which nearly occurred at the Three Mile Island nuclear power plant or that which did actually occur at Chernobyl? How does the cost for building a conventional power plant compare to the cost of a nuclear plant? This analytical and critical thinking fuels engaged, active learning, and engaged, active learning invariably enhances comprehension, retention, and test performance.

MEMORIZING INFORMATION

Being able to identify and recall important facts is clearly essential when preparing for tests. There are nine common memorization techniques:

- Writing information over and over.
- Reciting information over and over.
- Making a powerful visual or word association with the information. (e.g., seeing in your mind the peasants storming the Bastille under the heading "1789: Start of the French Revolution.")
- Categorizing. (e.g., listing the means for generating electricity.)
- Clustering. (e.g., creating a grouping or constellation of information that relates to an issue such as the social causes of the French Revolution.)
- Chaining. (e.g., creating a time line or track of information such as the events leading to World War II.)
- Cue response. (e.g., using a topic [cue] such as *lasers* and practicing associating everything that you know [response] about the topic.)
- Mnemonics. (e.g., creating a formula or acronym to remember information such as SOHCAHTOA to remember sine = opposite over hypotenuse; cosine = adjacent over hypotenuse; tangent = opposite of adjacent).

PREPARING FOR TESTS

Good students often anticipate questions that their teacher is likely to ask on tests. They have a sense of whether their teacher is primarily detail-oriented (e.g., the date when Fort Sumpter was attacked by the South) or concept-oriented (e.g., the social conditions that led to the War of Independence). They also know what types of tests their teacher prefers (e.g., short answer and multiple choice). They then gear their studying accordingly.

Effective methods for helping your child prepare for tests include:

- Have your child identify main ideas or concepts in her notes and textbooks. (These should be highlighted in a specific color).
- Have your child identify details and facts in her notes and text-books. (These should be highlighted in a [different] specific color.)
- Encourage your child to put the concept and main ideas on one side of an index card and the related details on the opposite side. (This will facilitate review and permit organization and reorganization.)
- Encourage your child to continually pose questions when she studies.
- Show your child how to coordinate class notes and textbook notes when studying.
- Have your child review previous tests to develop a sense of the teacher's testing style and to identify the types of mistakes she has made on tests in the past.
- Have your child use the identified important information to make up practice tests. (These tests should correspond to the types of tests her teacher gives and should include short-answer, multiple choice, true–false, and essay questions.) Then have your child answer her own test questions.
- Encourage your child to spend time studying in a controlled environment with a motivated classmate who, ideally, gets good grades. (This studying should not be used as an opportunity for socializing.)

TAKING TESTS

By providing your child with practical test-taking procedures and techniques, you can help improve her test performance. These include:

- Quickly look through all the questions before beginning so that you can gauge how much time you should spend answering each question.
- Be aware of the time constraints and be prepared to speed up if you're falling behind. If there's time left over at the end, you can review your answers to the difficult questions.
- Pay attention to details. Sometimes a single important fact will be wrong in an answer that you might be tempted to select. Be on the lookout for tricky questions.
- Don't get bogged down on difficult questions. Do the easy ones first and come back to the hard ones.
- Eliminate implausible answers in multiple choice questions if you can't immediately identify the correct answer. This will reduce the odds if you have to guess.

REDUCING TEST ANXIETY

Test anxiety can be incapacitating and can cause children to forget what they've assiduously studied. The following relaxation techniques can reduce your child's anxiety:

- Silently recite and repeat positive statements about doing well while you study.
- See yourself in your mind being calm and confident while sitting at your desk in class and waiting for the test to be handed to you.
- Close your eyes and slowly take several deep breaths as the test is being distributed. (Don't take more than three or four breaths, as this could cause you to hyperventilate and become dizzy.)
- Keep your eyes closed for a moment and form a mental picture of you looking at the questions, knowing the answers, taking the test, feeling self-assured, doing well, and feeling proud.

- With your eyes still closed, feel your body relax and feel the fear and stress flowing out. Imagine that your stress is localized in a particular place in your body—your chest, your throat, your stomach, etc. Focus on the spot and imagine the anxiety ebbing from it.
- Select an easy question to answer first.
- Silently recite and repeat positive statements about doing well as you take the test.

SOME FINAL THOUGHTS ABOUT SCHOOL SUCCESS

The fundamentals of academic achievement are not mysterious. Students who succeed in school are motivated. They want to learn and are willing to work. They think strategically and have a plan for getting from point A to point B to point C. They figure out how they learn best, and they deliberately develop a personalized study system that capitalizes on their natural learning strengths. They're organized. They establish goals and priorities. They know what their assignments are. They're able to manage the clock, schedule their academic obligations, and plan ahead. They finish their work, and they submit it on time. When they study, they identify important information and use practical methods to understand and assimilate this information. They derive pleasure from their achievements and take pride in their work. They're able to solve problems and handle challenges. They learn from mistakes, weigh the pluses and the minuses of their choices, apply basic cause-and-effect principles, bounce back from setbacks, and figure out how to overcome obstacles.

This book has focused on factors that cause children to underperform, and become resistant and ineffectual learners. It has provided you with a range of effective, hands-on strategies and techniques for positively reorienting your child.

Ideally, your child is now on a different track from the one she was on when you first began to read this book. Ideally, she has become a more enthusiastic learner. Ideally, her self-concept has been enhanced by her successes in school, and her expectations and aspirations have expanded. Ideally, your child is now working more diligently and is ready and willing to succeed academically.

If the desired changes in attitude, behavior, and academic performance have not occurred, don't throw your hands in the air and exclaim, "Well, I tried." There's more that needs to be done. The first step
in the process is to identify the remaining impediments. You may want
to review specific sections in this book that are relevant to these residual issues. If you don't believe that this review will be fruitful, it's
strongly recommended that you seek help from a qualified professional, such as a tutor, educational therapist, psychologist, or family
therapist.

You simply can't give up on your child! Figure out what needs to be
done to turn things around. If necessary, refinance the house or get a
second job so that you can provide this assistance, but don't throw in
the towel. If plan A doesn't work, you must switch to plan B, and if
plan B doesn't work, be prepared to switch to plan C. Providing help
for a resistant, learning-aversive child is vital. It is also the best investment that you can possibly make. This investment could literally transform your child's life, and it could also save you and your child
incalculable grief now and in the future.

At the end of the introduction to this book, I used a baseball analogy.
I wrote: "With your skillful and proactive intervention, your child will
be playing and winning in a new franchise, in a revised lineup, and in a
new ballgame. Trust me. It's doable." It is my sincerest wish that these
changes were indeed "doable" and that your trust was not misplaced.

Appendix:
Reproducible Materials

LEARNING MODALITY INVENTORY

	Yes	No	Not Sure
1. I learn best by reading information in textbooks, textbook notes, and lecture notes.	___	___	___
2. I can recall and understand information best when I can look at it.	___	___	___
3. Seeing a science experiment or a class demonstration helps me understand and learn the information.	___	___	___
4. I can remember information better when it's in diagrams, graphs, charts, and pictures.	___	___	___
5. When I can see information, it increases my interest, motivation, and involvement in what I am learning.	___	___	___
6. I learn best by listening to lectures, audio tapes, and spoken explanations.	___	___	___
7. I can understand and remember information better when I hear it.	___	___	___
8. Class discussions help me understand and learn what's being taught.	___	___	___
9. I can remember jokes and the words in songs when I hear them.	___	___	___
10. Hearing information that I'm expected to learn stimulates my interest, motivation, and active involvement.	___	___	___
11. I learn best when activities are physical.	___	___	___
12. I can recall and understand information better when I can move things around.	___	___	___
13. Doing experiments, drawing pictures, plotting graphs, making diagrams, or building models helps me understand what's being taught.	___	___	___
14. I can usually learn the steps to a dance or athletic plays by practicing them once.	___	___	___

15. Physical activities stimulate my interest, moti-
    vation, and involvement in what I am learning.   ___ ___   ___
16. I learn best when I am touching, holding,
    or manipulating what I need to learn.   ___ ___   ___
17. I can put something together without
    instructions.   ___ ___   ___
18. I can understand and recall how things
    work by handling them.   ___ ___   ___
19. I enjoy mechanical projects, and I can
    disassemble and reassemble objects
    with little difficulty.   ___ ___   ___
20. Hands-on activities stimulate my interest,
    motivation, and active involvement in
    what I am learning.   ___ ___   ___
21. I like to learn by figuring out how to
    do something on my own.   ___ ___   ___
22. I enjoy learning through trial and error.   ___ ___   ___
23. I don't like to follow written or
    verbal instructions.   ___ ___   ___
24. If I make a mistake, I learn from it and make
    adjustments so I can get it right the next time.   ___ ___   ___
25. I like to work independently.   ___ ___   ___

USING PREFERRED LEARNING MODALITIES

- Do you agree with what the inventory indicates about your preferred (or most natural) learning modality?
- Five primary learning modalities are described: *auditory, visual, tactile, experiential,* and *kinesthetic.* List these modalities in the order of your personal preference. Begin with your most preferred.

_____

_____

_____

_____

If you needed to study material that might require combining learning modalities, what would be your *preferred combination*? (Younger children may have difficulty handling this question. You will need to give concrete examples of how more than one modality might work in tandem.)

- visual/auditory
- visual/tactile
- visual/kinesthetic
- visual/experiential
  - auditory/tactile
  - auditory/kinesthetic
  - auditory/experiential
  - tactile/kinesthetic
- tactile/experiential
- kinesthetic/experiential

ORGANIZATION CHECKLIST

Code: 1 = Never 2 = Rarely 3 = Sometimes 4 = Often 5 = Always

My study area is neat and uncluttered. ____

My room is neat and uncluttered. ____

I make certain that I bring home the books and materials
I need to do my homework. ____

I have all the materials that I need to complete my
homework (pen, paper, dictionary, etc.) on, in, or
near my desk. ____

I have a system for filing previous tests, homework
assignments, book reports, etc. ____

I have labeled dividers in my binder for each subject. ____

I insert all returned papers in my binder in the correct
subject section. ____

I keep my assignment sheet in my binder. ____

I make certain before I go to sleep that I have put all
the materials I will need for school (completed
homework, textbooks, etc.) in my book bag. ____

I neatly place my books and other materials in my
backpack so that I can find what I need when I get to
school and when I return home after school. ____

DIBS

Define the Problem: _____

Investigate the Causes of the Problem: _____

_____

_____

_____

Brainstorm Solutions to the Problem: _____

_____

_____

_____

Select a Solution to Try Out: _____

_____

_____

_____

_____

_____

_____

REVIEWING THE STEPS FOR ORGANIZING A BINDER

#1. Insert your assignment sheet in the front of your binder.

#2. Use dividers for each of your courses.

#3. Label each subject.

#4. Label a section "Completed/Corrected Assignments."

#5. Label a section "Assignments To Turn In."

#6. Label a section "Miscellaneous."

#7. Place all school materials you want to keep (quizzes, tests, reports, course syllabi, reading lists, notes) in the appropriate subject category.

#8. Put dates on all material and insert them in chronological order.

#9. Tape your study schedule on the inside front cover of your notebook.

#10. Put another copy of your study schedule in a plastic sleeve and insert it in the front of your notebook.

#11. Punch holes in any papers you want to keep that do not have holes. Use reinforcements for important papers so that you don't lose them.

SOLVING ARGUMENTS AND CONFLICTS

YOU WIN WE LOSE

WE WIN YOU LOSE

YOU WIN WE WIN

GOAL-SETTING CHECKLIST

CODE: 1 = Never 2 = Rarely 3 = Sometimes 4 = Often 5 = Always

I aim for a specific grade on tests, essays, reports, and
homework assignments. ___

I target the specific grade I want to get in each
class at the beginning of the semester. ___

I develop a strategy for getting what I want. ___

I carefully plan the steps I must take to achieve
my long-range goals. ___

I make these steps my short-term goals (for example,
a B– on the next math test). ___

I use short- and long-term goals to motivate me
to work hard. ___

I periodically review my goals to remind myself
about what I want to achieve. ___

I periodically review my goals to make certain they're
current, realistic, challenging, and attainable. ___

I set new goals to replace the ones that I've already achieved. ___

I carefully examine and make revisions in my
step-by-step plan (short-term goals) if I fail to
achieve a particular goal. ___

I am proud when I attain my goals. ___

MY PERSONAL LONG-RANGE GOALS

Date:_____

1. _____

2. _____

3. _____

4. _____

5. _____

6. _____

MY SHORT-TERM GOALS

Date:_____

1. _____

2. _____

3. _____

4. _____

5. _____

6. _____

7. _____

8. _____

9. _____

10. _____

LONG-TERM SCHOOL GOALS

Date:_____

1. _____

2. _____

3. _____

4. _____

SPECIFIC ACADEMIC SHORT-TERM GOALS

Subject	Most Recent Report Card Grade	Grade I Want on My Next Report Card
Math	_____	_____
_____	_____	_____
_____	_____	_____
_____	_____	_____
_____	_____	_____

GOAL-SETTING IN SCHOOL

		Goal Attained?	
		Yes	No
Week #1:			
Weekly Goal:	_____	___	___
Daily Goals:			
Monday:	_____	___	___
Tuesday:	_____	___	___
Wednesday:	_____	___	___
Thursday:	_____	___	___
Friday:	_____	___	___

		Goal Attained?	
		Yes	No
Week #2:			
Weekly Goal:	_____	___	___
Daily Goals:			
Monday:	_____	___	___
Tuesday:	_____	___	___
Wednesday:	_____	___	___
Thursday:	_____	___	___
Friday:	_____	___	___

PRIORITIES CHECKLIST

Code: 1 = Never 2 = Rarely 3 = Sometimes 4 = Often 5 = Always

I know what I need to do to meet my obligations in school. ____

I identify the tasks that are most immediate or urgent. ____

I identify the steps that are required to achieve specific goals. ____

I order the steps required to achieve a goal in a logical sequence. ____

I create a ladder of importance when I am faced with
making choices about my priorities. ____

I create a logical and practical sequence for completing
tasks and obligations. ____

I place the most significant tasks at the top of my to-do list
and list the less important tasks below in descending order
of importance. ____

I eliminate the less important or urgent tasks at the bottom
of my to-do list when it's clear that I can't do everything. ____

I remind myself of my goals and priorities to avoid
any temptation to procrastinate or become lazy. ____

I check off each task or obligation when completed. ____

I periodically evaluate my priorities to make sure that they
are properly ordered and will help me achieve my goals. ____

I make adjustments in my priorities when targeted goals
are attained or when my goals change. ____

PRIORITIZING THE STEPS FOR WRITING A TERM PAPER

___ Write first draft

___ Choose a topic

___ Write notes on index cards

___ Go to the library

___ Make up a bibliography

___ Go online to find relevant information

___ Write down quotations on index cards

___ Examine relevant books about subject

___ Read material about topic in the encyclopedia, using either the actual volumes or CD encyclopedia software

___ Turn in the paper on time

___ Proofread for spelling and grammar mistakes

___ Revise and edit first draft

___ Put index cards in order

___ Incorporate quotations into first draft

___ Write final draft

PRIORITIZING STEPS FOR PACKING THE CAR

___Tent	___Sleeping bags	___Ground cloth	___Blankets
___Flashlights	___Toiletries	___Games	___Towels
___Water bottles	___Rain gear	___Camera	___Ice chest
___Rubber pads	___Cell phone	___Compass	___Sunblock
___Blankets	___Marshmallows	___Kindling	___Snacks
___Lanterns	___Clothes	___Matches	___Food
___Backpacks	___Hiking boots	___Binoculars	___Books

Handling Problems

Nicole felt that the walls were closing in on her. She hadn't cracked her earth science textbook for ten days. Not only had she not read the last two assigned chapters, but she had also fallen seriously behind in doing the lab work. In fact, she hadn't submitted her lab notebook in more than three weeks. The notebook, which was supposed to be submitted every Friday, would count for 30 percent of her grade in the course.

During class, Mr. Takeda made a point of asking Nicole where her lab book was, and she had made up an excuse that she wanted to recopy the three most recent write-ups because they were sloppy. She promised that she would hand in the notebook on Monday. Mr. Takeda scowled. This was not the first time that Nicole had failed to meet deadlines in his class, and he was aware of her propensity to make up creative excuses. At home that evening, Nicole added up her grades on her earth science tests and homework assignments and figured that she was currently carrying a C in the course. This grade would be significantly reduced if Mr. Takeda gave her an F on her lab notebook for the semester. Even if he didn't give her an F, she knew he would lower her grade on the three late write-ups when she finally submitted them. This assumed, of course, that she would actually get around to doing the write-ups. The problem was also compounded by the fact that Nicole hadn't read the last two assigned textbook chapters. Unless she blocked out time to read and take notes on the chapters, Nicole was certain that she would flunk the next exam.

The reason Nicole had fallen so seriously behind was quite basic—she was spending more than an hour and a half each evening talking on the phone to Curtis and spending another forty-five minutes sending instant e-mail messages to her girlfriends. Her boyfriend had graduated high school in June and was taking a year off from school to work and earn money before he enrolled in the local community college. As Curtis currently didn't have any homework, he would call Nicole three or four times every night, and they would talk for at least twenty-five minutes each time he called. Nicole realized that these conversations and her instant messages were leaving her virtually no time to do her homework, but the tenth grader hadn't been able to summon the necessary fortitude to tell Curtis that she had to limit the telephone conversations.

Despite her attempts not to think about her predicament, the realities were staring her in the face. She knew that she was at risk of not only failing earth science, but also several other courses. These Fs would pull her GPA down below 2.0 and she would have to go to summer school again if she wanted to graduate with her class.

Nicole's most urgent predicament was her lab notebook. She estimated that it would take her a minimum of four hours to do the three overdue write-ups, and she simply wasn't willing to sacrifice her nightly telephone conversations with Curtis or allocate the required time during the weekend to do the work. Nicole had too many fun things planned. On Friday night she and Curtis would either go to a movie or watch TV with friends. On Saturday and Sunday, they would hang out at the mall, and there would invariably be a party on Saturday night. And, of course, Nicole also had her regular homework that was due on Monday. These assignments were customarily left until ten P.M. on Sunday evening and were rarely if ever completed. "You don't have to be a genius to see that there just isn't enough time to do the stupid lab write-ups!" Nicole thought sullenly.

Nicole concluded that there was no way to extricate herself from the jam she was in. She certainly wasn't prepared to give up talking with Curtis on the phone or doing fun things over the weekend. The situation was hopeless, and Nicole decided that all she could do was let the chips fall where they may. If she flunked earth science, too bad. She would just have to go to summer school.

When her best friend told her that she had the perfect solution to the lab notebook problem, Nicole was eager to hear what she had to say. Emily had taken the same earth science course from a different teacher during summer school and had gotten a B. Since she had done all of the same dissections and lab experiments, she suggested that Nicole simply copy her lab book. As Mr. Takeda had never seen her lab book, Emily was certain that he would never figure out what was happening.

Realizing that the plan could solve her most immediate problem, Nicole decided to go ahead with it. But later that day she began to have second thoughts. She certainly didn't consider herself an angel, but she had never done anything like this before. Sure, she had occasionally glanced at a classmate's answers while taking a test, but what Emily was proposing would guarantee an F in the course if she were caught. She might even be suspended. What would happen if Mr. Takeda realized that she had copied another student's lab book? What would her parents say if he flunked her because she had cheated? One voice in her head said, "Do it! It's no big deal. I've cheated before, and there's no chance of getting caught." Another voice said, "This could be a major mistake. Mr. Takeda is going to going to catch on and nail me to the wall."

Nicole wrestled with what to do for the entire day. That evening she tossed and turned and had troubled sleeping. At breakfast her father saw that she looked troubled and inquired if anything was wrong. Nicole responded "No," and then she made a joke about her mom's runny scrambled eggs to throw him off the track.

When Emily told Nicole during first period that she had her lab book in her backpack, Nicole gritted her teeth and said, "I've decided not to do it." Emily looked at her friend as if she were crazy.

"That's really dumb, Nicole," Emily whispered.

"Yeah, I know. But I just can't do it."

"Then what are you going to do? You're gonna flunk the class for sure if you don't hand in your lab notebook."

"I don't know what I am going to do. I just can't take the chance. If I were to get caught, I would be in really hot water, and my parents would go ballistic. I'd be grounded for life."

"Well, it's your call," Emily commented incredulously.

"What an awful mess!" Nicole replied.

FOUR-STEP GOAL-SETTING SYSTEM

Step 1:
Challenge/Problem: _____

_____

Step 2:
Long-Range Goal: _____

Step 3:
Short-Term Goals: _____

_____

_____

_____

_____

_____

_____

Step 4:
Specifics: _____

_____

_____

_____

_____

_____

RECORDING ASSIGNMENTS CHECKLIST

Code: 1 = Never   2 = Rarely   3 = Sometimes   4 = Often   5 = Always

I know what my assignments are in every subject. ____

I write down important details such as page numbers,
   assigned problems, and specific directions. ____

I make certain that I know when my assignments are due. ____

I record all of the clues that my teachers provide about
   what will be covered on tests. ____

I use abbreviations that I can understand. ____

I note the due date for long-range projects such as
   book reports and term papers. ____

I write down the announced dates of all tests and exams. ____

I carefully read and carefully follow instructions on
   teacher-prepared assignment sheets. ____

I check off my completed assignments on my assignment sheet. ____

I make certain that I bring my completed assignments to school. ____

I make certain that I submit my assignments on time. ____

I keep my assignment sheet in a specific location in my binder. ____

Common Abbreviations:

ans = answer	exp = explain	prac = practice	r.w. = rewrite
b.r. = book report	fin = finish	prob = problems	sec = section
ch = chapter	F = final exam	prfrd = proofread	sen = sentence
comp = complete	form = formula	Q = quiz	sk = skip
crct = correct	h.i. = hand in	ques = question	sp = spell
d = due	hmw = homework	rd = read	st = study
df = define	h/o = handout	r.d. = rough draft	s.w. = show work
	imp = important	rp = repeat	T = test
E = exam	l = learn	rpt = report	T.P. = term paper
ess = essay	m/t = midterm exam	rr = reread	u = unit
ex = example	o/b = open book	rvs = revise	vocab = vocabulary
exer = exercise	p = page	rvw = review	wkbk = workbook

Symbols:

¶ = paragraph	+ = plus	− = minus	> = greater than
< = less than	# = number	@ = at	% = percent
$ = money	& = and	* = important	{} = combine
>> = leading to	≤ = less than or equal to	≥ = more than or equal to	≠ = not equal to
± = plus or minus	÷ = divide	× = multiply	? = question

Sample Assignment Sheet

SUBJECTS	MONDAY	TUESDAY	WEDNESDAY	THURSDAY	FRIDAY
Math	p 127–28 probs. 10–20 s.w. I form p 120 completed: X	rvw p 125–27 p 128–29 probs. 1–15 sw completed: X	completed:	completed:	completed:
Social Studies	ch 5 rd p 92–99 ans ques p 102 1–8 comp sen completed: X	begin research T.P. Fr. Revol. rd ch 5 p 131–40 ans ques p. 142 1–7 comp. sen completed: X	completed:	completed:	completed:
English	rd story p. 81–89 ans ques p 94 st vocab wrds p 95 completed: X	write 10 sen. voc. wrds. p. 61 prfrd. b.r. completed: X	completed:	completed:	completed:
Science	p 80–89 I forms p 87 completed: X	u 4 ans ques 1–8 p. 81 completed: X	rd 74–80 completed:	completed:	completed:
Tests & Reports	Math Q. Friday 10/17 u. 3 Eng. b.r. Mon. 10/20 completed: completed:	voc Q Thurs. 10/16 completed: completed:	completed: completed:	completed: completed:	completed: completed:

Practice Assignment Sheet

SUBJECTS	MONDAY	TUESDAY	WEDNESDAY	THURSDAY	FRIDAY
Math					
	completed:	*completed:*	*completed:*	*completed:*	*completed:*
Social Studies					
	completed:	*completed:*	*completed:*	*completed:*	*completed:*
English					
	completed:	*completed:*	*completed:*	*completed:*	*completed:*
Science					
	completed:	*completed:*	*completed:*	*completed:*	*completed:*
Tests & Reports					
	completed: *completed:*	*completed:* *completed:*	*completed:* *completed:*	*completed:* *completed:*	*completed:* *completed:*

PRACTICE ORAL HOMEWORK ASSIGNMENT

Social Studies:	Due Tues.
	Read pages 72–80
	Answer questions 1–7 pg. 81
	Complete sentences. Skip line between answers.
	Test on chapter 2 Friday
Science:	Due Wed.
	Read pages 82–91
	Know definitions of six words on page 93
Math:	Due Tues.
	page 52 problems 1–9
	page 53 problems 1–6
	show your work (not just the answers)
English:	Due Tues.
	Learn vocabulary words page 76
	Use each word in a sentence that shows you understand the meaning. Underline the vocabulary word.

SAMPLE MATH AND SCIENCE ASSIGNMENT HANDOUT

Math:	*Due Tues.*
	page 17
	problems 1–8 (show work)
	Due Wed.
	page 20 problems 1–12 (show work)
	Due Thurs.
	page 25
	problems 1–12 (show work)
	Due Fri.
	page 29
	problems 1–7 (show work)

Science: *Due Tues.*
                  Exercises page 60 1–8
                  Test Wed.
                  Due Wed.
                  Read pages 61–66
                  Exercises page 67 1–5
                  Due Thurs.
                  Pages 67–73
                  Exercises page 76 1–6
                  Due Fri.
                  Test

REVIEWING THE STEPS FOR RECORDING
AND COMPLETING ASSIGNMENTS

#1 Make certain that you record key details and directions (page numbers, problem or exercise numbers, due dates, and specific instructions).

#2 Use abbreviations that you understand.

#3 Use different colored highlighters to indicate assigned problems, due dates, and long-range projects on teacher-prepared assignment sheets.

#4 Pay special attention to the teacher's hints about what will be covered on quizzes and tests.

#5 Check off each completed assignment.

#6 Make certain you submit your completed assignments on time.

TIME-MANAGEMENT CHECKLIST

CODE: 1 = Never 2 = Rarely 3 = Sometimes 4 = Often 5 = Always

I begin my homework at a specified time every school night. ____

I don't need to be reminded by my parents to begin my homework. ____

I have a good idea about how long it will take me to do
    each assignment. ____

I set aside sufficient time to do my homework and study for tests. ____

I set aside sufficient time to check over my work for errors
    and silly mistakes. ____

I complete my assignments. ____

I hand in my work on time. ____

I allow enough time to proofread my written assignments
    and check my math homework for careless mistakes. ____

I schedule sufficient time to complete long-range
    assignments such as book reports and term papers. ____

I avoid crises by planning ahead. ____

I budget sufficient time to study for midterm and final exams. ____

I begin studying for exams several days before. ____

I study for at least twenty-five minutes at a stretch before
    taking a short break. ____

I resist becoming distracted when I study and do homework. ____

I interrupt my studying every few minutes. ____

I make reasonable adjustments in my study schedule based
    on past experience (for example, a bad grade on a test
    or a bad grade on a math homework assignment). ____

SIX-STEP TIME-MANAGEMENT SYSTEM

Step 1: Academic Obligations
APPROXIMATE PROJECTED DAILY STUDY TIME REQUIRED TO DO A FIRST-RATE JOB OF STUDYING

My Courses   Study Time Required

_____   _____

_____   _____

_____   _____

_____   _____

_____   _____

_____   _____

Total Daily Study Time: _____

Step 2: When I Plan To Do My Homework

Monday: _____

Tuesday: _____

Wednesday: _____

Thursday: _____

Friday: _____

Saturday: _____

Sunday: _____

SAMPLE WEEKLY STUDY SCHEDULE

TIME:	MON.	TUES.	WED.	THURS.	FRI.
7:20 A.M.–7:45 A.M.	Breakfast	Breakfast	Breakfast	Breakfast	Breakfast
7:50–8:20	School bus	School bus	School bus	School bus	School bus
8:25–2:50	School	School	School	School	School
3:00–3:30	School bus	School bus	School bus	School bus	School bus
3:30–5:00	Free	Free	Free	Free	Free
5:00–5:30	Biology	Biology	Biology	Biology	Free
5:40–6:10	Spanish	Spanish	Spanish	Spanish	Free
6:15–6:45	Dinner	Dinner	Dinner	Dinner	Dinner
6:50–7:30	English	English	English	English	Free
7:40–8:10	Math	Math	Math	Math	Free
8:25–9:00	History	History	History	History	Free
9:00–10:00	Free	Free	Free	Free	Free

Step 3: My Weekly Study Schedule

TIME:	MON.	TUES.	WED.	THURS.	FRI.

Optional color code if felt markers or crayons are used to indicate blocks of time:

[ ]_____   [ ]_____   [ ]_____   [ ]_____   [ ]_____   [ ]_____

Step 4: My Weekend Study Schedule

TIME:	SATURDAY	SUNDAY

Optional color code if felt markers or crayons are used to indicate blocks of time:

[ ]_____   [ ]_____   [ ]_____   [ ]_____   [ ]_____   [ ]_____

TWO WEEK GRADE-TRACKING EXPERIMENT

Method 1: Grade Recording Form

COURSE: _____

Homework:

Date _____ Grade _____ Date _____ Grade _____ Date _____ Grade _____

Date _____ Grade _____ Date _____ Grade _____ Date _____ Grade _____

Date _____ Grade _____ Date _____ Grade _____ Date _____ Grade _____

Quizzes/Tests/Exams/Papers:

Date _____ Grade _____ Date _____ Grade _____ Date _____ Grade _____

Date _____ Grade _____ Date _____ Grade _____ Date _____ Grade _____

COURSE: _____

Homework:

Date _____ Grade _____ Date _____ Grade _____ Date _____ Grade _____ Date _____

Date _____ Grade _____ Date _____ Grade _____ Date _____ Grade _____ Date _____

Date _____ Grade _____ Date _____ Grade _____ Date _____ Grade _____ Date _____

Quizzes/Tests/Exams/Papers:

Date _____ Grade _____ Date _____ Grade _____ Date _____ Grade _____ Date _____

Date _____ Grade _____ Date _____ Grade _____ Date _____ Grade _____ Date _____

COURSE: _____

Homework:

Date _____ Grade _____ Date _____ Grade _____ Date _____ Grade _____ Date _____

Date _____ Grade _____ Date _____ Grade _____ Date _____ Grade _____ Date _____

Date _____ Grade _____ Date _____ Grade _____ Date _____ Grade _____ Date _____

Quizzes/Tests/Exams/Papers:

Date____ Grade____ Date____ Grade____ Date____ Grade____ Date____ Grade____

Date____ Grade____ Date____ Grade____ Date____ Grade____ Date____ Grade____

COURSE: ____

Homework:

Date____ Grade____ Date____ Grade____ Date____ Grade____ Date____ Grade____

Date____ Grade____ Date____ Grade____ Date____ Grade____ Date____ Grade____

Date____ Grade____ Date____ Grade____ Date____ Grade____ Date____ Grade____

Quizzes/Tests/Exams/Papers:

Date____ Grade____ Date____ Grade____ Date____ Grade____ Date____ Grade____

Date____ Grade____ Date____ Grade____ Date____ Grade____ Date____ Grade____

COURSE: _____

Homework:

Date____ Grade____ Date____ Grade____ Date____ Grade____ Date____ Grade____

Date____ Grade____ Date____ Grade____ Date____ Grade____ Date____ Grade____

Date____ Grade____ Date____ Grade____ Date____ Grade____ Date____ Grade____

Quizzes/Tests/Exams/Papers:

Date____ Grade____ Date____ Grade____ Date____ Grade____ Date____ Grade____

Date____ Grade____ Date____ Grade____ Date____ Grade____ Date____ Grade____

Homework Grades (Sample Graph)

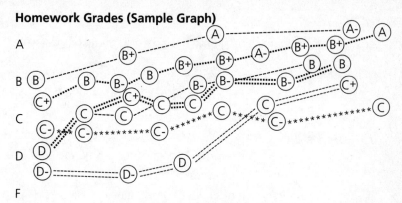

Date: 11/2 11/3 11/4 11/5 11/6 11/9 11/10 11/12 11/13 11/14

Code: English------ Spanish .... Biology ********* Math :::::::: Gov't ------

Test Grades (Sample Graph)

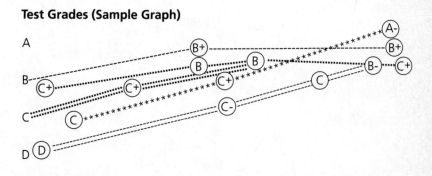

Date: 11/2 11/3 11/4 11/5 11/6 11/9 11/10 11/12 11/13 11/14

Code: English------ Spanish .... Biology ********* Math :::::::: Gov't ------

RECOMMENDED FORMULA FOR STUDY BREAKS

4th–6th Grade: Study and work conscientiously for a minimum of **twenty minutes** before taking a *five-minute break*.

7th–8th Grade: Study and work conscientiously for a minimum of **twenty-five minutes** before taking a *five-minute break*.

9th–12th Grade: Study or work conscientiously for a minimum of **thirty minutes** before taking a *five-minute break*.

DIBS

Define the Problem: _____

Investigate the Causes of the Problem: _____

_____

_____

_____

Brainstorm Solutions to the Problem: _____

_____

_____

_____

Select a Solution to Try Out: _____

MAKING AN AGREEMENT WITH MYSELF

A STUDY-SCHEDULE AGREEMENT

I, _____, agree to use the study schedule I created for a two-week trial period. I will keep track of my grades on homework and tests during this period. If after using the schedule for two weeks I decide that my schedule should be changed or fine-tuned, I'll discuss the changes with my parents. I understand that if I'm preparing for a test, I may need to set aside more time for studying before the test. If I do make adjustments in my day-to-day schedule, I'll use the revised schedule for a minimum of *four weeks*. During this period I'll continue to keep track of my grades. If I'm pleased with the results and my grades improve, I'll continue to use the schedule for the rest of the school year. I may make further adjustments every *four weeks* after discussing the proposed changes with my parents. Finally, I agree to keep to my study schedule without having to be prodded or reminded.

Signed: _____

Date: _____

Witness: _____

STUDY SKILLS INVENTORY

Code: 1 = Never 2 = Rarely 3 = Sometimes 4 = Often 5 = Always

1. I understand what I read in my textbooks.   ____

2. I can recall information I read in textbooks.   ____

3. I can recall information I hear in class.   ____

4. I can follow written instructions.   ____

5. I become confused when I study.   ____

6. I become bored when I study.   ____

7. I can identify important information when I study.   ____

8. I can recall key information when I take tests.   ____

9. I know how to take good notes in class.   ____

10. I know how to take good notes from textbooks.   ____

11. I can figure out what questions my teachers are likely to
    ask on tests.   ____

12. I can correctly answer multiple-choice test questions.   ____

13. I can correctly answer short-answer test questions.   ____

14. I can correctly answer true-false test questions.   ____

15. I can correctly answer essay test questions.   ____

16. I can correctly answer fill-in-the-blank test questions.   ____

17. I have confidence in my test-taking skills.   ____

Recommended Reading

Armstrong, Thomas. *In Their Own Way* (New York: J.P. Tarcher, 2000).

Gardner, Howard E. *Frames of Mind* (New York: Basic Books, 1993).

Garvey, William. *Ain't Misbehavin'* (Avon, Mass.: Adams Media Corporation, 1998).

Greene, Lawrence J. *Finding Help When Your Child Is Struggling in School* (New York: St. Martin's Press, 1998).

——. *Roadblocks to Learning* (New York: Warner Books, 2002).

——. *Study Max: A Program for Improving Study Skills in Grades 9–12* (Thousand Oaks, Calif.: Corwin Press, 2005). A study skills program for mainstream high school students.

——. *Study Wise: A Program for Maximizing Your Learning Potential* (New York: Prentice Hall, 2004). A study skills/life skills program for college students.

——. *Winning the Study Game* (Minnetonka, Minn.: Peytral Publications, 2002). A study skills/life skills program for special education middle school and high school students.

Levine, Mel. *One Mind at a Time* (New York: Simon & Schuster, 2003).

Shaywitz, Sally. *Overcoming Dyslexia* (New York: Alfred A. Knopf, 2003).

Bibliography

Armstrong, Thomas. 2000. *In Their Own Way*. New York: J. P. Tarcher.

Gardner, Howard E. 1993. *Frames of Mind*. New York: Basic Books.

Greene, Lawrence J. 1995. *Finding Help When Your Child Is Struggling in School*. New York: Golden Books/St. Martin's Press.

———. 1995. *The Life-Smart Kid*. Rocklin, Calif.: Prima/Crown Publishing Group.

———. 1995. *Winning the Study Game*. Minnetonka, Minn.: Peytral Publications.

———. 2002. *Roadblocks to Learning*. New York: Warner Books.

———. 2004. *Study Wise*. Upper Saddle River, N. J.: Pearson/Prentice Hall.

———. 2005. *Study Max: A Program for Improving Study Skills in Grades 9–12*. Thousand Oaks, Calif.: Corwin Press.

Shaywitz, Sally, M.D. 2003. *Overcoming Dyslexia*. New York: Alfred A. Knopf.

Vancouver Island Invisible Disability Association. 2003. *Learning Styles and Multiple Intelligences*. Web site. http://www.Idpride.net/

Index